MOLECULAR RED

MOLECULAR RED:

Theory for the Anthropocene

McKenzie Wark

VERSO

London • New York

First published by Verso 2015
© McKenzie Wark 2015

All rights reserved

The moral rights of the author have been asserted

3 5 7 9 10 8 6 4 2

Verso
UK: 6 Meard Street, London W1F 0EG
US: 20 Jay Street, Suite 1010, Brooklyn, NY 11201
www.versobooks.com

Verso is the imprint of New Left Books

ISBN-13: 978-1-78168-827-4
eISBN-13: 978-1-78168-828-1 (UK)
eISBN-13: 978-1-78168-829-8 (US)

British Library Cataloguing in Publication Data
A catalogue record for this book is available from the British Library

Library of Congress Cataloging-in-Publication Data

Wark, McKenzie, 1961–
Molecular red : theory for the Anthropocene / McKenzie Wark.
pages cm
Includes bibliographical references and index.
ISBN 978-1-78168-827-4 (paperback : alkaline paper) — ISBN 978-1-78168-
828-1 (electronic : US) — ISBN 978-1-78168-829-8 (electronic : UK)
1. Global environmental change—Social aspects. 2. Atmospheric carbon
dioxide—Environmental aspects. 3. Climate change mitigation—Philosophy. 4.
Bogdanov, A. (Aleksandr), 1873-1928—Criticism and interpretation. 5.
Platonov, Andrei Platonovich, 1899-1951—Criticism and interpretation. 6.
Haraway, Donna Jeanne—Criticism and interpretation. 7. Robinson, Kim
Stanley—Criticism and interpretation. 8. Labor in literature. 9. Nature in
literature. 10. Utopias in literature. I. Title.
GE149.W27 2015
363.738'74—dc23
2014043301

Typeset in Adobe Garmond by Hewer Text UK Ltd, Edinburgh, Scotland
Printed in the US by Maple Press

For Vera:
Hoc et cogitatione et realitate vera est.

Mother history's made monsters of the lot of us!
Andrey Platonov

All that is unhuman is not un-kind.
Donna Haraway

Contents

Preface

Workings of the world untie! You have a win to world!
—The Cyborg International

Disparate times call for disparate methods. Let's just say that this is the end of pre-history, this moment when planetary constraints start really coming to bear on the ever-expanding universe of the commodification of everything. This is the worldview-changing realization that some now call the *Anthropocene*. Let's not despair. Some of the greatest accelerations in the life of our species-being have happened in moments of limit, if never before on such a scale.

The Anthropocene is the name Paul Crutzen and others give to this period of geological time upon which the planet has entered. Crutzen:

> About 30–50 percent of the planet's land surface is exploited by humans . . . More than half of all accessible fresh water is used by mankind. Fisheries remove more than 25 percent of the primary production in upwelling ocean regions . . . Energy use has grown sixteen-fold during the twentieth century . . . More nitrogen fertilizer is applied in agriculture than is fixed naturally in all terrestrial ecosystems.[1]

It's not the end of the world, but it is the end of pre-history. It is time to announce in the marketplace of social media that the God who still hid in the worldview of an ecology that was self-correcting, self-balancing and self-healing—is dead. "The Anthropocene represents a new phase in the history of the Earth, when natural forces and human forces became intertwined, so that the fate of one determines the fate of the other. Geologically, this is a remarkable episode in the history of the planet."[2] The human is no longer that figure in the foreground which pursues its self-interest against the background of a wholistic, organicist cycle that the human might perturb but with which it can remain in balance and harmony, in the end, by simply *withdrawing* from certain excesses.

This is not the end of pre-history that the main currents of critical theory thought they would encounter. So perhaps we need some new critical theory. Or new-old, for it turns out that there was a powerful and original current of thought that was all but snuffed out in a previous, failed attempt to end pre-history. There may even be more than one. But the one I offer here in the first part of this book, "Labor and Nature," bears the names of two Russian Marxist writers, Alexander Bogdanov and Andrey Platonov.

Once we are equipped with this preterite thought, we can set it to work. In the second part, "Science and Utopia," we move from the cold and hunger of early Soviet Russia to the sunshine and plenty of California at the end of the twentieth century. The feminist science studies scholar Donna Haraway and the science fiction writer Kim Stanley Robinson are avatars of two approaches to thinking and writing at the end of this pre-history that echo and update Bogdanov and Platonov for our self-consciously Anthropocene times.

Common sense has it that the Cold War is over, that the Soviet Union lost and the United States won. While some would wish to hibernate in some "psychic soviet," the dominant mood is that regnant American-style capitalism won a global victory. The historic arc of *Molecular Red* is different. In this version, the collapse of the Soviet system merely prefigures the collapse of the American one. While the ruins of the first are real and poignant, the ruins of the latter have not quite been apprehended for what they are.[3]

A traveler among the antique ruins comes across the shattered visor of a rusting ship, half sunk in sand. Round the decay of this colossal wreck nothing beside remains; only desperation, boundless and bare. The name of this vessel has peeled off, but it might as well be named after Ozymandias, the fabled Egyptian king of Shelley's poem, and his challenge "Look on my works, ye Mighty, and despair!"

Beyond this rusting hull lies innumerable others. This is a modern ruin, mass-produced. And it is not just sand or time that ruined it. This dusted Martian landscape is one of the Seven Wonders of the World in negative. The vast and now gone waters that these ships once plied was the Aral Sea, which is less than a tenth of its former size.[4]

There were once pharaoh-sized statues here too. The Aral Sea is in what was once the Soviet Union, so perhaps the statues were of Lenin, pointing to a future rather remote from this one. But the ship itself is a wreck that recalls a power of a different kind: the capricious stubbornness of the natural world.

Cotton-growing actually began in this region when the American Civil War cut off Russia's cotton supply. After the revolution, Soviet engineers tapped the Amu Darya River that flowed into the Aral Sea as a water source for a cotton industry. The Soviets greatly expanded cotton production as an export crop after World War Two, and built vast irrigation projects to this end. Enormous quantities of water were an input, mixed with soil and seed and fertilizer, to grow cotton plants. The engineers knew the Aral Sea would disappear. Its fishing fleet was collateral damage, and so too perhaps were the many species of plant and animal now fossilizing here.

This is an example of what, after Marx, we might call *metabolic rift*.[5] Labor pounds and wheedles rocks and soil, plants and animals, extracting the molecular flows out of which our shared life is made and remade. But those molecular flows do not return from whence they came. The waters diverted from the Aral Sea to the cotton fields did not come back. As Marx knew, agriculture is a maker of deserts.

Marx's example of metabolic rift was the way nineteenth-century English farming extracted nutrients such as nitrates from the soil, which growing plants absorbed, which farmers harvested as crops, which workers in the cities ate to fuel their industrious labors, and who would then shit and piss the waste products out of their private metabolisms. Those waste products, including the nitrates, flow through run-off and sewers and pour out to sea. Whole industries for making artificial fertilizer would arise to address this rift—in turn causing further metabolic rifts elsewhere.[6]

The Anthropocene is a series of metabolic rifts, where one molecule after another is extracted by labor and technique to make things for humans, but the waste products don't return so that the cycle can renew itself. The soils deplete, the seas recede, the climate alters, the gyre widens: a world on fire. Earth, water, air: there is a metabolic rift where the molecules that are out of joint are potassium nitrate, as in Marx's farming example; or where they are dihydrogen-oxide as with the Aral sea; or where they are carbon dioxide, as in our current climate change scenario.

It used to seem as if exhausting the soil here or diverting water there were local problems. The Anthropocene is the recognition that some metabolic rifts are global in scope.[7] Nitrogen and carbon are on vacation from their old routines. Climate change already appears to be affecting the global distribution of water in profound ways. The Aral Sea experience of Soviet times is a microcosm of our now global experiment in metabolic rift. The draining of the Aral Sea was a kind of terraforming in reverse, making Earth into a Martian desert rather than Martian deserts into a new Earth.[8]

Marx: "All that is solid melts into air."[9] That effervescent phrase suggests something different now. Of all the liberation movements of the eighteenth, nineteenth and twentieth centuries, one succeeded without limit. It did not liberate a nation, or a class, or a colony, or a gender, or a sexuality. What it freed was not the animals, and still less the cyborgs, although it was far from human. What it freed was chemical, an element: carbon. A central theme of the Anthropocene was and remains the story of the Carbon Liberation Front.

The Carbon Liberation Front seeks out all of past life that took the form of fossilized carbon, unearths it and burns it to release its energy. The Anthropocene runs on carbon.[10] It is a redistribution, not of wealth, or power, or recognition, but of molecules. Released into the atmosphere as carbon dioxide, these molecules trap heat, they change climates. The end of pre-history appears on the horizon as carbon bound within the earth becomes scarce, and liberated carbon pushes the climate into the red zone.[11]

Powerful interests still deny the existence of the Carbon Liberation Front.[12] Those authorities attentive to the evidence of this metabolic rift usually imagine four ways of mitigating its effects. One is that the market will take care of everything. Another proposes that all we need is new technology. A third imagines a social change in which we all become individually accountable for quantifying and limiting our own carbon "footprint." A fourth is a romantic turn away from the modern, from technology, as if the rift is made whole when a privileged few shop at the farmer's market for artisanal cheese.[13] None of these four solutions seems quite the thing.

The first task of critique is to point out the poverty of these options.[14] A second task might be to create the space within which very different kinds of knowledge and practice might meet. Economic, technical, political, and cultural transformations are all advisable, but at least part of the problem is their relation to each other. The liberation of carbon transforms the totality within which each of these specific modes of thinking and being could be practiced. That calls for new ways of organizing knowledge.

Hegel, that great systematizer of knowledge, thought the French Revolution was a world-historical moment, but from our vantage point in time he was mistaken.[15] A world-historical event of considerably more general significance is the discovery of the totality of effects of human activity on its material support, on what we now call the *biosphere*.[16] All the products of any labor process have to be factored back into it, and for all of them. That's a task beyond any master-thinker or grand plan, beyond the magic of the market or computer modeling. How to think about designing the ad hoc practices for mitigating such a rift? *Molecular Red* sets itself the lowly task of gleaning some forgotten histories, neglected concepts, and minor stories that might usefully re-orient thought to such an agenda.

We are not short of big-picture stories, either about the fate of the October Revolution, or the grand epoch of unchallenged capitalism since the demise of the Soviet Union.[17] Here the left doesn't differ too much from the right. This is a drama of events that could be called the *molar*, where big-bodied entities clash, antagonist against protagonist. Meanwhile, the interesting processes might be more subtle and imperceptible—*molecular*. Felix Guattari: "The same elements existing in flows, strata and assemblages can be organized in a molar or a molecular mode. The molar order corresponds to signification that delimits objects, subjects, representations and their reference systems. Whereas the molecular order is that of flows, becomings, phase transitions and intensities."[18]

The molecular is less obvious but not more real than the molar. In the pores of those vast dramas of class and party, nation and history, there is another kind of story: the Carbon Liberation Front and the metabolic rift. It's a question of being able to perceive both molar drama and molecular gesture together, of not being too distracted by the stagecraft of the molar clash of embodied ideas.

How can knowledge and labor be organized to extract a *living* from nature when that very process produces secondary effects that undermine its own ongoing life? Taking on the Carbon Liberation Front requires not just actions of a number of different kinds but their integration. What we need is a kind of *low theory*, for designing integrated solutions on a collaborative basis, which includes many kinds of people's experience of the labors of the molecular.[19]

The unspeakable secret about climate change is that nobody really wants to think about it for too long.[20] It's just too depressing! Reading about it sometimes seems like helplessly watching some awful train derailment careen in slow motion. Rather, let's take this world-historical moment to be one in which to reimagine what the collective efforts of everyone who labors could make of the world, and as a world.

Here is the itinerary for *Molecular Red*: Our story begins with Alexander Bogdanov. Once Lenin's rival for the leadership of the Bolsheviks, he went on to elaborate and occasionally even try to implement a radical practice of knowledge. He took the core of Marxism to be the *labor point of view*. He thought that if labor was to organize the world, it needed to develop its own organization of knowledge, which he called *tektology*, and its own means of cultural development, or *proletkult*.

Bogdanov saw a positive role for ideologies as *worldviews* that overcome affective *resistance* to organizing the human side of collective labor. Drawing on the philosopher-scientist Ernst Mach, his own worldview is an *empiro-monism*, which took its metaphors from advanced labor practices, including the sciences, and refused all spiritual doubles to this world. He understood the emotional appeal of the spiritual and saw *utopia* as another way of motivating the needs and wants of labor in its collective tasks.

Bogdanov usefully delimits the category of *nature*. To him it specifies *that which labor encounters*. It's a focused yet open way to handle a term that can so quickly get out of hand. But Bogdanov still thought in terms of labor's domination over nature. Here we turn to Andrey Platonov, perhaps the greatest proletkult writer, but one who gave up writing in the worst years of the Russian Civil War to become an engineer. Nature appears as harsh and unforgiving in Platonov, and he grasps early on that as labor presses down on nature, nature presses down even harder on labor. Usually thought of as a fiction writer, I treat Platonov as a theorist not just of the point of view of labor, but the point of view of *comrades*.

For Platonov, we are comrades only when we face the same dangers. Those dangers start with famine and the struggle to produce an *infrastructure* that could undergird the grand projects of the early Soviet period. Platonov extends the idea of an organization of knowledge, by and for labor, into his vision of a *factory of literature*, able to collaboratively filter the everyday life of working people into an understanding of collective labor and its tasks.

Bogdanov was largely forgotten and Platonov mostly unknown

to those who created postwar versions of Marxism as a critical theory, the best known of which center on philosophy, cultural critique or normative political thought. In Part II of *Molecular Red* I pick up the thread of those writers who, while having little else in common with Bogdanov and Platonov, at least worked as they did on the borders between culture and the *sciences*, and across both critical and fictional writing. My central examples are the Californian writers Donna Haraway and Kim Stanley Robinson. Our themes also change here, from *Labor and Nature*, to *Science and Utopia*.

The synthesis of Ernst Mach and Karl Marx attempted by Bogdanov has few inheritors. I begin Part II with one of Mach's defenders, Paul Feyerabend, who finds Mach far from a simple-minded "empiricist" and rather a practitioner of an art of discovery, in which philosophy's tendency to high theory is muted, but the experimental rerouting of concepts from one kind of scientific labor to another is part of a *dada* method. It's a way of keeping the rather extravagant tendencies of language-work oriented toward matters at hand.

The central node onto which Feyerabend and everyone else in Part II is grafted is the work of Donna Haraway, who gives the metaphoric potentials of language a freer hand, rather like Bogdanov did in his tektology, even though Haraway stays very close to the biological sciences. Haraway usefully updates Bogdanov's account of worldview as both means and limit to organizing the world, and she confronts his concept of the labor point of view not only with a *feminist standpoint*, but also with its porous boundaries with other organisms, and with technology, not least in her famous concept of the *cyborg*. The cyborg refigures the imaginative possibilities not only for critical but also for utopian thought, in these times inextricably entangled with *techno-science*.

Two other writers influenced in various ways by Haraway help flesh out the cyborg point of view within a world made over by techno-science. Karan Barad's close engagement with modern physics shows Mach's tactics for thinking scientific knowledge at work. She introduces to the labor, or rather cyborg, point of view a close attention to the *apparatus*, as that which makes the *cut* between labor and nature in the act of producing knowledge.

Paul Edwards extends this concept of apparatus to that of the *knowledge infrastructure* required to collaboratively produce a science of the Carbon Liberation Front and its climate-changing effects. Here we witness the collaborative labor of scientists and technical labor producing a new worldview and overcoming resistances, both technical and ideological, on a global scale.

In the age of the Carbon Liberation Front, even sunny California can seem like a vision haunted in advance by its own ruins. No wonder critical theorists are now turning to past-times, reading Saint Paul for instance, as if there was nothing for it as Rome burns but to day-trip in the City of God. This is why, to conclude *Molecular Red*, I turn to Kim Stanley Robinson, whose majestic *Mars Trilogy* science fiction novels revisit the utopian practice of Bogdanov for the age of techno-science. I read these books as theoretical works. Robinson offers a mode of writing that really does confront this era of metabolic rift with a renewal of utopian thought, in which, strangely enough, science fiction turns out to be a kind of realism of the possible.

Like Haraway, Robinson takes us always to be cyborg beings embedded in techno-science. Like Barad, he is attentive to how different apparatuses make cuts that produce different objects and subjects of knowledge. Like Platonov, Robinson asks how such different subjects engaged in different struggles in and against their object-worlds can yet be comrades. Like Bogdanov, he refuses an over-arching high theory in favor of a low theory of negotiating between different worldviews.

What Robinson offers is something like a *meta-utopia*, a kind of writerly problem-solving practice for combining different visions of an endurable future. For at the end of the day, what Bogdanov and Platonov, Haraway and Robinson have in common is a critical and creative approach to the *selection* out of the past, into the future, of ways of life that know that only if our species-being endures can it be said to touch the real.

But now, a caveat: These are strictly amateur discussions of the languages of the sciences. They are not meant to settle disputes or provide an overarching philosophy, still less to proffer a humanist judgment on other modes of knowing. I take being a theorist writing about the sciences not to be a claim to any kind of authority but simply as permission to be wrong. Where these discussions of the sciences are wrong, the test is whether they can be *usefully* wrong, in providing metaphors or diagrams to test out in other fields of collective labor.

A theory for the Anthropocene can be about other things besides the melancholy paralysis that its contemplation too often produces. Here I think there's a place for what Platonov called *secondary ideas*. What can keep the larger project from becoming debilitating is getting to work on the kinds of knowledge practices that are useful in a particular domain. The particular secondary ideas that are the topic of *Molecular Red* are about selecting from within the archive those strands of Marxist theory for which the Anthropocene already appears as an object of thought and action in all but name.

Addressing the Anthropocene is not something to leave in the hands of those in charge, given just how badly the ruling class of our time has mishandled this end of pre-history, this firstly scientific and now belatedly cultural discovery that we all live in a biosphere in a state of advanced metabolic rift. The challenge then is to construct the *labor perspective* on the historical tasks of our time. What would it mean to see historical tasks from the point of view of working people of all kinds? How can everyday experiences, technical hacks and even utopian speculations combine in a common cause, where each is a check on certain tendencies of the other?

Technical knowledge checks the popular sentiment toward purely romantic visions of a world of harmony and butterflies—as if that was a viable plan for seven billion people. Folk knowledge from everyday experience checks the tendency of technical knowledge to imagine sweeping plans without thought for the particular consequences—like diverting the waters of the Aral Sea.[21] Utopian speculations are that secret heliotropism which orients action and invention toward a sun now regarded with more caution and respect than it once was. There is no other world, but it can't be this one.[22]

Most historical thought that takes ameliorating climate change seriously assumes one of two big-picture narratives, the first of which is *capitalist realism*.[23] This insists that there is no alternative, and we just have to stick with the program. If it takes the planet down with it then so be it. The alternative narrative imagines a kind of non-technical, holistic and spiritual alternative, often drawing its images from a pre-capitalist landscape. But as was already clear to Marx, this is *capitalist romance*, a story constructed within capitalism itself as one of the byproducts of its own momentum.[24] It is a kind of capitalist realism in negative, where we all ride bamboo bicycles, but it rarely ventures beyond an ideological mirroring of capitalist realism.

What we need then is an alternative realism. One which sticks close to the collaborative labors of knowing and doing. One which opens toward plural narratives about how history can work out otherwise. A realism formed by past experience, but not confined to it. This requires something of a reorienting of critical thought away from certain dominating tendencies: rather than a speculative realism in philosophy, a speculative fiction that makes no claims to be a spokesmodel for the object world, let alone the absolute; rather than an obsession with all-powerful capital and the phantasm of a pure redeeming communism, a working knowledge of the ways labor and nature confront and confuse each other; rather than a totalizing critique of technology as the acme of Western metaphysics, a frank acknowledgment of the entangling of our cyborg bodies within the technical.

What the Carbon Liberation Front calls us to create in its molecular shadow is not yet another philosophy, but a poetics and technics for the organization of knowledge. As it turns out, that's exactly what Alexander Bogdanov tried to create. We could do worse than to pick up the thread of his efforts. So let's start with a version of his story, a bit of his life and times, a bit more about his concepts, from the point of view of the kind of past that labor might need now, as it confronts not only its old nemesis of capital, but also its molecular spawn—the Carbon Liberation Front. Here among the ruins, something living yet remains.

Acknowledgments

Tiny bits of this book appeared previously in *Public Seminar*, *Occupied Times*, the *Los Angeles Review of Books*, the *White Review*, and in the book *Realism, Materialism, Art*. Thanks to Jeff Goldfarb, Naomi Goldfarb, Jack Dean, Evan Kindley, Ben Eastham, Tyler Curtis, Suhail Malik, and Jenny Jaskey.

Other bits were presented at the New School for Social Research, and the conferences Historical Materialism, Incredible Machines, and Post-Planetary Capital. Thanks to Inessa Medzibovskaya, Elizabeth Kendall Evgeny Pavlov, Mohammad Salemy, and Ed Keller. Special thanks to Kriss Ravetto-Biagioli and Mario Biagioli for inviting me to UC Davis, and introducing me to Kim Stanley Robinson.

Thanks to my research assistant and translator Anna Kalashyan and to my Eugene Lang College and New School for Social Research students, particularly Nash Petrovic and Ryan Richardson.

Molecular Red benefited enormously from some early editorial direction by Rowan Wilson, much careful editorial help from Leo Hollis, and the superior subediting of Tim Clark. A shout-out to Jessica Turner, Mark Martin, Sarah Shin, Huw Lemmey, Jacob Stevens and everyone who keeps the wheels turning at Verso Books.

Special thanks to David Rowley for making his translation of Bogdanov's *Philosophy of Living Experience* available, and to Donna Haraway for sharing some unpublished work.

Proceeds from the sale of this book go to support the Bogdanov Library, a project of the journal *Historical Materialism* dedicated to bringing out fresh translations of Bogdanov in English.

PART I
Labor and Nature

1

Alexander Bogdanov: Workings of the World

There is a magnificent photograph of the famous writer and Bolshevik sympathizer Maxim Gorky watching Alexander Bogdanov play chess with Lenin. It is 1908 and Lenin is visiting Gorky and his houseguest Bogdanov at Gorky's villa on the island of Capri. Bogdanov won that match, and according to Gorky, Lenin was not a good sport about it.[1] Gorky's attempt to reconcile Lenin and Bogdanov, the leading lights of the party, did not go well. Borrowing a line from *Hamlet*, Gorky accused Lenin of trying to play people like flutes. And yet of these three once-famous people, it is Lenin who is best remembered.

In the larger game between them, Lenin checked Bogdanov's designs on how to organize the theoretical, scientific, and practical stratagems of the workers' movement—and did so more than once. We rarely remember much about those whom the grand masters beat in the heat. Even though, when the masters are defeated in their turn, there might be something to glean from the faded tactics of the losers. Now that Lenin's world too is listed in columns of the defeated, perhaps we can pick through the strategies of his opponents and find things of value; now that it's time to build the world again, again.

Our species-being is as builders of worlds. This is the central proposition of all of Bogdanov's thought. Let's not concern ourselves just yet with what the boundaries of the "human" might be. It's a category endlessly caught up in differences and similarities with the categories of the animal, the angelic or the machinic.[2] Let's just think of us, for now, as Darwin might, as a *population*. And while we now know that all our writings may well be "read" by the machines of the security agencies, I will assume that the human is a population to which you, dear reader, most likely belong, and whose collective well-being is something you might care for. Bogdanov, who knew some Darwin, had more interest in the life of this species-being than in its definition.

Bogdanov's version of social democracy was always more about the self-organization of workers than about building a party to seize the state.[3] It was always more attuned to the struggle in and against *nature* to organize a way of life. Nature is of course an elusive category, prone to slippage between the material and the divine, between substance and essence.[4] As Bogdanov was well aware, different kinds of social organization produce wildly different images of it. Nature is for the moment then a category without a content. It means simply *that which labor encounters.*

Born in the industrial town of Tula in 1873, son of a school inspector, Bogdanov was educated at boarding school. Bogdanov: "Experience of the malicious and obtuse authorities there taught me to hate rulers and deny all authority. I was awarded a gold medal on completion of my studies."[5] He was first arrested in 1894, and arrested and exiled several times thereafter. Exile to Vologda in 1901 only furthered his political education, among the thriving dissident community there. Here he wrote one of the earliest and most widely used handbooks on Marxist economics.[6]

Nicolai Berdyaev: "He was a remarkable man, extremely sincere and utterly devoted to his ideas; but he had a rather narrow mind, and constantly engaged in finicky and sterile sophistry"[7]—including in disputes with Berdyaev, who was then retreating from Marxism, in which Bogdanov probably bested him with his sophisticated version of the same. In Vologda he met several other internal exiles whom he later recruited into the Bolshevik faction of Russian Social Democracy, including the future Commissar of

Enlightenment Anatole Lunacharsky, and the co-translators of Marx's *Capital*. He joined the Russian Social Democratic Workers' Party in 1899.

Like many activists in Russia at the time, he had little interest in or knowledge of the factional squabbles of the leaders of the party in European exile. He didn't meet Lenin until 1904, in Switzerland, when he was thirty-one and Lenin thirty-four. There Bogdanov was welcomed into the fractious conclave that was the Bolshevik faction of the party.

Back in Russia, he became Lenin's front man, and a Bolshevik representative on the St. Petersburg Soviet in the 1905 revolution. The legendary Bolshevik bank robber Kamo offers a colorful portrait of Bogdanov the revolutionary: "Krasin introduced me to a great man. Together they run the military-technical center for the Bolsheviks. You must understand that this man knows everything. He writes scholarly books, he makes bombs and dynamite. He also treats patients, you know, as a doctor."[8]

During the 1905 revolution Bogdanov was arrested again. In prison, he completed his first major philosophical work, *Empiriomonism*, and on his release sent Lenin a copy. In his Finland retreat, Lenin composed a long letter to Bogdanov on it. Bogdanov returned the letter, writing that in the interests of maintaining their political unity, he would pretend never to have read it. His alignment with Lenin disintegrated by 1907.

Three things were at stake.[9] First, Bogdanov opposed Lenin's rightward tack after the failure of the 1905 revolution. Lenin wanted the Bolsheviks to participate in elections, while Bogdanov wanted to keep the party underground and continue revolutionary work, and many in the party agreed with him.

Second, there was apparently also some squabbling over party funds. Bogdanov and the Bolshevik engineer Leonid Krasin had control over money raised through "expropriations"—bank robberies. It is hard to imagine Lenin having much tolerance for political or intellectual independence, but for both to then be combined with financial independence must have been particularly galling.

Third, the two men were never in agreement on philosophical matters. Lenin hewed closer to the "dialectical materialist" orthodoxy of George Plekhanov, who was aggressively opposed to the theoretical innovations starting to emanate from Bogdanov and his circle. Plekhanov once even wrote a polemic addressed to "Mr. Bogdanov"—as he refused to consider the author of such heresies a comrade.[10] Lenin and Bogdanov maintained unity within the Bolsheviks so long as they were agreed on tactics. When that unity broke down, the philosophical dispute came out in the open.

Bogdanov led the left-wing of the Bolsheviks against Lenin from 1907 to 1911. Lenin's position was a difficult one. Bogdanov may have had more support than Lenin among the Bolsheviks in exile, and most certainly among those still in Russia, which may be why Lenin attacked him on philosophical rather than political grounds. He took aim at Bogdanov's *Empirio-monism*.

Published in three volumes from 1904 to 1906, *Empirio-monism* addresses the impact on Marxist thought of the new physics, and the "spontaneous" philosophy that sprang from it, of Ernst Mach and others. For Mach, a scientific theory is just the most economical way of describing sensory experience. He withdrew the warrant for metaphysical speculation about what is real, beyond what can be said about what is observed. Bogdanov found in Mach a useful line of retreat from the would-be materialism of Engels and Plekhanov, which had raised the scientific theories of their time—only some of which would prove enduring—into metaphysical "laws."[11]

At a time of increasing repression within Russia and political crisis within the party, it rather puzzled militants that Lenin in exile was spending his time in libraries researching philosophical questions. The result of these labors was Lenin's lengthy polemic against Bogdanov and other "Machists," *Materialism and Empirio-criticism* (1909). Gorky thought this tract had "the sound of a hooligan," but it did the job.[12]

Being "philosophical" rather than political may have helped the book evade censorship. It certainly checked the influence not just of Bogdanov's theoretical innovations but also of his political line.

Lenin secured his expulsion from the Bolsheviks, and—whether intentionally or not—set the dismal precedent of trials of doctrinal orthodoxy, as if correct action on any and every issue required the correct "line" in philosophy.

Whether Bogdanov's political tactics would have been better than Lenin's need not concern us, but his *theoretical* tactics certainly had—and continue to have—merit, even if they diverged from the first principles of so-called "dialectical materialism." But then, as Gilles Deleuze once noted, the first principles in a philosophy are less interesting than the second or third principles.[13] Even with third principles, there's no end to the fruitless argument to be had.

Of more interest might be the kinds of *practices of knowledge* that can be built on a particular theoretical configuration. Stuart Hall: "Theory is always a detour on the way to something more important."[14] It is the contention of *Molecular Red* that Bogdanov offers, even today, a base on which to build a practice of knowledge for the era of the Carbon Liberation Front. Bogdanov retreated from the sterile attempts to construct a materialist metaphysics and took his stand on a realist approach to sensation itself, opening a path for thinking about the practice of knowledge as organized sensation. Such pragmatism seems timely again.

Alienated from Lenin on political, practical, and theoretical matters, Bogdanov, Gorky, and Lunacharsky formed their own faction. They ran two party schools in Capri in 1909 and Bologna in 1910, funded by Gorky's earnings as a celebrated writer and perhaps some expropriation funds Bogdanov still controlled. The Capri gathering was the moment when an intellectually open Bolshevism existed, if only for a brief moment.[15]

The Capri school didn't last. The students were arrested on their return to Russia; Bogdanov and Gorky fell out; Lenin patched up his relations with Gorky, while Lunacharsky drifted back under Lenin's spell. Alienated from his party, by 1909 Bogdanov considered suicide. He gave up politics in 1911 to concentrate on literary and scientific work. At odds with both Lenin and Gorky, with the Bolsheviks in disarray, Bogdanov watched from afar the long, slow counter-revolution that unfolded in Russia. It was in these difficult circumstances for the revolution, for the party, and for Bogdanov personally that he wrote, of all things, a *utopia*.

Bogdanov's utopia, *Red Star*, proved rather popular, and was a founding text of Soviet science fiction. It is the pole-star by which Bogdanov himself navigated the tempestuous times that were to follow. By attending to *Red Star*, we can understand something of Bogdanov's project and how it might be reimagined for the era of the Carbon Liberation Front.

RED MARS

"Well, you should write a novel for the workers," says Lenin to Bogdanov, "on how the predatory capitalists have despoiled the Earth and wasted all its oil, iron, lumber and coal. That would be a very useful book, Mister Machist!"[16] Or so Gorky recalled, or thought he recalled, from Lenin's visit to Capri. Much to Lenin's annoyance, Bogdanov's novel was rather more original and sensational than that.

The utopian fable *Red Star* (1908) and its prequel, the vampire story *The Engineer Menni* (1913), are didactic tracts that popularized Bogdanov's ideas about labor, nature and revolution. Both are set on Mars. Older and further from the sun, Martian life is less energetic than on Earth, less violent in its struggles, and more advanced.[17] The two books, taken together, are thought-experiments conducted in a parallel planet. Certain variables are missing—Mars lacks competing states—but in its essentials, pre-revolution Mars is not unlike where twenty-first-century Earth actually ended up after the victory of the Carbon Liberation Front.

In *Engineer Menni*, what drives the story is the tension between a vast, state-directed development project and the interests of finance capital. Martian capitalism is on the brink of crisis. Markets must expand, but there's nowhere left to grow. Menni the engineer proposes a canal-building project as the solution, a project so vast it will lead to whole new planetary spatial form. It will even alter the climate.

A delicate political compromise puts a state-run agency in charge, but this does not appease financial interests. Meanwhile, the workers are angry about the casualty rate that ensues from a particularly difficult stretch of terrain. Finance seizes on this as an opportunity to privatize the whole project. Their alternate route for the canal is through earthquake country. While the work is easier and there's a quick profit to be made, in the long run it will endanger whole populations along the shaky new route. The logic of accumulating capital, with its own special reality, dominates that of labor struggling in and against nature to build and maintain a habitable world.

The workers find toiling for finance capital worse than working for the engineer-dominated state corporation. Netti, a radical engineer, proposes a worker-engineer alliance against the one percent. He writes an exposé of corruption and incompetence on the project, and releases it to coincide with a general strike. Bogdanov wants to combine the interests of workers who labor directly with resistant matter with those who hack the information that organizes direct labor and a knowledge of nature.

But Netti's agenda is far more ambitious: "What must we do so that we ourselves can know and see, and not just constantly believe? Or is that impossible? Is it always going to be like it is now? And if it is impossible, then what is the use of living and struggling if we are to remain slaves?"[18] The worst form of slavery is believing instead of knowing, of taking on faith what hasn't been derived from the careful testing of what is sensed.[19] The goal is not just to throw off the vampire squid of finance capital, but to organize again the whole of labor and knowledge.

Red Star takes place after *Engineer Menni*, on socialist Mars. Gender equality prevails, if still patterned on a masculine norm. The Martians enjoy a liberated sexuality, free from repressive morality if not from emotional complexity. It is a vision rather like that of Bolshevik feminist Alexandra Kollontai. Martian medicine is of course advanced. They practice blood transfusion as a restorative therapy.[20] Bogdanov here has an uncanny intimation of posthuman techniques via which the tissues of the human body will pass transversally from body to body.[21] It is a field to which he will even contribute himself in the last stage of his own life.

On Mars, labor has become fully socialized. The human narrator can barely perceive what labor has become for the more advanced Martians: "To the outsider the threads connecting the delicate brains of the men with the indestructible organs of the machines were subtle and invisible."[22] Bogdanov's tract constructs a utopia of near-frictionless, computer-coordinated labor, to bracket off the class struggle of our own Earth, and show how it masks another struggle, between labor and nature. It is perhaps the earliest vision of a kind of cyber-communism as a new mode of production based on a more efficient and effective mode of information than the market.[23]

Bogdanov's utopia is not a Platonist stasis. The struggle in and against nature continues. As a Martian explains to the gob-smacked human visitor: "Happy? Peaceful? Where did you get that impression? True, peace reigns among men, but there cannot be peace with the natural elements."[24] Like H. G. Wells before him, Bogdanov grasped the significance of Darwin for utopian writing, which could no longer posit ideal states beyond the horizon of historical time. The utopian after Darwin had to be more of a storm-tossed ship than an eternal city on the hill.

For the Martians, the canal-building project came at a terrible price: "Only seventy years ago, when our coal reserves were exhausted and the transition to hydroelectric power was still far from complete, we were forced to destroy a considerable portion of our forests in order to give us time to redesign our machines. This disfigured the planet and *worsened the climate for decades*."[25]

That clearing forests could have a *local* effect on climate was understood at the time.[26] The doctor in Chekhov's *Uncle Vanya* (1897) gets in a whole speech about it. Bogdanov grasps the molecular relation between clearing and burning forests, changing the atmosphere and hence changing the climate, although of course he imagines the Martian climate to be essentially the same as the Earth's. What is not clear is whether Bogdanov was starting to grasp the global implications.

In their search for new sources of energy, the Martians' choice is to get it from Earth or from Venus. The former is technically easier, but involves the destruction of human life. Even socialist Mars contemplates extermination when it is running out of energy while trying to mitigate climate change. Fortunately their organizational culture is richer than that, and the option is not pursued. For Bogdanov, violence is a logical choice at lower levels of organization, but not at higher ones—a theme that will reappear in Robinson, and in Platonov in a far more desperate form.

The Martians are interested not just in science and technology but also in a new kind of art: the *tragedy of the totality*. Bogdanov: "The struggle between classes, groups and individuals precludes both the idea of the whole and the happiness *and suffering* implied by the notion."[27] The exploitation of class by class is one of the fetishes to be overcome in the struggle to organize the totality of human effort, in and against a world that resists the labors of our species-being. But there is no end to this more basic story, this natural history without end. Bogdanov uses the utopian literary form to write from the point of view of labor, but not limited to the labor point of view as capital limits and contains it. The happiness and suffering of the whole is at the heart of Bogdanov's whole teaching.

Labor has to aspire, through art and science, to the tragedy of the totality.[28] *Red Star* aims not just to equip the labor movement with some intimation of its goals, but to suggest that labor's struggle is in its origin and ends not fundamentally against the ruling class, but is rather the quest to find and found a totality within which to cultivate the surplus of life. Is that not still the great task of labor?

The systematic thought of forms and environments "was excluded from the minds of the old classes by the divisibility of their existence and the separateness and one-sidedness of their experience."[29] But this view of the joy and suffering of the totality is something toward which even the proletariat has to work. It has to overcome its own fetishes and understand not just its own activities but the totality of activities from the labor point of view. This was the project for which Bogdanov would later construct his tektology, which has the singular merit of finding a unique form for such an inquiry, even if the fate of that writing was decades of oblivion, thanks to Lenin and his successors.

It is notable that in *Red Star*, Bogdanov already has inklings of the workings of the Carbon Liberation Front and its relation to climate. He anticipates the possibility of Martian (and hence of human) generated climate change at a time when the theoretical possibility was starting to occur to climate scientists, even though the *infrastructure* did not exist yet for measuring or computing climate models.[30] The Martians of *Red Star* already possess a global knowledge concord, frictionless data gathering, and computational power that Earthly climate science would finally acquire by the late twentieth century. With that infrastructure in place, the Martians found then what humans have found only now—that collective labor transforms nature at the level of the totality.

In parallel to the writing of his utopia and its prequel, Bogdanov undertook two other important literary tasks. He was the general editor of the translation into Russian of all three volumes of Marx's *Capital*, which appeared between 1907 and 1910.[31] These would become standard translations in the Soviet Union—even if Bogdanov's name was removed from them. Soviet dogma would later ritually accuse Bogdanov of "idealist" heresies, but the fact is he knew his Marx better than most, and traces of Marx's metabolic thinking, especially from the third volume of *Capital*, show up in Bogdanov's thought.

Bogdanov also set to work redacting his empirio-monist philosophy into a compact volume. The result, *The Philosophy of Living Experience*, came out in 1913, around the same time as *Engineer Menni*. Bogdanov had by then given up on exile politics and returned to Moscow. In his more philosophical writings he would flesh out what was only implied in the science fiction novels: the worker and engineer alliance, the labor point of view, the neither dialectical nor materialist Marxism, and the qualified optimism about the task of revolution. And this is why it is important: given that we may still need some sort of revolution to head off the Carbon Liberation Front, these ideas may help us to equip ourselves with some other elements of Bogdanov's program.

THE PHILOSOPHY OF LIVING EXPERIENCE

The Philosophy of Living Experience sketches the program with which Bogdanov could move forward, out of philosophy into a new practice of knowledge.[32] Within philosophy, Bogdanov's thought is a species of *monism*, which holds that there is only one substance. But this is for him a point of departure from philosophy, since it has no special method for knowing it. *The Philosophy of Living Experience* is a step toward a *tektology*, a new way of organizing knowledge, and a new practice of culture, called *proletkult*. These are still key steps toward the practice of a molecular red knowledge of the kind we need today.

Bogdanov is not really trying to write philosophy so much as to hack it, to repurpose it for something other than the making of more philosophy. Philosophy is no longer an end in itself, but a kind of raw material for the design and organizing, not quite of what Foucault called discourses of power/knowledge, but more of practices of laboring/knowing.[33] The projected audience for this writing is not philosophers so much as the organic intellectuals of the working class, exactly the kind of people Bogdanov's activities as an educator-activist had always addressed. Having clearly read his Nietzsche, Bogdanov's decision is that if one is to philosophize with a hammer, then this is best done, not with professional philosophers, but with professional hammerers.

Bogdanov's practice is a *détournement* of philosophy for other purposes. Détournement, a term developed by the Situationists, refers to the practice of taking all of past culture and knowledge to be a commons, as always and already belonging to all of us.[34] If the Marxist tradition is a critique of bourgeois property, then property in knowledge is also an object of critique. It turns out Bogdanov had his own critique of bourgeois property in knowledge, and indeed some distinctive practices of détournement.

Bogdanov is not interested in what is unique to any given subjectivity, which is likely to be based on only very specific kinds of activity in the world. His interest is in two kinds of collective knowing: folk knowledge and scientific knowledge.[35] Both are in their own ways verified and corrected by forms of collective praxis. Take for example the folk knowledge embedded in proverbs. "Many hands make light work" is a condensation of the experience of collective labor, as is "too many cooks spoil the broth." Folk knowledge from a given stage of the development of organized labor about the capacities and limits of cooperation is embedded in the tension between these two incompatible proverbs.

Whatever their limitations, such proverbs might hold more organizational thought than certain kinds of formal philosophy. Professional philosophers have over time become detached from other kinds of labor and from everyday life. Philosophy becomes just the study of thought, and forgets its real subject, which is the entirety of human experience. To the extent that philosophy has responded to other kinds of activity, whether of labor or science, it has been by trying to subsume them or even legislate what is proper for them. A critical theory can become hypocritical theory if it attempts to dominate other forms of knowing from other modes of collective experience.

As great a work as Marx's *Capital* is, it is not the work of an individual author, but the product of collective experience. The author is the codifier of the social activity of a class:

> Marx utilized a huge amount of material that was gathered before him by both learned and practical people. He applied perfected methods of treatment, which were also partly created and partly prepared by the efforts of innumerable investigators. And he unified and tied together all the ideas that express the direction of the entire development of contemporary society. In a word, we have a conscious and systematic verification of the ideas of all existent collective experience, consciously and systematically organized according to collectively elaborated methods.[36]

Or, in short, the achievement understood under the rubric of "Marx" is not that of an individual genius, but of a collective process—a "science," broadly understood.

A *science* is that which comprehends the whole of a given domain of collective experience as fully as is possible within the social organization and technical apparatus of its time. The scientific point of view is that which corresponds to the highest level of development of an era. There are no universal or eternal forms. Bogdanov: "There can be no absolute and eternal philosophical truth."[37] Universals are projections beyond the limit of a given experience into a *worldview*, which may be expressed in literature or philosophy or religion.[38] This is not, however, a species of relativism. Some worldviews are more general than others. And while regression is possible, successful worldviews are usually more and more general, grasping more and more of a totality. A worldview overshoots the science of its time, and may either lead it or mislead it.

Science, philosophy, and everyday experience ought to converge as the proletariat grows. Bogdanov: "When a powerful class, to which history has entrusted new, grandiose tasks, steps into the arena of history, then a new philosophy also inevitably emerges."[39] Marx's work is a step in this direction, but only a step. Proletarian class experience calls for the integration of forms of specialized knowledge, just as it integrates tasks in the labor process. More and more of life can then be subject to scientific scrutiny. The task of today's thought is to integrate the knowledge of sciences and social sciences that expresses the whole of the experience of the progressive class forces of the moment.

Bogdanov: "The philosophy of a class is the highest form of its collective consciousness."[40] As such, bourgeois philosophy has served the bourgeoisie well, but the role of philosophy in class struggle is not understood by that class. It wanted to universalize its own experience. But philosophies cannot be universal. They are situated. The philosophy of one class will not make sense to a class with a different experience of its actions in the world. Just as the bourgeoisie sponsored a revolution in thought that corresponds to its new forms of social practice, so too organized labor must reorganize thought as well as practice.

The *basic metaphor* is the naming of relations in nature after social relations.[41] It can be found "at work" in the theory of *causality*, the centerpiece of any worldview. *Authoritarian causality* had its uses: it allowed the ordering of experience, and reinforced authoritarian cooperation in production. Worldviews that assume authoritarian causes when none were observed usually invoke invisible spirit authorities as causes. Horatio obeys Hamlet; Hamlet obeys his father's ghost. Matter is subordinated to spirit. Thus the slave model of social relations became a whole ontology of what is and ever could be.

Bogdanov makes the striking argument that religion was the scientific worldview of its time. The old holy books are veritable encyclopedias, somewhat arbitrarily arranged, on how to organize farming, crafts, sexuality or aged-care. This was a valid form of knowledge so long as an authoritarian organization of labor prevailed. But as technique and organization changed, "religious thinking lost touch with the system of labor, acquired an 'unearthly' character, and became a special realm of faith."[42] There was a detachment of authority from direct production. Religion then becomes an objective account of a partial world.

Bogdanov thinks it no accident that the philosophical worldviews that partially displaced religion and authoritarian causation arose where mercantile exchange relations were prevalent—among the Greeks.[43] Extended exchange relations suggest another causal model, *abstract causality*. Buyers and sellers in the marketplace come to realize that there is a force operating independently of their will, but operating in the abstract, as a system of relations, rather than acting as a particular cause of a particular event.

This is an advance on authoritarian causation, but it will in turn reveal its limitations in the light of more advanced forms of social organization:

> in exchange relations economic necessity—external to people and foreign to them—determines both their actions and the objective results of those actions. The nature and origin of economic necessity

will remain unknown to people because they find themselves struggling with other commodity producers in the marketplace, and they cannot see the social collaboration which is hidden beneath this struggle. Society as a laboring whole exists outside the boundaries of their thought; each producer can only see his separate, partial business. Thus producers are unable to understand the force of the social relation which hangs over them. They do not see the living *economic connection of people* and instead conceive of it as necessity—only empty, naked, abstract necessity without any concrete social content. This is how economic causality appears to the commodity producer.[44]

Nevertheless, philosophy remained a mix of authoritarian and abstract causal models. Within this mix, abstract causality was the progressive development. It posited an infinite set of cause-effect sequences governed by a necessity at once both logical and natural. Yet this causality remains abstract. It is often posited metaphorically as a law, as if nature itself was a judge banging a gavel.

Each successive worldview formalizes the experience of the class to which that experience belongs. Bogdanov's empirio-monism is based on the experience of labor, and points beyond the limits of exchange society. One of his more interesting arguments is that *both* idealist and materialist philosophies fall short of the labor point of view, as both approach the world as an object of contemplation. Idealism takes the organization of social relations as its model for thought, while materialism tries to bypass social relations and take the relations of the natural world as its object of contemplation.

Materialism at least has the advantage of being closer to labor as *praxis*, as living activity, and to be destabilized by the periodic developments of new natural scientific knowledge and new labor processes. The problem with materialism is that it tends toward purely abstract accounts of nature. It makes matter primary being, but as a thing apart.

Twenty-first-century materialisms are no different in this regard. Slavoj Žižek: "Materialism has nothing to do with the assertion of the inert density of matter; it is, on the contrary, a position which accepts the ultimate Void of reality—the consequence of its central thesis on the primordial multiplicity is that there is no 'substantial reality', that the only 'substance' of the multiplicity is Void."[45] Here are all the old vices. Here is authoritarian causation, in the form of a first principle, outside of labor, the everyday, or scientific investigation, not to be further questioned, a principle of which now philosophers rather than priests have some special knowledge.

Rather than such a contemplative materialism, Bogdanov, like Marx, wants an active one, an account based on the social production of human existence. Bogdanov: "Nature is what people call the endlessly unfolding field of their labor-experience."[46] Nature is the arena of labor. Neither labor nor nature can be conceived as concepts without the other. They are historically co-produced concepts.

The being of nature is not something a philosophy can dogmatically claim to know. It is not void, or matter; it is whatever appears as resistance in labor. Bogdanov changes the object of theory from nature in the abstract to the practices in which it is encountered and known: "The system of experience is the system of labor, all of its contents lie within the limits of the collective practice of mankind."

Take thermodynamics as an example. Industrialization runs on carbon. Demand for carbon in the form of coal meant that miners dug deeper and deeper. Pumping water out of deep mines becomes an acute problem, and so the first application of steam power was for pumping water out of mines. Out of the practical problem of designing steam-driven pumps arises the abstract principles of thermodynamics as a science.[47] Thermodynamic models of causation then become the basic metaphor for thinking about causation in general, extended by substitution to explain all sorts of things.

There are at least two levels of labor activity: the technical and the organizational. Both have to overcome resistance. Technical labor has to overcome the recalcitrance of matter itself. Organizational labor has to overcome the emotional truculence of the human components of a laboring apparatus. Its means of motivation is *ideology*, which for Bogdanov has a positive character, as a means of threading people together around their tasks. What the idealist thinker unwittingly discovers is the labor-nature of our species-being—ideology as organization and the resistance to it—a not insignificant field of experience, but a partial one.

Before Marx, neither materialists nor idealists oriented thought within labor. The materialists thought the ideal an attribute of abstract matter; the idealists thought matter an attribute of an abstract ideal. Both suffer from a kind of *abstract fetishism*, or the positing of absolute concepts that are essences outside of human experience and that are its cause. Bogdanov: "An idea which is objectively the result of past social activity and which is the tool of the latter, is presented as something independent, cut off from it."[48] This abstract fetishism arises from exchange society. Causation moves away from particular authorities, from lords and The Lord, but still posits a universal principle of command.

This is why Bogdanov takes his distance even from materialist philosophy before Marx, for it still posits an abstract causation: matter determines thought, but in an abstract way. Whether as "matter" or "void," a basic metaphor is raised to a universal principle by mere contemplation, rather than thought through social labor's encounters with it. The revival in the twenty-first century of philosophies of speculative objects or vitalist matter is not a particularly progressive moment in Bogdanovite terms.

The labor point of view has to reject ontologies of abstract exchange with nature.[49] Labor finds itself *in and against* nature. Labor is always firstly in nature, subsumed within a totality greater than itself. Labor is secondly against nature. It comes into being through an effort to bend resisting nature to its purposes. Its intuitive understanding of causality comes not from exchange value but from use value. Labor experiments with nature, finding new uses for it. Its understanding of nature is historical, always evolving, reticent about erecting an abstract causality over the unknown.

The labor point of view is a monism, yet one of plural, active processes. Nature is what labor grasps in the encounter, and grasps in a way specific to a given situation. Marx: "The chief defect of all hitherto existing materialisms . . . is that the thing, sensuousness, is conceived only in the form of the object of contemplation, but not as sensuous human activity, practice, not subjectively."[50]

The basic metaphor, the one which posits an image of causality, is just a special instance of a broader practice of thought. All philosophies explain the world by metaphorical *substitution*.[51] A great example in which Marx himself participates would be the way *metabolism* moves between fields, from respiration in mammals to agricultural science to social-historical metabolism. Substitution extends from the experience of either nature or labor as resistance (materialism or idealism). But in either case, progress in knowledge is limited. The result tends to be the thought of activity without matter or of matter without activity. This is the problem which "dialectical materialism" imagines itself to have solved, although it has done so only abstractly.

Materialism is concerned with a larger portion of experience and is hence more progressive and more general, but it still falls short of the labor point of view. Materialist thought evolves as the material base evolves. For Bogdanov, the history of materialism is the history of philosophy, for materialism in philosophy is a kind of labor unconscious.

How can thought get outside of its cloistered world, into the great outdoors? The dogmatic philosophers who preceded Kant had no trouble erecting various metaphysics of the absolute. Kant brought thought back to its conditions of possibility as thought, and barred the way to a direct knowledge of the thing-in-itself. Philosophy would no longer pronounce on what is, but rather on the limits to what can be known about what is. What can be known is what correlates with what a subject can know.

The limit to what a subject can know is henceforth the proper jurisdiction of philosophy. Kant put paid to philosophy's claims to a knowledge of the absolute, but in so doing substituted the image of philosophy as judge of the conditions of thinking scientifically at all. As such, philosophy trapped only an image of the labor specific to science, one caught in the correlation of the object of thought with the subject that thinks it, or some other dualism like it.

Actual sciences, little by little, began working through an *apparatus* capable of registering sensations that extended far beyond the scale and scope of the human. Science became not just a way of objectively recording what the subject senses, but of recording also what a subject could never sense: scales way below the molecular or above the solar system; times faster even than thought, or epochs billions of years before the perceiving subject—before this only life we know—existed.[52]

Bogdanov rightly saw Mach as pointing to a way out of Kant's legislative edicts. Mach and the empirio-critics fused the object and subject of knowledge into one substance—*sensation*. Quentin Meillassoux: "They acknowledged correlationism's discovery of a fundamental constraint—viz., that we only have access to the for-us, not the in-itself—but instead of concluding from this that the in-itself is unknowable, they concluded that the correlation is the only veritable in-itself."[53] It remained only for Bogdanov to connect sensation back to labor, to the experience of the collective and historical task of its production. This is the passage from the empirio-criticism of Mach to the *empirio-monism* of Bogdanov.

Empirio-monism will emerge as a synthesis of the philosophies of Marx and Mach, which Bogdanov takes to be the advanced forms of the point of view respectively of industrial labor and scientific labor. Or, in twenty-first-century terms, workers and hackers, where the latter includes all kinds of non-routine scientific, technical and intellectual labor, whose object is not determined in advance as it is in industrial labor.[54]

In Bogdanov's reading, the central category in Mach and his empirio-critical school is sensation, but not as individual sensation. Sensation is an undecidable assemblage of sense impressions and material forms. Bogdanov: "The empirio-critics strove to overcome the duality of things and psychical facts, to advance philosophical thought towards realism, towards living experience, from which it has been separated."[55] The only material with which knowledge works is sensation, and the goal of knowledge is finding an orientation within that experience.

All elements of experience are continuous with each other. The empirio-critic begins with the critical method of breaking experience up into elements, with the goal of describing integrated wholes. The basic metaphor of causality is *functional dependency*: this happens and then that happens. Bogdanov reads this basic metaphor in Mach as a materialist causality, but of a still rather abstract kind.

For Mach, knowledge *describes* experience and orders it, but it doesn't intend to change it. This worldview expresses the role of technical and scientific labor, particularly in the new research institutes of the time, and the emerging organizational role of the intellectual in production.[56] It is a world of intellectual workers, detached from that social labor with direct experience of the resistance of nature. Theirs is a fetishistic abstraction—an imagining of the resistance of nature in formal terms only, like in a lab experiment.

The scientist's experience of labor relations was still an authoritarian one. Hence the persistence of dualities of thought, of forms of idealism, and of the tendency to see the world as subordinate to abstract schemes. Mach's thought is still that of his class, although not in a simple way. It is partly limited to causal models drawn from the exchange relations of advanced capitalism. It is also partly drawn from the authoritarian habits in relation to that labor which works more directly on resistant nature in the laboratory.[57]

The kind of dialectical materialism in which Lenin so devoutly believed was not for Bogdanov a particularly plausible alternative to these sorts of spontaneous philosophy of the scientific and technical workers. The dialectic is an idealist residue within an otherwise active and materialist theory. Marx's dialectic was unreal and still abstract, imposed from without, falling short of a metaphor which could substitute for any and every experience of process. The dialectic is not a universal method, as Hegel and Marx still maintained. It is only a cognitive model taken from human organizational experience, and from a narrow realm of experience at that.

Bogdanov: "Idealism by its nature does not know real, sensuous activity."[58] German idealism came up with an active process, but it is an explanation which substitutes the logic of ideas for living practices. With Hegel it at least rose to the level of systematizing this zone of experience. Feuerbach tried to turn philosophy away from the self-developing idea to the self-development of the species-being of man in and against resisting nature.[59] But Feuerbach retreats to the petit-bourgeois scale of the family and affective life. He gets beyond individualism—even the individualism writ large of Hegel—but does not get to collective labor. He does not make the transit from molar to molecular perceptions of experience that comes with the labor point of view.

Labor as social activity, in and against nature, is what is central to Marx, not an abstract concept of material nature. He grasped that matter and activity are not just correlates but aspects of the same—monistic—process. He moves beyond Hegel's ideal contradictions to concrete forces at work. But his dialectic was still idealist. There is a limit to explaining the world through struggles of opposites, which substitute the form of linguistic relations for all other relations.[60]

While sympathetic to Joseph Dietzgen, the worker-philosopher, Bogdanov did not think it progress to retreat from Marx's engagement with Hegel to Spinoza, which resulted in an even more abstract and contentless monism. Dietzgen was, however, the source for Bogdanov's idea that there could be specifically proletarian class-forms of thought, or *proletkult*.[61] Dietzgen's achievement, like Marx's, is neither the dialectic nor materialism, but the *labor point of view*.

Bogdanov saved his critical attention for the so-called dialectical materialism of Lenin and Plekhanov, where "man and his consciousness are posited as the passive product of external matter. This is that reflective relationship which was characteristic of all old materialisms and against which Marx asserted himself. Matter is an object of human activity . . ."[62] The dogmatic insistence on the causal priority of matter as thing-in-itself places matter outside of experience. It becomes an article of faith. An authoritarian causal first principle—that the world is made of matter—is simply asserted.

This is contrary to the scientific worldview and practice, where a knowledge of matter is to be produced by experiment with an apparatus rather than through contemplation alone. Such scientific methods are not really explained by the dialectic. The problem with dialectical materialism is that it doesn't criticize the dialectic in the light of labor and scientific experience. The dialectic describes only a part of the organizational whole, the molar struggle for authority of rival ideas for organizing labor. It does not necessarily also explain labor's experience in and against nature.

Bogdanov's empirio-monism is a critique of the dialectic, but one which takes from Marx the active worldview and the collective experience of the proletariat. The starting point is a realistic view of activity and what resists it. The sensation of matter is a product of social activity, not a thing-in-itself. The practice of knowledge is to search for explanations of processes, and its aim is nothing less than *organizing the world*. Organizational processes can move from less to more complexity, but are not necessarily dialectical.

Bogdanov: "Elements of the dialectic may be found almost everywhere, but life and movement are not exhausted by them. Philosophy must, consequently, conceive of its task in the broadest and most general form: to research the bonds of the world process in order to discover all possible ways and means of organization. Such is the basic notion of Empirio-monism."[63] It is a low theory of the discovery and communication of potential forms of organization between different experiences in a comradely way.

The labor point of view calls for a thought which embodies its ambitions. Bogdanov: "Dialectical materialism was the first attempt to formulate the working-class point of view on life and the world."[64] But not the last. Strikingly, the labor point of view implies a new understanding of causality. The apparatuses of both modern science and machine production generate new experiences of causation. As in modern chemistry, labor can interrupt and divert causal sequences. Matter is not a thing-in-itself beyond experience, but a placeholder for the not-yet-experienced.

Bogdanov's example is the concept of energy, which is neither substance nor idea but whose discovery emerges out of the practical relationship of the labor apparatus to a nature which resists it. Energy is not *in* coal or oil, but an outcome of an activity of labor on these materials. Bogdanov: "Labor causality gives man a program and a plan for the conquest of the world: to dominate phenomena, things, step by step so as to receive some from others and by means of some to dominate others."[65]

Here Bogdanov retains a rather authoritarian worldview, but imposed on nature, rather than on a subordinate class. That there can be unintended effects of such interventions on a resistant nature has not quite occurred to him as a concept, even though he intuits it, as shown in the peak energy and climate change problems confronting his Commie Martians in *Red Star*. Bogdanov has not entirely overcome the authoritarian streak in his own activity. He may not be a Leninist, but he still thinks like a Bolshevik. His thought is marked by the organizational limits of his times. But then, as good Bogdanovites, we know all philosophies are bound to their era and do not touch the eternal. Or as Guy Debord once put it: "Theories are made to die in the war of time."[66]

TOWARD A COMRADELY POETICS OF
KNOWLEDGE AND LABOR

While rejecting Bogdanov's residual attachment to an authoritarian relation of collective labor to nature, his practices of organization still have something to recommend them, and are worth a little further elaboration. The elements of experience have to be not only efficiently named but also combined in new ways with a view to new or better labor processes. This is the seed of Bogdanov's idea of a practice of tektology. Neither a theory or a science, tektology is a practice which generalizes the act of substitution by which one thing is understood metaphorically via another.[67] It is a practice of making worldviews.

Rather than unconsciously using metaphors borrowed from authoritarian or exchange relations, the wager of tektology is that it might be possible to construct a kind of low theory whose purpose is to experimentally apply understandings of one process to other quite different processes to see if they can be grasped as analogous. It is a kind of détournement that works "sideways," from field to field, rather than from past to present.

For Bogdanov, labor is first physical, then mental. Physical labor is always social, whereas psychic labor is always negotiating the idiosyncratic philosophies of individuals. What is objective is what is socially agreed. A certain trade-off comes at this point if one thinks empirio-monism consistently. The physical world *as we know it* cannot be thought as preceding our labors upon it. The world is not absolute or eternal, even if, at each moment in the history of social labor, objective worldviews form that claim certain things are absolute and eternal.

What appears *objective* is the product not of thought alone but of the social labor apparatus of all kinds. Bogdanov insists that no "reality" limits social labor in advance, as limits are discovered in practice. Here he is expunging residues of the Gods, even from within materialism. A really consistent "materialism" cannot claim to speak of the nature of the world in advance of practices in and against it. Bogdanov: "the practical organization of labor effort precedes the mental organization of the elements of experience and produces it."[68]

As we shall see later, an example is the evolution of climate science. It has three elements: predicting the weather, modeling the climate, and the physics of how both weather and climate work. It took many decades to bring all three together. Gathering timely weather data from disparate locations and altitudes requires a huge, global apparatus. Crunching that data with an accurate model of the physics takes a vast amount of computational power. Data, communication, and computational resistances impeded the study of climate until the late twentieth century. At the base of our contemporary knowledge of climate, and climate change, is an evolution from discrete fields and technologies to a global climate knowledge infrastructure, requiring coordinated global labors, or in Bogdanov's terms, a kind of tektology.[69]

While our worldview is always partial and limited, bound by the labor practices of our time, some perspectives are better than others. Some correspond to more advanced, in the sense of more general, forms of labor activity. In Bogdanov's time, it appeared as if the industrial working class was the avant-garde of organizational practice. In our own time, Kim Stanley Robinson suggests that the scientific, technical *and* creative work of hackers occupies such a position. The Bogdanovite challenge is to think from the point of view of the most advanced, general and complex forms of social activity.

Labor may well take different forms than it did in Bogdanov's time, but his key method for making a low theory that passes between forms of labor may still apply. *Substitution* is the method of systematizing labor's various experiences. The means of organizing labor process A may turn out to be helpful for process B. Substitution is a kind of détournement, by which the formal properties of any given activity can become the experimental template for any other. The product of the sum of all labors belongs to the laboring classes as a whole.

So too the *conceptual product* of any particular encounter with resistant nature belongs to all, and can inform the invention of yet more kinds of organization through an experimental practice of substitution. Substitution is part of an experimental process for finding out which discoveries and inventions of labor can be generalized. The concept of fluid dynamics, which proved so useful for engineering A-bombs, is also at work in climate science, not to mention other fields of application. Bogdanov: "Substitution in general strives to replace lesser contents with greater, permitting more combinations in consciousness such that the material for processing will be richer, and, at the same time, to replace complexes more simple and strictly organized with less structured, less organized complexes such that the resistance to the processing activity will be less."[70]

Labor causality and substitution are two versions of the same proposition. No substitution is forbidden in advance. Each production of a causal series by labor points to other possible causal series. Bogdanov, who was not a particularly poetic writer, nevertheless advocates a poetics of knowledge formation. This will become his tektology, which is at heart a poetics of the experimental substitution of one relation for another which in turn has to be tested in practice. Not all substitutions will work. For instance, there is a limit to how much *metabolism* will explain about agricultural chemistry or the totality of collective labor.

Empirio-monism is a worldview that frees our species-being from external a priori forms. Philosophy codifies present reality and no other. It metaphorically substitutes a class interest and experience toward the world.[71] Philosophy is scientific when based on collective experience. From the labor point of view, philosophy is not of especial interest as a high theory, a specialized domain which produces knowledge of the world through the systematic production of relations within language. Rather, it can become a low theory, whose task is to extract from particular labor processes those diagrams of form and relation that might have experimental application elsewhere.

Or rather, this low theory is what replaces philosophy now that its Gods—authoritarian and abstract causality—are passing from the objective reality of the world as labor makes and remakes it. Philosophy is not the form of knowledge with which we need ultimately be concerned. It's a step toward something else. Bogdanov: "No effort of thought can gather and organize the parts of a shattered body into a living whole. Philosophy cannot work miracles."[72] The detour of critical theory through philosophy can come to an end, not because the problems of philosophy have been "solved," but because in the Anthropocene labor and science have other problems. Not the least of which is the challenge of the Carbon Liberation Front.

The form of knowledge that the present requires is determined by forms of social labor and the kinds of resistance it encounters. Automation requires knowledge beyond immediate experience. Bogdanov thought that as automation advanced, all workers would become more like engineers, and also more like artists—like the Martians in *Red Star*. In the Bogdanovian future, workers cease to be workers, organizers of their particular labor alone, but become co-creators of the whole of social organization. The science and poetics of organization become the tools for changing the world, superseding philosophy.

Bogdanov did not anticipate deskilling, or the counter-attack via which capital used technology to prevent the accumulation of knowledge by workers in the workplace.[73] He did not anticipate that the ruling class would so effectively co-opt the surpluses of time and information, let alone of life. Bogdanov's thought appears limited to his time in at least three respects.

First, it is limited by the furthest advances of industrial labor of the science of the time. Second, Bogdanov expunged authoritarian relations within proletarian knowledge and labor practice, but not between labor and nature. Third, tektology clearly implies the dissolution of philosophy as the system-building of the master thinker into a low theory that is collectively and collaboratively produced, and yet Bogdanov cannot quite stop himself from engaging in a system-building that overshoots the limits of his own core principles. Still, he makes a great case for empirio-monism as the last *necessary* philosophy, and tektology as the beginning of something else.

For labor to becoming self-organizing is for labor to acquire not just a knowledge of technical labor but also to take over the functions of organizational labor from the bourgeoisie. Labor has to acquire its own practices of coordination on larger and larger scales. The Russian revolutions of 1917 directly posed the problem of just how much of the social formation organized labor could claim to manage, and how. Before a *tektology* of organizing the material world can apply, a *proletkult* has to emerge within which workers acquire for themselves the confidence to organize the world.

In the era of the Carbon Liberation Front, tektology prefigures a pressing need to coordinate the social labor of confronting metabolic rift. Proletkult prefigures the no less pressing need to elaborate a new folk knowledge of cooperative labor's abilities, limits, and challenges.

RED HAMLET: FROM SHAKESPEARE TO MARX

Something is rotten in the October Revolution. Bogdanov was not alone in this suspicion. It was shared by many of the Russian and European left.[74] Bogdanov worked both in and against the new Soviet state. His critique of the course of events was uncannily accurate, even though his actions were, in the end, futile. His biographer calls him Red Hamlet, and like Hamlet, he had to glide through the superstructures of a new world with rotten roots, speaking in riddles, while the old mole labored away below, undermining it.[75]

One of Bogdanov's more engaging bits of journalism is actually about Shakespeare's *Hamlet*, in which he illustrates how the proletariat can usefully read the classics of the past to help it act within its present condition.[76] It is still a good statement of the Bogdanovite practice of détournement. It has the added charm of functioning as an allegory of Bogdanov's own fate in the Soviet Union. How intentionally he meant it to be read as such we may never know. It remains an allegory for our times, too.

Hamlet is a soul torn between love and struggle. Bogdanov: "What should be done to restore harmony to the soul rent asunder by the sharp conflict between its deepest and sublimest need, and the imperious demand dictated by the hostility of his environment?" The proletariat too has this problem: it wants harmony and unity, but has to struggle with the rift between exchange value and use value. "Little joys have been given it, and great is the thirst for them; but even that little is constantly threatened with destruction or deformation by the inevitable elements of social hatred and anarchy."

By contrast, Hamlet's life has been a good one. Study abroad made him a cultured man, and he has the love of Ophelia.[77] But upon returning to his native land, horror grips him. He finds his family destroyed, his country shattered, a traitor on the throne, the good old customs breached, not honored. Even his mother is in the camp of the enemy. Something must be done, but what? Is he able to accomplish it? He has to be not just an aesthete, but an activist.

Hamlet must resort to tactics hostile to his nature. Bogdanov: "Here is the essence of the tragedy. The struggle demands from Hamlet a resort to cunning, deception, violence and cruelty; but these are repulsive to his mild and refined soul. And more, he has to direct them against his nearest and dearest." This, he cannot do, at least not directly:

> His hand, which is raised for the blow, is stopped; the inner struggle paralyses his will, the momentary resolution gives way to hesitation and inaction, time passes in fruitless meditation—the result is a deep duality and for a time even the wreck of his personality: everything is confused in the chaos of unavoidable contradictions, Hamlet "becomes insane."

An ordinary person would have been crushed in such a situation, yet Hamlet becomes the activist-aesthete, "the champion of the harmony of life." He becomes the example within the everyday that another life is possible. He enacts the good life. "The organizational problem is solved, the artistic idea has been clothed in form." He wagers against the brief, violent time of intrigue with the long loops of everyday culture.

Most prophetically, Bogdanov writes in conclusion: "Hamlet, it is true, perished; and in this the great poet is objectively right, as always. The enemies of Hamlet had this advantage: while he was gathering the forces of his soul, they acted, and prepared everything for his destruction." Bogdanov too will die from a poisoned point.

What Bogdanov constructs within the emerging Soviet spectacle is proletkult, a sort of counter-spectacle, which can say the unsayable while it can still be said, just as Hamlet had his players do. He refuses what he once loved. He refuses to join a world given over to intrigue. He writes the lines, but it is the part of the historical actor, the proletariat, to figure out how to play them. The play's the thing, with which to catch the conscience, not of the king, but of the proletariat itself.

On several key points, he called it: The struggle against capitalism is not the same as the struggle for socialism. The Bolshevik seizure of power in 1917 was premature. Revolutions can be regressive as well as progressive, leading to less rather than more complex organization. The Bolshevik's coercive policy of war communism was no different to the expediencies of other wartime states and was not a step toward socialism. War communism turned the worker's party into a soldier's party. Labor should neither be militarized (Trotsky) nor Taylorized (Lenin). While the peasants had to be appeased, the long-term alliance should be between workers and technical personnel. It is not enough to learn from advanced capitalist culture; socialist forms have to be invented within and against it.[78]

Bogdanov recasts Hamlet's role for a different time in not only creating a counter-spectacle, but in mapping out a pedagogy for how proletarian culture could become self-determining. The task of proletarian culture is the détournement of the past rather than the rejection or admiration of it. The overcoming of bourgeois modes of organization requires a broader grasp of organizational forms. The proletariat had to learn for itself the history of organizational design. This provides the key protocol for how to read the culture of the past.

Shakespeare's *Hamlet* can be usefully read as a work from the last days of the feudal world. It has a double form: the molar form presents a struggle between an illicit hierarchy and a legitimate one, against the backdrop of military maneuverings. On the molar level, the king is to his minions "a massy wheel, fix'd on the summit of the highest mount, to whose huge spokes ten thousand lesser things are mortised and adjoin'd." The molecular form is Hamlet's perception of a quite different organization of matter: "A man may fish with the worm that hath eat of a king, and eat of the fish that hath fed of that worm." Hamlet's madness is in seeing through the huggermugger of courtly mischief to this other scale of organization which knows no ideal hierarchies.

Even the feudal aspect of *Hamlet* does not destroy its legacy for the proletariat. What can be extracted from a Bogdanovite reading of its worldview is something like what Raymond Williams calls a *structure of feeling* of a feudal mode of organization.[79] This is what it feels like to organize the world through authoritarian relations that present themselves as divinely inspired. The play's merit is more than "to show you how a king may go a progress through the guts of a beggar." Or, to show the vanity of that authority that would "go to gain a little patch of ground that hath in it no profit but the name." It might teach as well that no matter what the form of state, "the readiness is all."

It is not as if authoritarian forms belong only in the past. Their study can speak to the present in illuminating ways as well:

> It also becomes clear why the patriarchal petit-bourgeois and peasant family is so attached to religion, to the "law of God"; and at the same time we can see the great danger in the way of social progress that this fecund seed of authoritarianism may represent if it is preserved. A new light is shed upon the role of party leaders, on authorities and the significance of collective control over them.

Marx begins the process of the détournement of the past from the labor point of view, starting with bourgeois economics and its petit-bourgeois critics from Feuerbach to Fourier. Bogdanov: "All this received a new form and was arranged in new combinations, it was turned into a tool for the building of a proletarian organization." Marx extracts molecular flows, of concepts, of evidence, out of the old molar world view of the old ruling class. He continues in no tradition. Quite the reverse. He appropriates textual materials into the labor point of view from the extant discourses of his time.

Marx is not a philosopher or an economist or a sociologist and still less a theologian. He détourns from all of the above, ignoring property and propriety and paternity in the process.[80] He begins a new practice of knowledge from a novel point of view. Bogdanov continues in that vein. He is not faithful to Marxist writ, but détourns Marx and the modern life sciences from the labor point of view, with the same disregard for property and propriety and paternity.

If the proletariat wants different modes of organization to bourgeois ones, then there is a lot to learn from forms of organization that were as different to the bourgeois modes as the proletarian ones aspire to become. "And who else, if not the great and skillful artist, can lead one into the very depths of an alien organization of life and thought?"[81] Bogdanov was perhaps not skilled enough an artist to describe Martian organization, but he was a good enough organizer to create the space where it might come into being of its own accord—the Proletkult movement.

FROM MARX TO PROLETKULT

After the October Revolution, Proletkult had an uneasy relationship with the Commissariat of Enlightenment, headed by Anatole Lunacharsky, Bogdanov's old friend and former comrade of the Capri school days.[82] The Commissariat took over the cultural and educational activities of the old Tsarist state. Proletkult, on the other hand, was interested in a specially proletarian culture. While Lunacharsky was not unsympathetic to Proletkult, his support or tolerance could only be partial. The biggest problem of his ministry—and its biggest success—was in raising levels of literacy. He lent support to a variety of factions and groups on the cultural left, of which Proletkult was only one.

Among the Bolshevik leadership, only Bukharin was at all supportive. Lenin most notably was not. Since Proletkult received its budget from the Commissariat of Enlightenment, and hence from the Bolshevik-controlled state, its desire for an autonomous proletarian culture was always compromised. Still, for a time it aroused considerable enthusiasm, and not least among class-conscious workers themselves. Bogdanov nearly got his version of the counter-spectacle to happen within and against the Bolshevik one.

For Bogdanov, scientists, artists, and philosophers are "organizers of experience" and the proletarian revolution should in turn organize their labors in a certain way.[83] If culture grows out of particular experiences within the relations of production and exchange, then the proletariat could not simply adopt or adapt bourgeois culture. Proletarian culture needed developing, not just as new content within the old forms, but as a new form of culture altogether. Most centrally, proletarian culture had to develop organically out of the experience of collaborative labor. The ethos of bourgeois individualism had grown out of competitive market relations; the ethos of proletarian collaboration would grow out of the sophisticated self-organization of labor in the most advanced industries.

This was hardly an academic question. The Russian Revolution faced an impossible decision in 1917. Put crudely: The proletariat could be mobilized to seize control of strategic assets, but if it moved quickly and alone, its leaders faced the challenge of making a revolution without the help of specialists, technicians, and others of the educated class. This was the Bolshevik policy. The Menshevik policy, at least in its more cogent moments, was to take it slow, to try to forge a united front between the proletariat and the intelligentsia—not unlike what transpired in Bogdanov's imaginary Martian revolution. With the October Revolution, the Bolsheviks seized the initiative, but as a consequence took control of a state and an economy with barely the means to run them.

Proletkult created a network of studios in both the arts and the sciences (although they worked best in the arts). The aim was self-governed activity on the part of workers rather than propaganda or consciousness raising. Proletkult sought liberation from fetishes such as authority, subjectivity, and property. Bogdanov even thought this might be easier in Russia, where everyday life was barely touched by bourgeois norms.

Proletkult was a movement with a mission: to *change labor*, by merging art and work; to *change everyday life*, by developing the collaborative life within the city and changing gender roles and norms; and to *change affect*, to create new structures of feeling, to overcome the emotional friction of organizing the labor that in turn organizes nature around its appetites.

Realizing Proletkult's mission was the aim of a threefold practice:

Creativity—to overturn the fetish of the individual creator; to reveal the role of the unconscious in creation. The newspaper was the model of a collective creativity. One might note that all significant Marxists were also great journalists, and often editors and publishers as well, starting with Marx himself.[84]

Collectivity—to work in groups and express the sensations of group life. Bogdanov did not however want to submerge singularities. His is rather the community those who have nothing in common.[85] His Martians, for example, were far from indistinguishable numbers, and their cooperation is imperfect.

Universalism—to break down the division of labor. This raised the problem of professionalism: should Proletkult have professional artists? When the going gets weird, as it did in the civil war, even as weird a writer as Andrey Platonov could turn pro, although in the end his professional success was meager. Professional specialization remained a conceptual problem for the whole life of the movement.

Proletarian culture is not an end in itself, and in this regard Proletkult is different to most flavors of workerism. It can tend to a certain fetishism of its limited perspective, rather than trying to expand out toward the most general account of the experience of the world. The violent rejection of bourgeois culture is no better than naive atheism. It is not able to put up anything as an alternative. The proletariat needs a point of view through which to assimilate the past. Proletarian détournement is not then a matter of picking out the bits that seem "revolutionary." The proletariat should be self-developing rather than self-mythologizing.[86]

Bogdanov anticipates those who, like Henri Lefebvre, move the focus of proletarian self-determination from the space of the factory alone to the space of everyday life in the city as a whole.[87] The city provides the situations for the development of the labor point of view. It is in the city that the worker can discover that in the struggle against the elements for existence the individual is a node in a web. On their own, workers are powerless playthings of external forces.

The city extends the time and complexity of cooperative action, but it has its limits: "while the masses are gathered in the cities, they become removed from nature. The latter reveals itself to the proletariat only as a force in production, not as a source of live impressions."[88] The proletariat has to learn a more systematic way to organize its experiences.

Bogdanov co-authored a textbook of political economy that came out in 1919, and appears as his major contribution to pedagogy during the revolution.[89] It must have seemed somewhat counterintuitive to Bolsheviks at the time, in its stress on the revolutionary force of capitalism and its role in the development of the forces of production. The discussion centered on the development of an organic social system. As the pioneering Bogdanov scholar Ilmari Susiluoto puts it: "He had set his sights centuries ahead. He could not, therefore, provide exact advice on how a new society should be built. The ideal should be implemented through a prolonged period of learning, in the process of which the collective experience would raise the awareness of the people to a new level."[90]

Bogdanov thought a major area of proletarian learning had to be around new energy systems. Fossil fuels were limited and nonrenewable. Tides and winds had to be harnessed as energy sources, as well as the "internal energy of the atom." The power of the atom would also be a stimulus to more cooperative forms of government.

That cooperative form of government was more a form of what he elsewhere called the *biregulator*, where two systems regulate each other. In this case the two systems are labor and nature, and their relationship one of statistical automation. Bogdanov:

> Since all goal oriented human activity is organizational in character, the organization of natural elements for the benefit of society is a technical process; the organization of experiences is a process of consciousness; the organization of human forces in society is an economic process. All of these join together in principle to form a single organization of socio-productive energy.[91]

The deficit of organizational intelligence made the formation of a proletarian culture, of a new type, a pressing agenda. The prevailing position in the Bolshevik Party was that the political revolution abolished the class basis of culture and made all of the cultural inheritance of the past common property.[92] Bogdanov insisted that culture wasn't just "content" that could be poured into a new form. Culture was itself a series of forms which had a definite class character. The proletariat had to struggle for its own form of culture, which Bogdanov saw as an extension of the commons of collaborative and experimental practice embodied in industrial labor at its most sophisticated.

Proletarian culture had to be more than bourgeois novels and symphonies mass produced for a mass audience by a "socialist" culture industry. It also had to be more than an extension of the Bolshevik propaganda of the revolutionary period, bringing consciousness from without. Proletarian culture should rather grow out of the laboratory that is labor, and the labor that is the laboratory.

This was also different to the avant-garde modernism that flourished in the early days of the Soviet Union, which confined innovation to questions of literary or plastic form. Bogdanov wanted to revolutionize the relations of production of culture, not just literary form or affective content.[93] Proletkult did not mean this or that modernist style of poem or painting. It meant the collaborative production of art, culture, even science, by and for the proletariat itself.

Proletkult was popular in the civil war period, although this may have been in part because the spaces Proletkult commandeered had food and heat.[94] It rapidly became a mass movement, and together with the trade unions, it provided some semblance of balance to the power of the Bolshevik Party within the state. When the civil war turned in the Bolshevik's favor, and the party had less need of equivocal allies, the power of both the unions and Proletkult were seriously curtailed—although that of the Cheka, or secret police—not so much.[95]

Like the French Revolution before it, the Russian Revolution called for an enlightenment, and like that earlier one, it was to be about not just particular ideas but new modes of practicing knowledge. Bogdanov thought a specifically proletarian encyclopedia a worthy project, to redact the sum of existing knowledge with a new kind of reader in mind.

Bogdanov's most ambitious plan for Proletkult was in higher education, and for a brief period he managed to organize a program along the line of his empirio-monism and tektology. In 1919 the Proletarian University opened with 450 students. It was based on the experiments of the Capri school, and had some of the same teachers. It was aimed at adult students, and stressed the equality of teacher and student. It offered a concentrated curriculum that included the basics of both social and natural sciences. Its goal was not just to transmit knowledge but to transform selves. It was not so much a liberal arts college as a social arts college, seeking close alignment with the workplace rather than distance from it.

But with the eclipse of Proletkult, this too was taken from him. Bogdanov kept some of his academic and administrative posts, but the proletariat was not to have its own independent mass organization. Like many other non-Bolshevik intellectuals of the left who had managed to stay out of the hands of the Cheka, at least for now, he was exiled in the university.

Proletkult artists and writers are not as well remembered as other currents from the heady early years of the Soviet Union.[96] Much of what Proletkult achieved is still buried in the archives, waiting for the moment when a collective and common culture can recognize its own precursor. In the meantime, there is at least one writer who emerged out of Proletkult whose work is undeniably great in that recognizably bourgeois form—the genius. The work of Andrey Platonov does not mark the achievement of a new organization of perception and communication (although as we shall see, he proposed one). But he does at least open the door to a new practice of it by his particular example. Platonov is what could be made out of the ruins of what Bogdanov proposed for Proletkult.

While Bogdanov was not to get his own university, his plan for how to organize it, and how it might train the proletariat for the work of this world, remains. And it is still a striking model of how to organize labor and knowledge for interesting times—such as our own. Bogdanov's most extraordinary achievement, however, was his tektology. It is a way of organizing knowledge for difficult times, such as the times of total war, revolution and civil war that Bogdanov experienced, and perhaps also for the strange times likely to come in the twenty-first century, courtesy of the Carbon Liberation Front.

The labor point of view advances along three axes. The first is empirio-monism, a détournement of philosophy aimed at finding in it some practices of organization. The second is proletkult, and the organization of labor through the affective attractions of culture. And the third is tektology, and the organization of the nonhuman world—to which we now turn.

FROM DIALECTICAL MATERIALISM TO TEKTOLOGY

Bogdanov belongs to that generation whose thought responds to the shock of the Great War, when "the command of the most insignificant individual . . . directed millions of people into an unprecedented hell of iron and dynamite . . ."[97] He served as an army doctor during the war. A distressing time, and not least because his training was mostly in psychiatry, not in cauterizing the bloody stumps of severed limbs. Experience taught Bogdanov what a crude form of organization the military was in his day.

Bogdanov: "The world war turned out to be the greatest school of organization."[98] He had written his *Empirio-monism* volumes before and after the 1905 revolution. His second great series of inquiries, the *Tektology*, began in 1913 but received a great impetus from the war and the 1917 revolutions.[99] And just as he had summed up his earlier inquiries in *Philosophy of Lived Experience* (1913) so too his inquiries in tektology resulted in the synthesis of *Essays in Tektology* (1921). The former is a philosophical program for the revolution to come; the latter is an organizational program for a revolution that has come to pass.

Bogdanov thought that the stalemate produced by the February 1917 revolution bespoke a social formation with only a rudimentary organizational capacity. Even on the left, the differences among the rival forces created a deadlock that could only be resolved by force. Thus the *Tektology* is a program for a higher level of organization. If such abilities were not to be found within the Bolshevik state, then Bogdanov could at least formulate a program for higher education that might one day achieve it. He was not without success, for "Bogdanovites" populated key economic and technical bureaux until the time of Stalin.[100]

The word *organ*, from the Greek via the Latin *organum*, can mean a tool, but also a part of the body. The seed of Bogdanov's thought is contained within the metaphorical leap of this primary term. A tool is an external organ of a body; an organ is an internal tool of a body.[101] And as to what then defines a body, when its organs can be outside and tools can be inside—that then gets rather interesting. "If several workers work at one machine, then as far as their system of collaboration is concerned, their relation to this machine, which binds them together, is an internal connection of the system, although this is a relation to a spatially external object."[102] What is inside and outside a system can be different to what is inside and outside an object or body. As we shall see, troubling kinds of fetishism can arise out of perceiving the body and not what organizes behind its appearance.

Bogdanov conceived of organization very broadly, even if part of the impetus was his particular experiences of it: "splits in organizations which occur in the political and cultural life of our epoch, which is full of contradictions, would probably be less frequent, if the leaders always clearly understood that in a partial and temporary separation is inevitably concealed a tendency toward a deeper and irreversible one."[103] It's an observation which could apply to the split between Mensheviks and Bolsheviks, or the further splitting of the Bolsheviks between Lenin and Bogdanov, both of which proved irreconcilable divergences.

In the cultural and scientific domains, Bogdanov wanted to equip the proletariat with the courage and the skill to understand the given world and realize its capacity to transform both that world and itself. Even before the October Revolution of 1917, he saw power not just as a matter of insurrection and seizing or smashing the state. His abiding interest was in the "fate of forms," their emergence, persistence, and dissolution. Bogdanov was a writer in and against his times.[104] He was not in favor of Lenin's seizure of power in October. He viewed with alarm the militarization of the party and state during the civil war.[105]

This stems from the different relation Bogdanov and Lenin had with the proletariat. If, as Gorky put it, the worker was to Lenin what iron ore was to the ironworker, Bogdanov was fascinated by the flux of collective *affect*:

> their strength now crystallizes into an unexpectedly mighty, triumphant transport, now spreads and dissipates into an elemental apathy; at times the success of the boldest plans is achieved with astounding ease, at others it is gained only through the most stubborn and intense efforts. Because of the changeability and instability of the environment, our politician develops a point of view and methods which include shades of utopianism and adventurism.[106]

This might be partly self-criticism, but may also be directed at Lenin, who took the shift of the masses toward the Bolshevik position in late 1917 to be an historical alignment rather than a situational convergence.

Bogdanov's was quite a different way of thinking to Lenin's partisan splits and political leaps: "The working class carries out the organization of things in its labor, and the organization of its human forces in its social struggle. It must connect the experience of both fields into a special ideology; namely, the organization of ideas. Thus, life itself makes the proletariat an organizer of a universal type, and the organizational point of view is a natural and even necessary tendency for it."[107] The only difference between political and economic organization is that the latter is usually more predictable.

The *Essays in Tektology* are the intellectual component of Bogdanov's quiet struggle within the revolution over its fate, and as such are a discourse on forms. Tektology, he said, is "consciously practical."[108] Bogdanov:

Assume that in this case some sensitive and experienced political figure has captured the essence of the situation by the *analogies* which he knows personally from life or history. But he is able to transmit to others neither his knowledge as a whole nor his practical sensitivity, and, therefore, his conclusions are not convincing to others. And, perhaps, the most vital elements would continue to expend their energies in the wrong direction, against the turning point of the wheel of history. Only a scientific organization of experience permits a real proof of such conclusions.[109]

Bogdanov's aim was not a "scientific socialism," but a socialism of science. Based not only on his own experience but on extensive reading in the general scientific literature available at the time, *Essays in Tektology* is essentially a pedagogy in how *forms* emerge, evolve, interact, and decay. Bogdanov treats form as a category entirely independent of scale: "Is it really possible that the same laws can be applied to combinations of cosmic worlds and biological cells, living people and etheric waves, scientific ideas and energy atoms?"[110] He sees exactly this metaphorical work of substitution as an organizing act in itself. It is a prototype of the organizational view of the universe. Tektology first proposes a metaphorical jump from one scale or form of organization to another.

Metaphor is the tektology of the everyday, a movement in language that recognizes the connection and relation of all things, but it has to be subject to verifiable experiment. While more positive about metaphor than Mach, Bogdanov is aware of the possibility that the substitution of ideas from one scale of organization to another that abounds in tektology might be no more than metaphorical.[111] Old habits of thought can lead to false analogies. A bee hive is not presided over by a "queen," for instance. Nevertheless, language arises out of communal labor, and reason arises out of language. Language is where reason *works*.[112] So one of the methods of tektology is to trace metaphor back to the process of its production.

Tektology can also speculatively draw organizational principles out of the particular sciences. "The methods of all sciences are for tektology only modes of the organization of material supplied by experience."[113] Tektology is not a philosophy but a method of organization. It is a very different idea to that of setting up some version of "dialectical materialism" as the universal guarantor of particular knowledge practices. Nevertheless, tektology does have some basic operating assumptions, crystallized out of scientific, political, and everyday life experiences—not least of its founder.

Nature is the first organizer, and the human is just one of its organizational products. Everything is organized in some manner and in some degree. "Complete disorganization is a concept without meaning. It is, in reality, the same as naked non-being." Once we break through the "membranes of fetishism," we discover that "mankind has no other activity except organizational activity, there being no other problems except organizational problems."[114] And indeed, there is no more useful way of thinking the human than as a self-organizing population.

When the whole is more than its parts, there is organization; when there is less, there is disorganization. Bogdanov's concept of organization excludes the positing in advance of a purpose, which he defines as a fetishism. Organization is as organization does. There are no goals or gods. Tektology "is just as alien to morals as it is to mathematics."[115] Mathematics is not ontology; tektology is not theology. Rather, it struggles against the residues of Platonism old and new, ontological and theological.

Tektology diagrams organizational forms and situations, but there are only particular organizations. There's no prior unity or ultimate synthesis, no permanent harmony that they subtend or intend. Not even the revolution can forge a unity of the disparate natural and social forms as if by fiat. Even *Red Mars* has an imperfect way of organizing labor and nature, which can't prevent the exhaustion of fossil fuels or the attendant effects of the Carbon Liberation Front. For Bogdanov, a political revolution is not the solution to anything. It merely enables the problem of organization to be posed. There can be no victory over the sun.[116]

Marx showed how private property and the wage relation turn particular and concrete labors into abstract labor.[117] Concrete labors interact with nature and each other in particular ways, but are subsumed into the same commodity form. The commodity form is not the only form with which to organize the concrete via the abstract. There is another way that concrete labors are connected, and it is via the transfer of techniques. Steam power, for example, arose in one branch of industry (mining) and was transferred to others. Just as there is technology transfer, there is also *tektology transfer*. Forms of organization can migrate from site to site. Tektology is among other things a pedagogy for this other practice of synthesis, outside of the wage relation and the commodity form. Tektology's movement is "towards a monism of organizational experience."[118]

Tektology "was excluded from the minds of the old classes by the divisibility of their existence and the separateness and one-sidedness of their experience."[119] Once the bourgeoisie is surpassed, and with them the fetish of market competition within relations of exchange as the sole recognized organizational principle, tektology can begin in earnest. The bourgeois thinks in terms of the profit on an investment in competition with others; the worker thinks about the enjambment of his or her labor with those in the adjacent lines of the labor process. This for Bogdanov is the basis in everyday life for the organizational outlook. All that comes from without is the pedagogy for realizing what the worker already knows.

There is a pessimism in Bogdanov that is sometimes lacking in his Proletkult followers. Full organization is not possible, and "there is no absolutely harmonious combination."[120] While organizational forms can be improved with conscious study and practice, they are not perfectible. Red Mars has in the end to face up to extinction (and does so in high-phallic style by sending the "seeds" of its culture off on rockets into space). There's a note that pervades Bogdanov's writing where he appears as a detached observer of his own fallibility: "Sometimes it is possible in the same system to observe factually all the transitional steps from the higher organization to the deepest disorganization; as happens, for example, with the gradually unfolding quarrel between close collaborators or between spouses."[121]

"The basic significance of tektology lies in the most general statement of questions." It refuses the unstated demand of the Leninist revival in the West of the twenty-first century, which repeats Mao's slogan "put politics in command" but means by it "put philosophy in command," and takes philosophy to be the language of an ideal state, if not to come, then at least legible in utopian moments such as that of 1917. "Tektology rejects as fruitless scholasticism the . . . philosophical theory of cognition which aims to investigate conditions and modes of cognition not as vital, organizational processes among other processes, but abstractly, as a process which differs essentially from practice."[122] A materialist philosophy is a contradiction in terms, for as philosophy its materialism remains contemplative. Tektology, as a monist approach to knowledge, organizes it. Materialist philosophy is new wine in old bottles; tektology seizes the bottle factory and makes it a cooperative.

Ideologies are not so much "false consciousness" as the "true" limited consciousness of particular modes of organization. For example, dualist beliefs, which separate spirit and matter, are org-charts to authoritarian power, which separates the leader from the led.[123] Or, to give another example: the doctrine of marginal utility, based on the subjective evaluations of atomized units, diagrams the possessive individualism of the market economy and private property. And while he was hardly explicit on the topic, one might imagine that Bogdanov perceived the Bolshevik faith in sacrifice in the name of history as an accurate ideological map to an authoritarian state embarking on a period of primitive accumulation in the context of a hostile peasantry, an exhausted working class and surrounded by imperialist enemies.

Viewed via tektology, the labor theory of value is not true where marginal utility is false, it is rather a form which anticipates a different kind of organization. All those categories that economists—even progressive ones—find superfluous, such as surplus value, use value, and labor power, point to the intractable externality within and against which any economic organization tries to contend.[124]

Call it "nature," but it is a nature that can only be known through particular organizational forms and processes. "For tektology the unity of experience is not 'discovered' but actively *created* by organizational means."[125] An ideology is a mode of substitution specific to a mode of production. Bogdanov finds the roots of this organizational approach to ideology in Marx, "but Marx did not posit the question in a general form."[126]

Marx at least puts three related things on the agenda: the problem of the organization of collective labor, the problem of social needs, and the problem of nature's intractability. Marx's thought is relentlessly metonymic, showing how parts emerge out of wholes and are made back into parts of a transformed whole. His thought is horizontal and historical. Bogdanov's thought is relentlessly vertical and metaphorical, jumping from one whole to another, showing how one whole differs from another.[127]

The result is strange and beautiful sentences, worthy of Platonov, such as: "Conjunction is the assimilation of nourishment which sustains an organism and of poison which destroys it, soft embraces of lovers and mad embraces of enemies, congress of workers in the same trade and a close fight of antagonistic detachments."[128] In so many respects a "bad Marxist," Bogdanov has the singular merit of opening up a whole dimension that is present in a subordinate way in Marx's thought. His is a non-standard Marxism in that it addresses a set of phenomena that includes what Marxism is traditionally thought to cover within a larger domain, but not in the form of a dialectical materialist philosophy.

Marx: "Capitalist production . . . only develops the techniques and the degree of combination of the social process of production by simultaneously undermining the original source of all wealth— *the soil and the worker*."[129] Bogdanov might add two things to this. First, the undermining of the wealth of the soil is obscured for a time by the undermining of the worker. The depletion of the soil—the Phosphorous Liberation Front—emerges only belatedly as a problem for capitalist organization. The solution came firstly by way of "guano imperialism," and then through the development of the chemical industry.[130] The molecular elements stripped from the soil are replenished from elsewhere, at least for a time, and yet the metabolic rift continues.

Second, Bogdanov's concept of these undermining forces operates in a more abstract way. An organization is only as durable as its weakest component. That which disorganizes it could even be molecular. "People . . . are capable of the collective creation of fortresses which can withstand any living enemies but they are not yet able to guard themselves against geological and, even less so, against cosmic crises. We must, therefore, study the question within the limits of its relative solution."[131] If social organization is weakened by the Phosphorous Liberation Front at one moment, it may be the Carbon Liberation Front, or the Nitrogen Liberation Front, at another. The point is not this or that constraint, but that organization has to be thought more generally in terms of such constraints. Marx:

> Large landed property reduces the agricultural population to an ever decreasing minimum and confronts it with an ever growing industrial population crammed together in large towns; in this way it produces the conditions that provoke an *irreparable rift in the interdependent process of the social metabolism*, a metabolism prescribed by the natural laws of life itself.[132]

In the Russia of Bogdanov's time, shifting the population from agriculture to industry seemed an intractable problem. In the twenty-first century, when the global urban population may now outnumber the rural for the first time, talk of "large towns" rather than a *planet of slums* seems quaint.[133]

Still, in his own way, Bogdanov grasped the problem of the *metabolic rift* between economy as organization and nature as environment, as his fable of the Martians makes evident. Tektology was meant to be a design practice for organizing organization, conceived under very real conditions of scarcity and disorganization, but under no illusions that a rosy and harmonious future lay ahead. The Anthropocene makes Bogdanov our contemporary, and the tektology worth a closer look.

TEKTOLOGY AS METAPHORIC MACHINE

At the core of tektology is a handful of concepts: environment, conjunction, linkage, ingression, disingression, boundary, crisis, selection, equilibrium, egression and degression. There is always an *environment*: Bogdanov brackets it off at first to simplify the exposition, in which the primary term is *conjunction*. Before systems can interact, merge or destroy each other, or in short for there to be any kind of tektology, there is first their conjunction. Systems mesh at the margin. Nothing is entirely discrete. This is the basic principle of Bogdanov's monism.

The breaching of a *boundary* starts a conjunction: "revolution is . . . a breach in the social boundaries between various classes . . . ; the boiling of water, a breach of the physical boundary between the liquid and its atmosphere; the propagation of a living cell, the creation of a vital boundary between its parts which acquire independence; death a breach in the living bond of an organism . . ."[134] Cooking is a conjunction of fire and water, labor is a conjunction of "the tender cells of the brain" with aggregates of steel. It is even "possible to coordinate the efforts of two workers who happen to be at the two opposite sides of the earth" by means of a "sufficient number of telegraphic stations."[135]

Linkage is the forging of connections between the elements of different systems, in the zone where they overlap. *Ingression* is the formation of a new system out of that linkage. *Disingression* is the decline of the conjugated system, a situation where these systems "mutually paralyze each other."[136] An *equilibrium* is the stabilizing of a boundary between the two disingressive systems, such as the front line between two armies (and it is entirely characteristic of Bogdanov to think of two contending armies as one system). A *crisis* appears where the linkage of systems produces a disequilibrium.

Bogdanov wants to broaden the meaning of the term *selection* both toward events in the non-living world and events in human culture.[137] All of these are domains for "natural selection," although not of the same kind. There is selection when the climate changes, as some species perish and others thrive. There is selection when a town catches fire, as the stone buildings survive and the wooden ones burn. There is selection in the way the awn on an ear of barley enables it to not only stick to but work its way up the sleeve of a peasant walking across a field.

Conservative selection governs the preservation or destruction of an organization in relation to an environment, where that environment is unchanging. Environment here means the "totality of the external influences under which a system finds itself, but taken exactly in relation to it."[138] Where the organization survives, it is in equilibrium with its environment. But there are few, if any, unchanging environments, so the concept is a stepping-stone to the idea of progressive selection and of dynamic equilibrium, or the preservation of forms in changing environments.

Progressive selection is a change in the number of elements in a system that maintains a dynamic equilibrium with a changing environment. For instance, a drop of dew on a leaf is exchanging molecules of water with the atmosphere. Under certain conditions of temperature, pressure, and humidity, the molecules lost from the drop and those adhering to it are the same. If this was maintained, then it would be a situation of conservative selection. But all of these variables can change, and with them the exchange of molecules between the drop and the atmosphere. Progressive selection prevails, and from the point of view of the droplet, its effect can be positive or negative. It can either add or lose elements from its system. Moreover, the effect is not merely quantitative. If the droplet is diminishing, its form becomes more and more ovoid; if it is growing, it becomes less ovoid and flattens. If it grows some more, then the conjunction of water vapor within the liquid droplet, linking the new molecules with the existing form, may result in a disingression, where a boundary forms and the droplet splits in two.

Bogdanov anticipates those like Franco Moretti who find evidence for a process of selection working also in cultural forms. A culture retains those ideas "which correspond to the permanent and common conditions of its life."[139] The domain of culture operates according to parallel processes of selection as other domains, although it has its own specific forms of tektological movement. "Cognition operates with complexes which are much more plastic; and its field, which has as its base the same field of physical labor, expands much faster and easier. Therefore it develops its chain of ingressions correspondingly faster and easier . . . cognition has long ago arrived at the idea of a continuous connection of all that exists, at the idea of a 'universal ingression.'"[140] Culture opens toward the totality. But it does so in a rather open-ended way.

Tektology as organized labor experiments with the poetic substitutions of universal ingression, to propose social and technical forms, from among which history will select. This was the program intended for the Proletkult labs, and it might not be a bad one for twenty-first-century design practice either. It begins with a kind of détournement of existing forms, then experiments with their application in other domains, before testing out prototypes in situations where users select the most useful and discard the least useful.[141]

What is selected for in the life of organizing ideas is what in the past has enabled collective being to survive. Nothing guarantees that such ideas have eternal survival value, and in any case selection works negatively. Images, metaphors or concepts are preserved "which correspond to the permanent and common conditions of its life, and those disintegrate and disappear which are in opposition to them; this is the selection of social complexes."[142] Even the permanent and common conditions of life can change, however. The question remains of how ideas that in the past were selected out might be tried again under changed conditions.

The main question for Bogdanov is: how to build a program of knowledge oriented not only to survival but to growth in organizational capacities in relation to an environment. Particularly problematic here is that one can't always know in advance where the environment is going to make itself felt. "The total stability of a system in relation to its environment is evidently a complex result of the partial stabilities of its various parts in relation to those influences which are directed against them."[143]

Education based on the assumption of conservative selection can specialize to meet what it knows to be the challenges of maintaining equilibrium in a given environment. But "conservatively formed organisms are stable only in a conservative environment."[144] If the relation to the environment is one of progressive selection, it is much less easy to predict the points at which equilibrium might fail. "What can these hothouse plants put in opposition to the severe blows of actual reality?"[145] A different kind of knowledge is called for, one more flexible and adaptable, which can meet the challenge to survival at any point.

Bogdanov thought that the "replacement of conservative social structures by structures carrying the seeds of progressive development" calls for new kinds of knowledge:

> when comparing two different political or cultural organizations existing within the frame of the same society, it is possible to conclude that one of them is structurally better adapted than another, i.e. more structurally stable. But if social conditions undergo an unusual change, such as a revolution, war or economic crisis, then the correlation will generally turn out to be different, sometimes quite the opposite.[146]

And probably not knowable in advance, outside of historical praxis.

What is revealed in the moment of victory in 1917 is for Bogdanov quite the opposite of what Bolshevik optimism expected to find there. "Capitalism with its crises provides a mass of examples of hidden contradictions which accumulate under conditions of 'prosperity.'"[147] Underneath the quantitative expansion of capital are underlying vulnerabilities. It's a system built on the assumption of conservative selection, which has specialized to meet predicted challenges. It isn't prepared for some rather less predictable ones that war and revolution might uncover.

In theory at least, the victorious proletariat of 1917 no longer confronts the bourgeoisie as a class, but confronts another boundary. The environment with which it has relations appears in a new form.

The entire environment of life on earth, the entire environment in which mankind acts and evolves, with its usual amplitude of fluctuations in the various conditions of its astronomical, atmospheric and other cycles, may be considered as limitedly-changeable; and this means exactly the environment in which changes are scientifically considered in advance, either in their totality or in broad summary conditions.[148]

If the revolution really is the moment of proletarian victory, then those boundaries that are both biospheric and molecular at the same time could come into view—and at the time still appear to be limitedly changeable.

Science and labor together confront the problem of identifying and refashioning the weak points in the interaction of social and natural systems. What changes is that flexibility is needed not just for anticipating and healing internal ruptures within the social, but for ruptures between the social and its external conditions of existence, and not always at sites that are known in advance. This is the field of operation of tektology.

The Soviet Union of the civil war period found itself in an environment of progressive selection. Social relations came apart at the most unexpected places. Everything had to be learned again. One of the main challenges was famine. Bolshevik boot-strapping fell back to earth repeatedly on the inability to make much improvement on the struggle to extract agricultural surplus from the land, and indeed their policies repeatedly made a bad situation even worse, as Bogdanov had predicted. The reversal of policy in 1921, when "war communism" was abandoned in favor of the New Economic Policy, is a striking example of how quickly the struggle within and against nature can ramify through the whole social organization. Bogdanov: "the chain will break at its weakest link."[149]

In *Red Star*, Bogdanov anticipated the possibility that the weakest link would be not so much energy for organic systems but energy for inorganic ones. The Martians destroyed their forests to fuel their industries, and changed their climate. While Bogdanov does not foresee human-engineered climate change as the likely challenge to equilibrium in the *Essays in Tektology*, he certainly understands the dynamics of climate as a system and the kinds of disruptions it can cause: "Climate change occurs in a country: it becomes colder. Of the animals and plants inhabiting it, some are able to endure this change and survive; others perish. As a result, the organization of life on a given territory is regulated in accordance with new conditions."[150]

Animal and plant life are part of a system characterized by both divergence and complementarity. *Divergence* is a refinement of the Epicurean concept of the swerve and a primitive attempt at a concept of a chaotic system. Small variations in initial conditions can lead to divergent transformations of otherwise almost identical systems. Small variations in otherwise comparable states in the weather produce wildly diverging patterns with a short space of time. Or, over a much larger time scale, plants and animals are two of several forms of life that started to diverge from initially small variations on a common ancestor, starting some 3,500 million years ago.

Selection favors some forms over others, no matter what their origins, and in particular those which form relations of *complementarity* with each other. So it is with animal and vegetable life. These two forms of organism diverged a long time ago, but their relation is one of complementary difference. Plant metabolism requires carbon dioxide as an input and produces oxygen as an output; animal metabolism requires oxygen as an input and produces carbon dioxide as an output. Their fates are linked.

Bogdanov understands life as part of a self-regulating system, although not necessarily one that will always find equilibrium. The cyclical exchange of carbon dioxide and oxygen:

> forms a basis for complimentary correlations between life as a whole—the *biosphere*—and the gaseous cover of the earth—the atmosphere. The quantity of carbon dioxide is maintained at a definite, stable level. If, due to the development of animal life, forest fires and also a *discharge of carbon dioxide in volcanic processes or from other*

sources, there is an overproduction of carbon dioxide, then the growth of plants immediately intensifies at its expense, and the surplus is absorbed.[151]

And vice versa. Remarkable for his time, Bogdanov has some understanding of the biosphere as a system. His struggle for a monist practice after philosophy has all been leading up to this threshold. The concept of the biosphere calls for a new worldview.

Philosophical monism and the cooperative point of view of labor point Bogdanov toward a symbiotic view of evolution, although in no sense does he see it as an intentional or teleological system.[152] Rather, it is an argument from the principle of selection. Any system that endures is likely to be self-correcting within given parameters, as is the systematic interaction of the atmosphere, biosphere, and lithosphere of earth. "Thus the regulation of their quantity by conjunctive couplings between the three spheres is a basic condition for the maintenance of a stable, on average, level of their temperature."[153] In the *Essays*, Bogdanov grasps the carbon cycle, but has now forgotten the possibility he canvassed in *Red Star* of the destabilizing effect of the Carbon Liberation Front.

The early Soviet Union is a microcosm in which a revolutionary society, no longer bound by the old laws of private property, nevertheless had to confront "the cognitive struggle with nature," or rather struggle(s) with(in) nature, and under difficult conditions.[154] It is a microcosm for us in the twenty-first century, for the Carbon Liberation Front will bring with it a widening metabolic rift, destabilization, and reduced circumstances. As for what forms of social organization will emerge, that is anybody's guess. Or perhaps not a guess. Perhaps tektology has a perspective on the fate of social forms in the Anthropocene.

This brings us to the concepts of egression and degression. *Degressive* systems are skeletal, often a matter of a waste product externalized, as with the skeletons of animals. It is not always hard like an animal skeleton. A squid's ink is a degressive system. So too is the surface tension of water. Interestingly, so too is writing.

Meaning exceeds the sign, but the signs "protect from decay the living plastic tissue of mental images."[155]

Egression is a system of sub-systems, one of which predominates. There's a protocol of interaction, within which one sub-system influences the others more than the others influence it. One could call it leadership, which may or may not be permanent. If the environment remains constant, and all the sub-systems are in the same environment, and one sub-system is better organized than the others, then "egressive difference" can only increase. Power accrues to the leading sub-system. "During revolutionary epochs, the process of conversion of organizations with an embryonic egression, in the form of a hardly noticeable authoritarianism, into organizations of fully expressed egression, strict authoritarian discipline and 'firm rule', appears quite frequently and quite vividly."[156]

Environments aren't constant, however, and equilibrium is usually dynamic. The environment can become more or less favorable, and in consequence selection can become positive or negative. In either case the better organized sub-system has the advantage. If the environment is favorable, it is enriched faster. Under negative selection it loses ground less quickly than the other sub-systems.

What comes together in tektology is molecular and biospheric thought. The war, revolution, and civil war ripped the veil away long enough for Bogdanov to see through to another way of organizing knowledge and practice. He was no enthusiast. He clearly saw the problems the Bolsheviks had set for themselves. He distanced himself from their authoritarian worldview, their new idealisms, their militarization of everyday life, and their instrumentalizing of labor. He was inclined as they were to champion labor's struggle in and against nature, even though elsewhere in his work he had already developed the concept of the biosphere and the feedback loop between the molecular rifts labor opens up and the planet as system. The arrest of Bogdanov in 1923 led him to focus more narrowly on scientific work, putting an end to the evolution of his larger frame of thought.

BLOOD EXCHANGE

By the time the *Essays on Tektology* came out in 1921, Bogdanov's position was a precarious one. Bukharin, under orders, attacked him in print. He was packed off on a trade mission to London by his friend Leonid Krasin to keep him out of harm's way. While in London he caught up on the latest in blood transfusion theory and technology. This was a topic of longstanding interest to Bogdanov—his Martians practiced it. He set up a small and rather secret group to experiment with it upon his return from London. His arrest came in 1923, when he was accused of leading the opposition group Worker's Truth. While his writings may have influenced such groups, he denied all involvement. The secret police interrogated him for two weeks in the basement of the Lubianka prison.

By 1924 Bogdanov was conducting experiments in which blood transfusions were simultaneous exchanges between two parties. The idea was that blood was a collective resource of the body, which could in turn be collectivized between bodies. The physiological basis of this was shaky. Nor did Bogdanov know modern scientific method. The lack of control conditions rendered his results meaningless. Yet it appears that he really did help Krasin recover from a case of anemia in 1925.

Krasin was not the only communist leader who suffered from anemia at the time. A veritable epidemic of exhaustion was passing though the Bolshevik leadership. Holding a monopoly on state power while sending not just your enemies but also your friends into exile or prison came at a cost. The leading circles of the party created their own private healthcare system, in part to deal with this endemic exhaustion. In 1926 Bogdanov got his own institute, whose mission was to develop blood transfusion techniques for sustaining the health of the party leaders. His institute was not approved in the usual way and stood outside the now very extensive scientific apparatus of the Soviet Union. More scientifically rigorous researchers in the field ignored it.[157]

Bogdanov died in 1928 as a result of a blood exchange with a student who had an inactive form of tuberculosis. He received a state funeral. Bukharin delivered the eulogy, although the meaning of this was rather obscure.[158] Having Bukharin preside may not have meant that Bogdanov was accepted as part of the party, but rather that Bukharin was joining Bogdanov among those who were already excluded from it. By 1929 his institute had been named after him, but had at the same time become a properly scientific one, and part of the establishment of a modern blood transfusion regime. Stalin invested resources in transfusion as part of his mobilization and militarization of the whole of society.

Attempts are sometimes made to make Bogdanov a precursor to Stalin, but this is itself a smear campaign of the Stalinist type. It is true enough that when Stalin was consolidating his power he mobilized the rhetoric of the cultural revolution that sounded a bit like Proletkult. But this was a top-down power play, not Bogdanov's self-organization of labor from below. In any case, Stalin quickly abandoned such rhetoric once it had served its purpose.[159]

It is also true enough that Bogdanov thought that acquired characteristics could be passed on by an organism to its offspring. But this was a common error among Darwinists even in the early twentieth century. A proper synthesis of Darwinian selection with Mendel's genetics had yet to be thought through (and would come, incidentally, from Marxist biologists in both the Soviet Union and Britain). Bogdanov is not to blame for the persecution by Stalin of Vavilov and other genetic scientists, and the elevation of the fraudulent but seemingly "dialectical materialist" work of Lysenko to scientific respectability.[160]

The legacy of Bogdanov lived on not in philosophy or science so much as in engineering culture. Some of the leaders of Lenin's electrification program were Bogdanovites. Platonov, as we shall see, went from Proletkult to hydro-engineering to an extraordinary synthesis of the literary and technical aspirations of the Proletkult movement. While not a major figure in his day in either technical or literary circles, Platonov now looms large as not only a great witness but also a great theoretician of his age.

That Bogdanov fell out with Lenin does not make him a Stalinist. On the other hand, it made him a non-person to the

Western Marxists who thought that they were returning to an authentic Leninist thought prior to Stalinist falsifications. The revival of Marxist thought by the New Left, which consolidated the canon of Western Marxism as we now know it, also selected against Bogdanov. Its interests were largely in grafting political and cultural theories onto Marxist political economy, and it looked to Lenin, Trotsky, and to Marxist philosophers in the West for the resources for this.[161] In the twenty-first century, when of all the liberation fronts it is the Carbon Liberation Front that is ascending, perhaps Bogdanov is the point to which to return.

Here our method can itself be a tektological one. For tektology, even superseded organizations may have their uses. "In this sense, tektology will preserve and save for mankind much of its labor, crystallized in the verities of the past. Undoubtedly, contemporary verities will also become obsolete and die in their time; but tektology guarantees that even they will not simply be discarded and will not be converted in the eyes of future generations into naked, fruitless illusions."[162] It's hard not to see in this statement, poignant given the circumstances in which it was written, a Bogdanov who is appealing to future readers, appealing, dear reader, to you. The *Essays in Tektology* are science fiction in reverse: not the present writing about the future, but the past writing to the future. Bogdanov wrote for the Martians, and the Martians are us.

At its most expansive, tektology makes not only all humans comrades, but all things comrades:

> But what is the origin of the tektological unity itself? The more science develops, the more it is revealed that this unity is nothing else but the result of a genetic unity, that in it is expressed the bond of origin, although this bond is quite remote. It unfolds to the entire universe *of the experience accessible to us*; and the formal convergence is being thereby reduced to a more indirect real convergence.[163]

The qualifying clause is quite important. An absolute unity of being can be posited as a worldview, and both science and labor discover through praxis the particular tektological forms via which all things embrace and transform each other, but a praxis can never be perfected. Our finite nature limits us. It is enough of a struggle for our species-being for it to survive those relentless pressures of selection that would erase it. This might be a particularly key point now that it is our own science, and our own labor, that sets loose the Carbon Liberation Front, which makes progressive selection progress at an ever faster clip.

The tektology can be read as a first, perhaps premature attempt at a *systems theory*. Bogdanov's systems are curiously less autopoetic than they are what Donna Haraway calls sympoetic.[164] While systems theory never quite became a science of science, it did spawn a series of metaphors and techniques which migrated sideways from science to science, illuminating systems and structures. Tektology is then not so much a failed attempt at a science of science as an intuition about a certain kind of "sideways" organization of knowledge in the world.

Bogdanov thought the great task for collective labor was the organizing of the world. That meant finding methods of coordinating across the division of labor other than commodity exchange. What he came up with is a model for a kind of experimental practice where the concepts developed in one labor process can be metaphorically substituted into others, and tested there in practice.

The labor and knowledge practices of Bogdanov's time were far too slender an infrastructure for such a tektology. The means simply didn't exist for comradely sharing of qualitative experiences from particular labors. There is a certain poignancy in Bogdanov's death from blood sharing. Neither the sharing of biological materials nor the sharing of conceptual materials was yet possible. Tektology, like blood exchange, was utopian.

And yet, as we shall see in Part II, the far more advanced technoscientific infrastructures of the twenty-first century do indeed support all kinds of substitutions between fields, and not just of a metaphorical kind. In a relatively new field like climate science, it is certainly possible to see echoes of many of Bogdanov's premature insights—and not least about atmospheric carbon. Not the least reason to restore the memory of Bogdanov's work is that he already anticipated the systematic and organizational problems that would confront working people in our time.

What of Bogdanov's other organizing idea: proletkult? Like tektology, it did not come to pass in the Soviet Union. But we do have at least one extraordinary instance of what proletkult could have been, in the work of Andrey Platonov. Attention to Platonov's major works, long buried in the Soviet archive, can help us think through certain follies to which Marxist and other critical theories are still prone, and toward a revised critical apparatus for the era of the Carbon Liberation Front.

Part of Bogdanov's originality was to insist that the central tenet of Marx's work is not dialectics or materialism or the critique of political economy, but the labor point of view. Bogdanov grasped the central role in Marx of what Deleuze calls the *conceptual personae*.[165] Marx, as Bogdanov reads him, thinks capital through the persona of the worker. The worker-persona both maps out, and constitutes, in its relation with other class personae, particularly its antagonistic relation to the capitalist-persona, the space of Marx's thought. The worker-persona is not a product of the author's mind, as the persona and the author are also mutually constituting. Personae are not so much novelistic characters as embodiments of concepts, even though the personae may at the same time have a certain affect and a certain appearance that attaches to them.

What Platonov will add to this persona of the worker is the persona of the *comrade*. He does not simply assume a universality of the worker point of view, as is sometimes the case in Marx and Bogdanov. He is interested in the struggle to become comrades together. For Deleuze, personae carry with them possible modes of existence. While Platonov writes both appealing and terrifying comrades, they are all integral to his thought, which is precisely the thought of the space between these various incarnations of the comrade. To understand Platonov, then, is to understand what is between comrades as a plural but not universal point of view.

2

Andrey Platonov: A Proletarian Writing

SON OF PROLETKULT

Famine and war appear on the first page of Platonov's great (anti) novel *Chevengur*. The old woman Ignatevna can cure children of hunger. She feeds them a broth of grass and mushrooms. They fall asleep and never wake up, "dry foam flecked on their lips."[1] She will take an old skirt or an iron for her services. There is not a lot to look back fondly on from the time of the Tsar.

The peasants leave their village to beg, or for the front. Pavlovich stays behind, living on boiled grass. He makes in wood all the things that used to exist in metal. He even makes an oak frying pan. He brings water to the boil in it slowly so the wood doesn't burn. He understands the material constraints on wants. He listens to a locomotive, off in the distance, but it stops.

Every page of Platonov contains condensed emblems of the Soviet experience. On the one hand, peasants and workers and their ways, doing and making, and the sensations that arise out of their labors. On the other hand, agents of the revolution, some noble idealists, some sinister hacks, and their fantastic exhortations. He stages close encounters of these comrades with each other, usually far from the center, in the village or the countryside, or the far, far east.

From the point of view of the high-minded Leninism of the Soviet state, it is like a game of telephone. What we get is not the governing universals of the philosophy of the center, but how minor characters in the provinces mix signal and noise to suit their own situations and experiences. In Platonov we touch that highfalutin language only from beneath. His personal party line is rather like that of the comrade who said to me once that "the party should stick to the working class like shit to a blanket."

Platonov was born into the working-class family of a metal worker for the railways in the provincial city of Voronezh. He grew up in one of those raw interzones between the industrial and the agricultural that are characteristic of early industrialization.[2] As the oldest of ten kids, he had to work to help support the family from an early age. He supported the Bolsheviks from the start of the revolution, and was briefly a party member, but a more lasting influence was Proletkult. He became something of a provincial success as a journalist, poet and story writer. The local Proletkult organization even sent him to Moscow for a congress, at which he heard Bogdanov speak.

While an accomplished writer of stories, Platonov's most striking works are a series of anti-novels or anti-novellas. Taken together, they are an allegorical history of the Soviet Union. *Chevengur* stretches from the revolution, through the civil war and war communism, to the New Economic Policy of the early 1920s. *Foundation Pit* tells the story of Stalin's forced collectivization of agriculture, beginning in 1928. *Happy Moscow* turns on Stalin's 1934 statement, after the completion of the first five-year plan, that "life has become merrier."[3] *Soul* escapes the imminent era of the great purges by traveling east, and confronts the whole history of the revolution with a fable of its failure and redemption in Turkmenistan.

Platonov's writings lend themselves to multiple readings. I leave it to others better qualified to account for his distinctive use of the Russian language, his cosmist or theological themes.[4] My reading concentrates on three things, read through three series of figures: his *historical allegory* of the revolution; the *everyday quality* of that history; and a kind of *tektology* that arises from his distinctive method of constructing proletarian prose. In the rather limited sphere of the production of writing, Platonov actually pulled off in a minor way something of what Bogdanov suggested, even if Bogdanov himself would have been rather perplexed by the results.

The first of these three readings—historical allegory—is mediated in turn by three figures, who no doubt literally loomed large over Platonov his whole adult life: Marx, Lenin, and Stalin. His play *Fourteen Little Red Huts* presents condensed versions of all three. About Marx, the intellectual says: "All his life he was looking for something serious and laughing at the current nonsense of every event." The peasant replies: "you're lying, man of science! Marx didn't laugh at us—he loved us, in advance and forever."[5]

This Marx addresses two classes, hacker and worker, as both critic and savior. One of Platonov's abiding themes is a Bogdanovite one: who is Marx to the proletariat? Marx's *Capital* traces an allegorical descent into hell of the worker who passes through the factory gates, out of the realm of circulation and equality into the inferno of production.[6] Platonov's world is a hell beneath that hell, of non-production, of bare want, but his proletarian is a being that speaks rather than being spoken of, opening a fissure in the Marxist canon, between high and low.

Fourteen Little Red Huts is set on a distant collective farm, over which presides a scarecrow, pointing into the distance. While this straw-man Lenin points to the remote future, in the near present the "class enemy" steals the livestock and even the children. The collective farm chairperson declares that: "We are poor here, we have no one except Stalin." Yet as the intellectual has already told her: "It's our fate not to be heard."[7] Lenin is present, but has no effect, while Stalin is absent, and yet his effects are everywhere.

The second series of three figures through whom I want to read Platonov are witnesses to a quite different disenchantment, that of postwar consumer capitalism: Henri Lefebvre, Raoul Vaneigem, and Guy Debord. Lefebvre inaugurates a critique of *everyday life* and its various alienations. This critique entails "relinquishing the traditional image of the philosopher as master and ruler of existence, witness and judge of life from the outside, enthroned above the masses, above the moments lost in triviality . . ."[8] Today's Leninoid philosophers and the Stalinist apparatchiks of the past join hands in denying low theory, emergent from below, and the Marx to be found there who loved us, in advance and forever.

Lefebvre's discovery, or rediscovery, of everyday life takes an even more pointed form with his apprentice, Raoul Vaneigem: "People who talk about revolution and class struggle without referring explicitly to everyday life, without understanding what is subversive about love and what is positive in the refusal of constraints, such people have a corpse in their mouth."[9] That might be a perfect epigram for Platonov, with a tad less love, and rather more corpses.

For all the apparent modernism of his prose, Platonov is the writer of the material practice of popular sense-making. Platonov's method, in a word, is détournement, the collective labor of unmaking from below the language of those above. Platonov's workaday characters have a naive genius for lifting the seal off official languages, whether of church, state or party, and using them as lubricants for the machinations of their own concerns, even if their use of it is no longer always dialectical. Language is material, but not a final means with which to grasp other kinds of materiality. Debord: "Whatever is explicitly presented as détournement within formulated theory serves to deny any durable autonomous existence to the sphere of theory merely formulated."[10] Language is just one kind of materiality among others.

Platonov describes one of his techniques of détournement in his story "Among Animals and Plants," his oblique account of the gulag:

> Federov preferred to choose pages at random—now page 50, now page 214. And although every book is interesting, reading this way makes it even better, and still more interesting, because you have to imagine for yourself everything you have skipped, and you have to compose anew passages that don't make sense or badly written, just as if you too were an author.[11]

Here he perfectly describes the *literary communism* discovered by Lautréamont and practiced by the Situationists, which erases a false idea and inscribes in its place the correct one. Platonov's détournement of the socialist realism of the 1930s might not be a bad guide to what is to be done with the capitalist realism that is the only acceptable language of our own time.

The third reading of Platonov is via our three rebel Bolsheviks of Capri: Gorky, Lunacharsky, and Bogdanov. As in Gorky, everything in Platonov begins and ends in labor. Gorky: "The music of toiling men drew me down the Volga. Even now it has an intoxicating effect and I remember very clearly the day when I first became aware of the heroic poetry of everyday life . . . My soul was brightened by the desire to spend my whole life in that half-insane rapture of work."[12]

Like Lunacharsky, Platonov thought socialism had to be more, rather than less, than a religion. Lunacharsky:

> To me, the revolution was a stage, inevitably tragic, in the world-wide development of the human spirit toward the "Universal Soul," the greatest and most decisive act in the process of "God-Building," the most striking and definite deed in the realization of the program which Nietzsche had so felicitously formulated when he said, "there is no sense in the world, but we ought to give sense to it."[13]

Much in Platonov reads like a running critique, in and against that sentiment. God-Building is surprisingly easy; actual building is relentlessly hard.

His relation to Bogdanov is rather more interesting. His key works can be read as pressing even further the pessimistic note in Bogdanov: the impossibility of designing a *dynamic equilibrium* of human and natural processes. His is a writing that always returns to the entropic, to the residues that can't be recycled into a molar narrative line. There are hints in Bogdanov of how everyday subjective experience appears from the point of view of tektology, but it is Platonov who pursues the tektology of the everyday to its logical conclusions.

Platonov: "There is a kind of link, some kinship, among burdocks and beggars, singing in the fields, electricity, a locomotive and its whistle, and earthquakes—there is the same birthmark on all of them and on some other things too . . . Growing grass and working steam engines take the same kind of mechanics."[14] What ensues is a strikingly poignant and subtly molecular account of everyday proletarian life, among rocks, animals, and plants—as comrades.

Platonov's early stories and journalism were caught up in the utopian fantasies of the technical overcoming of material constraints typical of Proletkult, if not of Bogdanov. He wrote about cloud seeding to alter the weather, and dynamiting a hole through the Urals to warm Siberia. Platonov responded to the practical as well as the utopian side of Bogdanov. In the wake of the terrible drought and famine of 1921, Platonov left journalism to study engineering and work on electrification. In 1924 he was working with considerable energy on land reclamation projects in his native Voronezh region. His own praxis as an engineer led him to a critique of what Susan Buck-Morss calls the *Soviet sublime*.[15] Given that similar plans are one response to the Carbon Liberation Front, both his experience and his writings are pertinent to our time as well.

The great literary theorist Viktor Shklovsky met Platonov at this time. He has little to say about Platonov's character—they didn't hit it off—but he left a memorable portrait of his work. "All these rivers we studied in our geography books . . . do not exist. They are overgrown with rush. If you push the rush aside, the ground underneath is wet. Platonov dredges the rivers."[16] There's no water, sometimes for forty kilometers; the villagers work all night at the well with their buckets. The peasants plow their fields using cows. Platonov straightens rivers, drains swamps, spreads lime to counteract the acidity of the soil. The dams are made of dirt and clay, and constructed in the winter when the ground is frozen. "Comrade Platonov is very busy. The desert is advancing."

Platonov somehow gets an orchard to flourish. Water flows to the trees down chutes on wooden stilts. Oats grow around the trees to prevent the rabbits from eating the fruit. There's no motor. The screw pump, of the kind designed in ancient times by Archimedes, is worked by hand. Platonov: "Given the agrarian over-population of the village and the famine in Voronezh . . . there's no motor cheaper than the village girl. She requires no amortization." (Or so Shklovsky says he says.)

Shklovsky: "Platonov understood the village." His work went well. In 1926 Moscow summoned Platonov to join the central land reclamation effort. He was sent to the restive Tambov region in 1927, but had less success there.[17] Back in Moscow, and with Gorky's support, he became a writer again. His attempt to leave literature, this experience of technical labor and of the real revolution in the countryside, is part of what makes his return to writing great.

Proletkult opens the possibility of writing to Platonov, but technical labor tempers Proletkult's raw enthusiasm with its constant encounters with recalcitrant nature. As Bogdanov had already shown, language overshoots most other kinds of material in its malleability. Tektological wholes are not so easily made with other stuff. The tragedy of the totality is the recognition of the gap that can open between them. Collaborative labor is the work of narrowing the gap, even if it can never be fully closed, rather than making a fetish of the difference.

In his (anti)novellas, Platonov sketches a history of the revolution not so much from below, as from *below the below*.[18] It is not just that the usual bourgeois characters of the novel are absent or in the margins. His characters are barely even proletarian. They are often orphans, landless, wanderers—typical figures of the actual period. Lenin had worn out the working class in revolution and civil war. These déclassé characters were the actual base of the social formation.

Platonov is the great writer of our planet of slums.[19] He saw beneath the sheen of socialist realism to the disorganization of labor beneath, like an old mole that undermines the surface. His work is like an allegory for what lies unseen under our own capitalist realism. The difference is that socialist realism at least felt obliged to acknowledge the reality of labor as subject if not the reality of the object of its labors. Platonov got critical purchase through attention to those personae closest to the struggle to wrest a surplus from nature.

Bogdanov gives us the tragedy of the totality from the point of view of those whose job it is to try to grasp that totality. Platonov sees it from below the below. He sees the tragedy of attempting and failing to get anything to work at all. His is a writing of residues and remainders. The era of the Carbon Liberation Front calls for both kinds of work, on the totality and on its failures and fissures.[20] Bogdanov and Platonov, taken together, are our contemporaries, then. The revolution they witnessed is an allegory of the weird times to come.

But let's not get ahead of ourselves. First: a reading of Platonov, through the protocols of historical allegory, everyday life, and tektology, which extract from the interplay of his comradely conceptual personae a plurality of concepts and figures for our situation.

CHEVENGUR AS HISTORICAL NOVEL

Chevengur can be read as two linked (anti)novellas, the first of which is an epic historical novel of the war, revolution, and civil war as seen from below the below. The characters are—like Marx's worker in *Capital*—conceptual personae caught at the same time within the exogenous struggle of nature and the endogenous struggle within the social formation.[21] The difference is that there is no social formation. There is no capitalism, and nothing has replaced it. The comrades struggle to create the base for the dream of Lenin's leap.[22]

Early on in *Chevengur* we meet with Pavlovich, who lives without music, but loves mechanical things. He loves only the finished thing, made by labor, which had begun its independent existence. "Machines were his people, constantly arousing within him feelings, thoughts and desires."[23] He has discovered all on his own a kind of labor that is not alienated—the synthesis of art and work to which Proletkult aspired. Nature troubles him as something quiet and sad, "some sort of forces acting without return."[24]

When he finds the child Prokofy begging, his love of machines blows away in the wind. From then on Pavlovich finds it hard to work without love and just for the wages. Tinkering with mechanical things only appears to assuage his own sadness, but doesn't really, as the sadness of the child still exists.

Pavlovich is a foster-father to Sasha Dvanov, who also works with him on the railways, but has a different attitude to the technical. "Sasha was interested in machines as he was in other moving and living things. He wanted more to feel them, to live their lives with them, than to find them out."[25] Dvanov wants to enter into the relations, not the things, and views all relations as parts of tektological wholes. The machinic is not a thing apart for Dvanov, but rather part of our species-being, a matter of organization.

Dvanov is a reader, while Pavlovich learns through his hands. "No matter how much he read and thought, some kind of hollow place remained ever within him, an emptiness through which an undescribed and untold world passed like a startled wind."[26] There is no logos, no logic common to word and world, whereby word can grasp world entire and as an object of contemplation. Words are just one of the forms of matter of the world, and perhaps even less helpful as a praxis than other kinds, like Platonov's land reclamation work, although that too will reveal its disappointments.

The war with Germany convinces both Pavlovich and Dvanov of the uselessness of the government, perhaps of all governments. And Pavlovich's beloved trains just seem to make war possible. The machine isn't free. The revolution is to Pavlovich the path of least resistance, easier than war. Dvanov's affective experience of the revolution is a layered one. "In the melody of the bells he heard alarm, faith and doubt. These same passions are also at work in revolution, for people are moved not only by cast-iron faith, but by shattering doubt as well."[27] A revolution is not just a leap of faith.

Pavlovich takes Dvanov in search of the most serious party. One party sounds like Mensheviks. They say "happiness is a complicated article, and not in it is man's goal, but rather in historical laws."[28] Pavlovich prefers the Bolsheviks. "Probably this would be the smartest power, which would within the year either completely build the world, or else raise up such a fuss that even a child's heart would grow tired."[29] Nonetheless, Pavlovich is more skeptical than Dvanov about these Bolsheviks. It was the workers and soldiers who made the revolution. What do we need a party for, he asks, let alone a state? He thinks the people can organize itself for itself.

The Bolsheviks send Dvanov to see if socialism has popped up anywhere of its own accord. After all, the people have nothing but each other now. "Dvanov remembered various people who wandered among the fields and slept in the empty buildings at the front; maybe those people in fact had already bunched up in a gulley somewhere, out of the wind and the government and there they lived, content with their friendship."[30] Such things actually happened. The comradeship of the war and civil war sent many landless, displaced former soldiers and wanderers off to make their own communes and organize their own lives. Platonov never loses a basic solidarity with that revolutionary structure of feeling.

One part of Dvanov's revolutionary feeling comes from Pavlovich, and is technical in nature, like improved irrigation: "He thought of the time when water would begin to glisten in the dry uplands. That would be socialism." But he is skeptical about the transformative power of the technical, which aligns with a whole ontology: "Nature had no gifts for creation . . . it succeeds through patience."[31] In history, as in natural history, selection erases all that is not fitted to endure. Communism for Dvanov combines raw comradeship in the face of common hardship with the technical overcoming of scarcity. These turn out to be compatible aims only in certain situations. State and ideology get in the way; machines go off their rails, and not everything can be redeemed at once. In Platonov, there is no shortcut to enduring happiness.

In the countryside during a civil war, "where there's mud we've got peace."[32] Friction, fog, and sheer distance get in the way. Locomotives collide head-on, while the engine drivers look on helplessly. The new Soviet state loves harvests, and while the peasants now have their land, they prefer to make stills from old machine-gun parts and brew moonshine. Dvanov encourages them to take over the landowners' estates. There's more than one civil war going on.

Captured by an anarchist band, Dvanov is rescued by Kopenkin, who "could have set fire to all the immobile property of earth with conviction, so that within man would remain only reverence for one's comrade."[33] He is an old man who had never paid much attention to his own life, living on "unreasoned hope" rather than bread. He is not the party and still less the government, but a natural force. His mount is Proletarian Strength, not a noble charger, more the kind of horse with which you pull up stumps.

In his cap is a picture of Rosa Luxemburg, whose portrait he once stood before in a district party office. "He had looked at her hair and imagined it as a mysterious park . . ."[34] She is to him like a mother, and yet also like a woman who died in childbirth. On that day when he first saw her image, he killed a kulak who had incited the peasants to attack a Bolshevik grain requisitioner. Kopenkin is the book's queer libido, its cod-Don Quixote, but not its central character.

Platonov dispenses with the residues of what Bogdanov would call "authoritarian organization" that adhere to Cervantes. Something keeps Dvanov from adopting Kopenkin's quixotic zeal. In a fever, a sick Dvanov's dreams of things. "Little things like boxes, shards, felt boots, and jackets turned into huge objects of enormous size and poured down on top of Dvanov."[35] They enter his body. He fears they will rip open his skin. The Bolsheviks' problem isn't just the masses, it is the intractable mass of things. In his madness Dvanov knows this, while Kopenkin, in his, does not.

Dvanov thinks communism is about getting water onto the steppes, and imagines this, in the spirit of Charles Fourier, as a kind of aesthetic perfection of the biosphere: "Because of the cultivated grain the earth will be shinier and more visible from other planets . . . and then too the water cycle will get stronger and that will make the sky bluer and more transparent."[36] He is still stuck at this stage with an image of nature as a thing to be contemplated rather than as a taciturn object against which to labor.

Dvanov thinks the revolution is about both subjects and objects, which he has learned from Pavlovich and Kopenkin respectively, but he does not yet know how hard it is to organize them, let alone how to organize part-objects or quasi-objects. He learns such things through experience, but tends to be a bit literal minded. A banner quotes Marx: "The revolution is the locomotive of history." This only makes Dvanov think of clapped-out old freight trains.[37] Taking metaphors literally is a sort of tektology in reverse. Bogdanov's interest was in the poetic suggestiveness of processes, of how the sensation of one might open up onto the diagram of another. Platonov is more attuned to the difficulties a metaphoric leap encounters when brought back into a material practice. The "locomotive" in the slogan "the revolution is the locomotive of history" is already an idealized one. Dvanov, like Platonov himself, is rather more knowledgeable about actual locomotives, which, at the time of the civil war, are in a very poor state indeed.

Kopenkin rides into what is not much more than a one-horse village. As an act of self-authorized revolutionary justice, he redistributes the nags from the rich to the poor peasants. One formerly rich peasant cracks wise: so the former rich, now poor, should get the foals when they are born, from the former poor, now rich. Such subaltern wiliness only enrages Kopenkin.[38] He does not see the futility of redistributing such impoverished resources, or that a simple leveling is not in itself communism. There can be no equality of heterogeneous things and hence no equality of the subjects with which they are inextricably connected. The peasant, more canny than Kopenkin, predicts a failure of productivity. There's a tension between Kopenkin's theological desire for equality in poverty and Dvanov's techniques for increasing the total wealth.

Like Quixote, what makes Kopenkin an enduring character is that sometimes his madness works, and yet is still madness. Another village does no plowing because they are too busy with their meetings. Here Kopenkin's remedy is actually a wise one. He prescribes *even more meetings*. Sometimes the remedy with someone pretending to be ill is not to contradict them but rather to persuade them they are really *very* ill.

The exhortations of the Bolshevik press don't much impress Dvanov and Kopenkin. They are only confused by talk of "Kronstadts of excess."[39] It is perhaps 1921, and the Bolsheviks have put down the mutiny of the revolutionary workers and sailors of Kronstadt, once the arsenal of the revolution, and yet Dvanov and Kopenkin are deaf to the signals of what it must mean. Kronstadt was a clash between the interests of the working class and those of the state, in which the Bolsheviks—Trotsky included—sided with the state. It is no accident that this is when Dvanov and Kopenkin meet Pashtinev.

They find him in a forest—perhaps the forest of Rosa's hair. Pashtinev is a more earthy character than Kopenkin. He thinks the revolution ended in 1919, when the German working class failed to topple the bourgeois state. He lacks Kopenkin's avenging mission, although his communism is, if anything, even more egalitarian. Of Trotsky, he says: "What comrade is he of mine, if he's commanding everybody?"[40] In Platonov, authoritarian organization is continually questioned, from below.

For Pashtinev it is all over. The law has come: "Armies, governments, and ways of life have come and gone, but to the people they always said the same thing . . . 'Stand up, get back in the ranks, you start work on Monday.'" He lives on "volunteer plants." He alone knows that the land can't be given to the peasants, because "the land is self-made, so that means it's nobody's."[41] Dissolving the fiction of particular private properties abolishes with it the more abstract fiction that the earth is there for us, to be arraigned around our wants. Pashtinev probes the limits of the Proletkult worldview.

A village blacksmith, loyal to his village and an enemy of everyone else, explains: "It's a sly business. First you hand over the land, then you take away the grain, right down to the last kernel . . . The peasant doesn't have anything left from the land any more except the horizon."[42] The communist horizon: the party abolished the heavens, and has not (yet) replaced them. But it has abolished the old base as well, leaving only the distant line between. Ideology is switching polarities, from vertical to horizontal; from earth as a fallen image of the divine, to a present as an imperfect realization of a future. The absolute of the eternal heavens gives way to the absolute of time itself: History as absolute. In this wavering moment, before socialist realism has made the communist horizon the new Godhead, Platonov's smith—an intermediary character between peasant and worker—still has the capacity to question it.

Kopenkin replies to the smith that the peasants want to leave the workers with nothing to eat while they make homebrew with the grain. Platonov's sympathies are not with the peasants. This is the other civil war, of town and country, over who gets control of the agricultural product. Dvanov and Kopenkin are supposed to be agents of the city in this civil war, but the peasants think of Dvanov and Kopenkin as neither dangerous nor necessary. They don't order forced labor, and Kopenkin uses state decrees for cigarette papers. They are the self-made revolutionaries of a self-making revolution, remote from St. Petersburg and Moscow.

When Dvanov goes to the city, it looks to him as if the Whites have taken it. No longer a fortress of the revolution, there is even food in the shops. The New Economic Policy (NEP) is taking effect, even if comrades in grain procurement are still getting killed. But things have not quite gone back to the old ways. "Now all the people knew that it is difficult to grow grain, that a plant lives as tenderly and complexly as a man . . . People had learned many things previously unknown. Their professions had expanded, their sense of life had become social."[43] At least for the moment, they see beyond the fetishism of the market.

With food in their bellies, people feel their *soul* and as a consequence particular appetites return. Elsewhere, Platonov defines soul as "an individual violation of a general trend of reality that is unique as an act and for that matter the soul is alive. I apologize for the old terminology—I developed a new meaning to it."[44] Soul always exists in sufficient quality and quantity. It's a question of whether surplus life enables one to feel it.

In the city, Dvanov meets up with comrade Gopner, who wonders whether food and revolution can coexist: "we are all comrades only when there is identical trouble for everybody."

Gopner is technically minded, but he thinks machines are quantifiable and life isn't. He has the approved Hegelian language to hand: "We're not objects now, we're subjects."[45] Still, it's the object world that will be the trouble. The light in the district party room pulses. Gopner knows that the drive belt for the dynamo at the power plant is not working smoothly. With no light there's no Bolshevik meetings. The molecular corrodes the infrastructure of the revolution, which is held together by a few skilled workers like Gopner—and Platonov.

When told of the NEP, Pavlovich declares: "So it's a lost cause then." The objective conditions won't allow Lenin's leap, and "what doesn't ripen in the correct time was sown in vain." It is in the context of the apparent retreat represented by the NEP that they encounter Chepurny, who claims to come "from communism," even though to Gopner that sounds like "a village named in memory of the future."[46] Constructing socialism is difficult enough on such a shallow base, so Chepurny's claim to have over-leapt it into the communist developmental stage is both crazy and appealing.

In a détournement of Marx's restrictively humanist formulae for stepping toward communism, "from each according to his abilities, to each according to his needs," Chepurny describes communist Chevengur as a place where "the blessings of life, the precision of truth, and the woe of existence all arose of their own accord in correspondence with their need."[47] These three realms, and the possibility of selecting a new tektological mode of their dynamic equilibrium, are Platonov's whole quixotic quest, and from the revolution to the start of the NEP he thought it might just be possible.

CHEVENGUR AS UTOPIA

The retreat of the NEP marks a break in the text, where the historical (anti)novella breaks off and steps into what Slavoj Žižek calls a "gnostic-materialist" utopia.[48] As in Bogdanov, in Platonov it is the failure of revolution which prompts the utopian mode. Chevengur is where those imbued for life with the comradeship of the civil war can find a way to live on in that spirit—a not untroubled affect as we shall see—while town and country realign their interests within that strange NEP-space of state-directed capitalism. What Debord called the *concentrated spectacle* governing the commodity form on the Soviet plan is close to hand.[49] *Chevengur*, and within it the almost-utopian place of Chevengur itself, preserves Platonov's sense of a struggle for another life foreclosed, where life, truth, and matter might evolve together.

From afar, the Chevengurians look like "people on vacation from imperialism."[50] For all its apparent placidity, Chevengur is a product of civil war. The violence there is hardly unique or unprovoked. The Whites kill the Reds; the Reds kill the Whites. Some "bourgeois" hoard so much grain and salt in their ceilings that they cave in—trusting in a superstructure that would not hold such providence. The Reds arrange a "second coming" for this bourgeoisie, who shall be granted the heavens, although not in this life.[51] The everyday life of utopia is founded on force, and in this regard it is *exactly the same* as any other everyday life.

Chevengur is a town that ate its scapegoat to share equally in guilt, and now "it reeks of some raw god."[52] During the Capri years, Lunacharsky and Gorky advocated God-Building, through which the proletariat would come to deify itself. Like George Sorel's myth of the general strike, it was a class-based inflection of Feuerbach and the civil religion of the French Revolution, the doctrine of that Marx who loved us in advance and forever. It does not escape Platonov's attention that while faith is a common bond, it also signals an originary violence; or that idolizing the leaping proletariat severed from its material conditions of existence, the subject without the object, is just a kind of fetishism.

Chepurny's communism is more that of the landless than of the peasants: "Chevengur doesn't collect property, it destroys it."[53] Chevengurians don't labor for an abstract, invisible common good, but for "close, comradely people." Even private family relations seem to have been abolished: "We don't have wives. All that's left is female companions."[54] It's the utopia of the landless, the displaced, rather than the utopia of hacker and worker cooperation in *Red Star*. In Chevengur, they have mobilized the sun, the world-wide proletarian, and they live off the surplus power of the solar base. Now that "the soul had been made the main profession," there's little to eat.[55] They prefer communism to labor discipline. Communism should be biting; sorrowful, but shared.

Boris Pilniak, Platonov's friend and collaborator, left his own portrait of the kind of men who might come together in a place like Chevengur:

> Here slept Communists who had been called to duty by war communism and discharged by the year nineteen hundred and twenty-one, men of arrested ideas, madmen and drunkards, men who, living together in a cave and working together unloading barges, sawing firewood, had created a strict fraternity, a strict communism, having nothing of their own, neither money nor possessions nor wives: their wives had left them.[56]

None of the Chevengurians have read Marx. Their communist manifesto has four theses: sun and soil; water and wind. The tektological unity of these elements is somewhat abstract. "Chepurny could not bear the mystery of time, so he cut short the length of history by the rapid construction of communism." The time of decay, of disorganization, the natural history of time, is simply erased by the absolute time of the communist horizon. "Dvanov guessed why Chepurny so wanted communism. Communism is the end of history and the end of time, for time runs only within nature, while within man there stands only melancholy."[57] In Platonov, as in Bogdanov, there can be no *end of history*, because natural history does not end. That is the tragedy of the totality.

Platonov writes brilliantly of the natural world of the steppe, with a kind of solar tektology of the effects of summer daylight: "the sun leaned dry and hard into the earth, and the earth was the first to falter in the weakness of its exhaustion, and began oozing the juices of grass, the dampness of loam, and disturbing the entire fibrous expanse of the steppe, while the sun only grew more tempered and strong from its tensed, dry patience."[58] And of daylight's passing: "The sun departed, releasing the moisture of the air for the grass. Nature became a deeper blue and calm, purged of the noisy solar laboring after the general comradeship of languished life."[59] The Chevengurian revolutionaries could not quite mesh their wants with this world of living and dead matter. The earth is not the equal of the sun; life is not the equal of the earth.

Nothing was planted in Chevengur for three years, and so the wheat and thistle propagate by themselves, and work out their own equilibrium, of three to one. The human and inhuman have not found their relation. Chepurny "touched a burdock. It too wanted communism. The entire weed patch was a friendship of living plants . . . Let the wild grasses grow in the streets of Chevengur, for just like the proletariat, this grass endures the life and heat and the death of deep snow."[60] But Chepurny's communism has leapt against the wind and has not found a way to endure.

The mark of the impasse in Chevengur is that it lacks women. Chepurny thinks that sex and reproduction are "an alien and natural matter, not a human and communistic one. Woman was acceptable for the human life of Chevengur in her drier and more human form, but not in her full beauty . . ." He wants "women of course, but please . . . you know . . . just barely, so there's just a tiny bit of difference . . ."[61]

For the Chevengurians, women trouble the boundary between the actual natural world of water, earth, and air agitated by the sun, and the communism of the fantastic leap, for which the sun is an emblem but not a tangible and tactile force. The comrades are a rather homosocial lot, perhaps even homosexual: "Deprived of families and work . . . all the sleeping Chevengurians were forced to animate nearby people and things in order that they might reproduce and lessen the life which accumulated in their stuffy bodies."[62]

When the women finally arrive they are frightened. In the revolution and the civil war, they are used to being abused by men, and always right away. There weren't long speeches first, like here in Chevengur. At best, "they had exchanged their bodies, their places of age and blossoming, for food . . ."[63] The men realize that the women are orphans too, like them. They want the women to become the mothers and daughters of the men; they want the men to become sons and fathers of the women. They want to end orphanhood for everyone. But the women don't really believe the fraternal and paternal feelings of the men. Women are the public irony of the eternal sphere.

Those gathered in Chevengur are the "miscellaneous," as they might actually be called in Soviet administrative language, who have even less than proletarians. If the definition of the proletariat is those who have nothing but their own kin, then the miscellaneous are a kind that lack even that. They are orphans; they are nobody's. They had no mother to protect their little bodies from the world, and no father to be a "first comrade" and lead them to other comrades. Their powerlessness is their indifferent strength. If one can keep living then everything else is still possible.

Chepurny is one of two leading communists of Chevengur. The other is Prokofy, the former beggar-boy, who has rather more authoritarian inclinations. For Chepurny, the party belongs to the proletariat; for Prokofy, the proletariat belongs to the party. "Revolution is our job and our duty," Prokofy says, "all you have to do is listen to our orders, and then you will stay alive and things will go well for you."[64]

Chepurny grasps that "the enemy used to live among us head-on, but we got him spit out of the revolutionary committee and now in place of the enemy we got the proletariat, so either they've got to be spit out too, or else the revolutionary committee is unnecessary."[65] He naively thinks that Prokofy is still his comrade, and cannot imagine that he himself will be on the side spat out. Only the sinister Prokofy has complete information about the objects and subjects gathered in Chevengur. He has taken an inventory of his future estate.

When Dvanov and Kopenkin, Gopner and Pashtinov come to Chevengur, they are skeptical. The death of a child shakes all these comradely conceptual personae. Dvanov had only intended to go to Chevengur and then return to people who were barely alive to help them. Gopner quickly sees there's no labor being performed.

Pashtinov thinks the leap was worth taking but it failed. Kopenkin may be a rather idealistic communist, but his Rosa is always out of reach, always buried in an alien land. It is a ghost that moves him, like the ghost of Hamlet's father, only this ghost possesses no paternal authority over him, but is rather a mother and daughter, a lover and most of all a comrade.

It is the evening of Chevengur, and the fall is coming. Still, they labor to try and make it work. Kopenkin harnesses Proletarian Strength to the plow. Gopner and Dvanov try to improve irrigation. They use oak crosses from the "bourgeois" cemetery for building material. While a rather disturbing clay statue of Prokofy has appeared, Gopner and Dvanov merge art and design into a practice of the productive object. Some of their inventions are rather impractical. They attempt to generate solar power but it never quite works. Platonov reverses the tenets of *productism*, perhaps the most radical artistic tendency of the time. In Platonov's version, rather than artists bringing the aesthetic to labor, he has workers bringing their labors to the point of becoming art.[66]

In order to protect and not exhaust his communism, Dvanov cultivates the *secondary idea*: "Now he feared the expansion of his calm spiritual sufficiency and wished to find another, secondary idea by which he might live and which he might spend and use, leaving his main idea as an untouched reserve, dipping into it but rarely for his happiness."[67] So he works on irrigation, on food security. No matter how spiritual the communist leap of faith, it only lives on in people's bodies, and bodies have wants. The secondary idea preserves against the melancholy that attends the first, whether it be the impossibility then of achieving communism—or the impossibility now of confronting the Carbon Liberation Front. The secondary idea does not dream backwards from the absolute time of a future horizon. It works outwards, from a particular present situation, looking for lines out of cramped spaces.

Even Chepurny learns from his new comrades, and not least this concept from tektology: "Chepurny had discovered one comforting secret for himself: that the proletariat does not admire nature, but rather destroys it, with labor." No romantic greening of labor here; *Chevengur* isn't pastoral. The problem of organizing labor and nature is precisely their difference, their heterogeneity to each other. Not least because the time Chepurny foreshortens is the time of disingression and decay. There is only nature without ecology.[68]

This nature is recalcitrant, enervating, unpredictable, only ever partially known, and if known at all, known badly, through the metaphors of the time. It has no ecology, in the sense that it is nature without guarantees. It has no necessary tendency to stability or order, no bias toward homeostasis. Its history is a history of metabolic rifts, of varied cosmological, geological, and biological causes. God is dead, and so too is ecology. Disingression awaits. Stabilities are temporary and haphazard organizations. Platonov lacks even Bogdanov's tenuous belief that selection selects for equilibrium.

Serbinov the party bureaucrat arrives, investigating a 20 percent drop in land under cultivation. He is a sad sort, an enervated timeserver, and yet he writes in his diary: "Man is not meaning, but a body filled with passionate veins, ravines of blood, mounds, openings, satisfaction, and oblivion." And: "History was spawned by a base failure who invented the future in order to exploit the present."[69] These insights into want and time are private. Serbinov is like a stone in the river, the revolution flowing over him while he stays sunk to the bottom by self-regard.

In Chevengur the amount of grain growing has actually risen. Chepurny's unitary town plan, which moves the houses about in close formation, had the unintended consequence of letting grasses grow in the streets.[70] The technical improvements of Dvanov and Gopner might actually work. But the hint of a possible victory is purely local. The Chevengurians labor freely for each other, not for the state. It's a strange kind of comedy, this season of reconciliation with the world.

The report to headquarters that Serbinov writes about these happy, useless, ungovernable people may well be the text of Platonov's *Chevengur*: "It had turned out intelligently and ambitiously, hostile and sarcastic both toward Chevengur and the capital."[71] It is not clear whether it is Serbinov's report or Prokofy's scheming which is Chevengur's undoing. It is not clear whose soldiers come, although the Chevengurians can only shout "Cossacks! Cadets!"—as if their only enemies could be the Whites.[72] They kill all the Chevengurians with a machine-like precision. Prokofy is left with an empty town.

FOUNDATION PIT: IMPOSSIBLE INFRASTRUCTURE

That dead and living matter might find an alignment with the revolutionary ideal is a possibility still open in *Chevengur*, no matter how much violence and waste attends the attempt to forge the revolution of everyday life. In *Foundation Pit* such possibilities are foreclosed. Platonov was one of very few writers who had seen first-hand what a disaster Stalin's forced collectivization was, from travels in the countryside in his technical, rather than writerly capacity. The civil war was finally settled, and at the peasants' expense, in a bloody liquidation.[73]

Foundation Pit is a détournement of Zola's *Work* and Stalinist "production" novels.[74] It is the great work on the intimacy of violence and spectacle. But rather than comfort bourgeois sensibilities in our own time, the effect is really the reverse, for the same critique applies now as then. This excavated underworld is, if not the foundation of our own world, then of one of its precursors. Capitalist realism is not that different to socialist realism: both are saturated in idealist fantasies about immaculate goals. The difference is that in capitalist realism these are mostly invoked to sate private wants, for shiny cars and condos.

Socialist realism had a phantasmal conception of the infrastructures beneath its gleaming communist horizon. Capitalist realism's relation to its conditions of existence are no less attenuated. The drought of 2012 obliged American farmers to feed their dairy cattle ice cream sprinkles, gummy worms, marshmallows, fruit loops and cookies. These varieties of high fructose corn syrup products were cheaper than the corn American cows would usually eat.[75] Neither socialist nor capitalist "realism" has much to say about the molecular struggle of labor in and against nature, although socialist realism at least had to acknowledge that labor exists.

Meet the new boss, same as the old boss: Voschev the worker stood still in the middle of production and thought about a plan for the shared and general life—and so they fired him. He is told happiness will come from materialism, not from meaning, even though he says—playing the game—that if he comes up with a plan for life it will improve "productivity."

Voschev is, by his own account, "a vain attempt by life to attain its goal." He is a ragged-trousered Hamlet. His soul has stopped knowing truth. He doubts the necessity of the world. Thought no longer engages the worlds of living and lifeless matter in a viable project. He finds a leaf on the ground and puts it in his sack. He will keep it and remember it, find out for what it once lived and has now perished. He "collected every kind of obscurity for memory and vengeance," as "documentary proof of the planless creation of the world."[76] In a world that really is topsy-turvy, where truth is a remnant of falsehood, Platonov, like Voschev, creates a salvage-punk practice for gathering the relevant ephemera.

He goes out into the "speechless existence," where "only faraway water and wind inhabited this darkness and nature, and only birds could sing the sorrow of this great substance." Voschev finds a building site where a small band of workers dig an enormous foundation pit for a future House of the Proletariat. The most energetic of the workers is Chicklin, but even he knows the job is probably futile: "This job's a killer. And time will eat up all the use."[77]

The House of the Proletariat, a great superstructure raised over a massive base, is Prushevsky's idea. He is a Bogdanovite of sorts, who thinks the soul is the surplus warmth of life. But is it an inevitable surplus? He tackles the relation between matter, life, and soul with a bit of tektological thinking culled from his experience of everyday life: "He could see how the topsoil rested on a layer of clay and did not originate from it. Could a superstructure develop from any base? Was soul within man an inevitable by-product of the manufacture of vital material? And if production could be improved to the point of precise economy, would it give rise to other oblique by-products?"[78] Prushevsky does not trouble himself for long. He goes about his work with a sort of tender indifference. He concerns himself only with "eternal matter," that against which every engineer labors.

Safronov is also a technical worker and also has his doubts. "If one looked only at what lay below, at the dry pettiness of the soil and the grasses living in the very thick and in poverty, then there was no hope in life; a general, universal unprepossessingness, along with people's uncultured gloom, perplexed Safronov and shook the ideological directive in him."[79] Unlike Prushevsky he cannot still his soul by working only on dead matter. His calculations of nature are turning him gray. "He pictured the whole world as a dead body, judging it by those parts he had already converted into structures."[80] He tries to imagine the base on the model of the superstructure. He is too aware of the rift between a sorrowful nature and the relentless optimism of the five-year plan. They are not the same kind of organization.

In Prushevsky, "the passion of reason is the pull toward death."[81] Prushevsky concerns himself only with dead matter; Safronov consoles himself with the thought of the leap beyond it. Both avoid the third layer, the problem of life, on which Voschev dwells, if not always morosely: "Sadness is nothing . . . it means that our class senses the whole world."[82] Voschev's wager is on the comradeship of shared sadness. He extends Proletkult's self-assumed task of organizing the whole world of production to production's by-products and externalities, including its odd affects.

At night, the workers lie side by side, exhausted. At least their dreams remain their own: "Various dreams come to a laboring man at night—some express a fulfilled hope, while others foresee a personal coffin in a clay grave—but daytime is lived by everyone according to the same stooped method, through the endurance of a body digging the earth in order to plant into a fresh abyss an eternal stone root of indestructible architecture."[83] Labor is the only really shared part of human experience in Platonov. Ideology is always, strangely, idiosyncratic. Everyone détourns universals in light of particular experiences. In Platonov's world, even Bogdanov's *Red Star* could not offer the Sorelian myth of a universal horizon for everyone.

In an abandoned tile factory, a child cares for her dying mother, who was herself the daughter of the former owner. The child is not sure if her mother is dying from being bourgeois or from death. The workers from the pit find the orphaned girl and bring her to their shelter to care for her. Some of them nod approvingly at this child who spouts aggressive slogans and seems to know more about comrade Stalin than about her own mother. Safronov calls Nastya "the substance of creation and the aim and goal of every directive," and, rather more ambiguously, "our future object of joy."[84]

The workers dig the pit ever deeper and wider. It is as if no base could ever support the extravagant superstructure promised as the substance of the plan. Voschev alone seems alert to the ontological crisis. Base, dead matter supports the living, and life supports the soul, each a meager surplus of the layer below. But if the soul can't expand itself to the point of immersion in the whole world, then the world cannot be organized. Its efforts remain partial and futile, and life slips back into the boring emptiness of dead matter. Time not only has no end or goal but does not even permit the passing on into the future of temporary reserves against entropy: "Endurance dragged on wearily in the world, as if everything living found itself in the middle of time and its own movement; its beginning had been forgotten by everyone, its end was unknown, and nothing remained but a direction to all sides."[85] Another world is possible, and it is exactly the same as this one, just a variation among variations.

The failure of the plan, its alien quality over both the dead and the living, prompts only Voschev to attempt some other relation to being. Even Chicklin, the pure proletarian digger, gets caught up in a peculiar ideological fervor. Chicklin says to Voschev: "Who is it that exists in the world—the party or you? Who is it that is?" Voschev is caught in the nightmare spectacle of a being he knows to be false, but whose existence cancels his own possibility of being as anything but refuse or worse—a "wrecker." Voschev waits in vain for the Celestial Party to advance on its own ontological rift. "When would a resolution be passed there to curtail the eternity of time and redeem the wearisomeness of life?"[86]

However, the dominant reaction is Safronov's, which is to double down on the leap: "We no longer feel the heat from the bonfire of the class struggle." The exhaustion of the working class and its old revolutionary vanguard has come to pass. Safronov says in despair: "Ay, you masses! It's difficult to organize you all into the gruel of communism. What do you bastards want? You've worn out the entire vanguard, you vermin!"[87] Even Bogdanov's transfusions could not keep this vanguard going.

Safronov volunteers to assist with the forced collectivization of a nearby village into the General Line Collective Farm, and he and another are killed for their troubles.[88] The civil war between town and country is being fought to its bitter conclusion. Chicklin assumes within his body all the undone tasks of his dead comrades. If Voschev keeps an archive of the forgotten thing, Chicklin tries to preserve at least a fragment of lost human labor, but in both cases it is in vain. The living and the dead have their own organization and it isn't the plan.

Presiding over the collectivization is a character known only as "the activist," who for all of his outward personality seems to have evaporated into the letter of the plan. The activist imagines he is the "most ideological worker in the district superstructure." Yet he is troubled from time to time by the anguish of life, even as he gets the benefits of future time on credit by being in the vanguard. "Is truth the due of the proletariat?" asks Voschev.[89] The activist offers what's left of the proletariat agitation without truth, a perpetual and futile motion which produces its own apparent truth out of itself but is void of any basis in the tektological forming and deforming of life out of matter. The activist even thinks the wind is out to sabotage the plan. And of course, in Platonov's sense— wind as eroding time—it is.

The peasants are mostly nameless and faceless in *Foundation Pit*, as they were to the Stalinists, but they are not voiceless. As one peasant describes the situation: "There's no jam in the middle. It's total collectivization—no joy for us!"[90] Another mourns for the trees, which he feels are his own flesh, and which will no longer be part of his being once they are collectivized. Another correctly predicts that some form of the old property relations will be the only result of forced collectivization. It isn't the people who will own the land, but Stalin and his factotums.[91]

And yet the peasants slaughter their own livestock rather than lose it. "Cows and horses were lying in these yards, their carcasses gaping and rotting—and the heat of life accumulated through long years beneath the sun was still seeping out from them into the air, into the shared wintry space."[92] Platonov conjures the eerie sight of an untimely plague of flies, a swarm of black dots on the white snow, the seasons out of joint.

A strange fur grows on proletarian bodies. Perhaps it is related to the "last unknown proletarian," a bear who works at the smithy. The bear, or the hammerer as he is also called, is taken around the peasant huts to sniff out kulaks.[93] He denounces peasants who really did exploit him. It is time, as Nastya says, to "liquidate the kulaks as a class." Not: liquidate the kulaks, as a *class*. That is, abolish class distinctions between rich and poor peasants. Rather: liquidate the *kulaks* as a class. Meaning, liquidate them all physically. The activist has a raft made so they can be "liquidated" by floating them off, down the river, "organized for eternity."[94]

Nastya the innocent ideologue asks: "Have you made a collective farm here for Stalin?" In a notorious article called "Dizzy With Success," Stalin put the blame for the mass murder of kulaks, the destruction of livestock, and the inevitable famine on his underlings. In *Foundation Pit*, the decision is sheeted home where it belongs. The activist will be denounced as a wrecker. The bear pounds the iron in the smithy into ruins. The poor peasants dance madly after the kulaks leave. They have been rendered numb by events. "We sense everything, only not ourselves," the assembled collective says to Chicklin.[95]

The activist draws up his accounts of the collective farm. He measures inputs and outputs. He decides who has worked how much and who receives which wages. But Voschev has his own information. He collects objects which are the worn traces of human life and labor. They might be the tokens of another tektology, of an impossible organization, by which "soul" might stand for that which organizes living labor in and against dead matter for shared life. In the absence of which they are rather tokens now only of "vengeance through the organization of eternal human meaning—on behalf of those who are now lying quietly in the earth."[96] Both the activist and Voschev make their reckoning gifts to Nastya. Voschev's is a sack of "rare toys, not for sale anywhere"—those worthless fragments of lost lives that cannot be commodified even in the topsy-turvy concentrated spectacle of the Stalin era.[97]

For Voschev the futile, destructive laboring of the bear is a witness to the absence of truth. Truth cannot call itself into existence by tugging on its own bootstraps. The result is just a fake ontology, an unsupportable being that destroys the clay on which it stands. And yet there's nobody left to mourn the passing of truth from this world, its becoming unreal and spectral. As Voschev says over the dead activist: "So that's why I never knew meaning! It wasn't just me you sucked dry, you arid soul, it was the whole of our class! And we were left to ferment like quiet dregs, and to know nothing!"[98]

Nastya's heart grows tired and she dies, and Chicklin buries her in the depths of the foundation pit. In a weird way Platonov's own faith that some sort of communism might not be impossible is buried in the depths of *Foundation Pit*. His act of witness is not just a moral one. The future House of the Proletariat really is sheltered in here, but in its depths, and in death. While this is in many ways his bleakest text, certain things remain. Voschev still feels the absence of truth in both soul and body. He still has the fallen leaf to remind him.

HAPPY MOSCOW: SUPERSTRUCTURAL PEOPLE

If *Foundation Pit* is about the endless labor to produce an infrastructure, then *Happy Moscow* is about mostly "superstructural" people, living high up in city apartments.[99] It is a portrait of the cream of the first Soviet generation, with no memories of capitalism or the Tsar, whose lives are insulated from much of Stalinist reality. Most of the characters are technical intellectuals, the proto-hacker class, Bogdanov's people, successful and renowned.[100] This is the era of Stalin's second five-year plan. If the first was all about basic industry, the second pays at least some attention to leisure and consumer goods, produced in quantities sufficient at least to reward those faithful to the regime.

Life has become happier, Stalin has declared, but not for Platonov. Among other things, *Happy Moscow* is—astonishingly—a critique of commodity fetishism written right from the heart of the socialist second world. The revolution has become a manic repetition of production and consumption, where the common project of labor yields only solitary consumer satisfactions. "The spherical hall of the restaurant, deafened by the music and the howls of the people, and filled by the tormenting smoke of cigarettes and the gas of squeezed passions, seemed to revolve, every voice in it sounded twice, and suffering kept on being repeated."[101] Can there really be even the beginnings of a socialist base if the symptoms of capitalism are appearing in the superstructures? Stalin has to deliver rising living standards, for he has taken away everything else.

Platonov gathers most of his characters for an event at the Young Communist League. Many famous engineers gather, as well as artists, understood at the time as "engineers of the soul." Who will sit next to whom at the communal table? "What they really wanted was to sit next to everyone at once." Platonov does not doubt the intentions of his art and tech hackers, only the efficacy of their methods. They want the shared life, but they cannot find it. "They all knew, or guessed at, the sullen dimensions of nature, the extensiveness of history, the length of future time and the true scale of their powers; they were rational and practical people, not to be seduced by empty delusion."[102]

Like Dvanov, they live at best on secondary ideas, at worst, stuck where they are by what Lauren Berlant calls a *cruel optimism*, their own private desires impeding them. Certain music, particularly Beethoven, calls the characters to the great project of finding and building the common life. It is the "last dream of a heroic world."[103] The music excites the common space of the air, but is heard in individual and fragmentary ways.

Like so many Platonov characters, Moscow Chestnova is an orphan. She was raised by the state and trained as a parachutist, because she likes wind and sun. She is a bit like Dvanov, a pure revolutionary spirit caught up in events. She wants to stand by the accelerator of the locomotive, not experiencing life but making it. She embodies the labor point of view. "Her heart could have regulated the course of events," but it doesn't.[104] She is more object than subject of history.

There is an ascetic side to Platonov, much more characteristic of a certain strain of Russian intellectual of his time than of our own. There is a distaste for sexual love in particular, and hence a queasiness about women, whom he takes as tokens of it. But in *Happy Moscow* he is onto something that still speaks to our time: that the obsession with the couple, and the sexual love mixed with romance that legitimates it, are at best stand-ins and at worst obstacles for shared life. Moscow's dérives, wandering the city, and her serial trysts, are attempts to find both the uses and the limits of love. Marriage is not the answer. She "began to love just one sly man who kept a tight hold on her, as if she were some inalienable asset."[105]

As in *Foundation Pit*, Platonov takes literally Marx's notion of an economic infrastructure below and a cultural superstructure up above. Only here the story is not about the endless task of building a base, but about the other Stalinist desire: to occupy the heights above such a base immediately. This is why Moscow is training to be a paratrooper, going higher even than the newly sprouting towers of her city. The aircraft, rather than the locomotive, is the gleaming new technological image of historical momentum.

One of Platonov's most striking images is of Moscow lighting a cigarette while testing a new parachute technology. Descending from an aeronautical superstructure toward the earth, a solipsistic pleasure distracts her. The webbing catches alight and she has to pull the reserve 'chute to make it. "So world, this is what you are really like! . . . You are only soft so long as we don't touch you!"[106] She glides past the boundary separating technology and catastrophe. She gets fired from the Air Corps upon landing for having an attitude of luxury rather than modesty toward nature. There lies Platonov's whole critique of the Stalinist twist upon Bolshevik volunteerism, of Stalin's attack on the earth from above. The leap has its own vanity.

Moscow tries not to repeat that selfish turn in her wanderings on the surface, looking for a way to share life that is neither too airy nor too earthy, too merry nor too sad. She is the spirit of the commons, "she belonged to nobody," she is a "living truth."[107] But perhaps her solution to the riddle of the shared life is just to keep trying to live it: "She wanted to take part in everything and she was filled by that indeterminacy of life which is just as happy as its definitive resolution."[108]

The conceptual personae that Moscow encounters on her wanderings play out variations on the struggle for the shared life. Bozhko is a dedicated shock-worker by day. By night he writes letters to proletarians all over the world—in Esperanto. He sits at his desk under portraits of Lenin, Stalin, and the inventor of that artificial common language. But he also puts up smaller pictures of nameless people from all over the world.

Bozhko works in the Weights and Measures Office, as did Platonov for a time when he could not publish. He wants the people to have accurate measures of their labor so there will be no more riots on the collective farms, as if it were just a problem of measure for measure. He picks up every crumb so the country can thrive in its entirety. He generously pays for Moscow's tuition at flying school, and is very proper with her, but after her visits, "Bozhko usually lay face down on the bed and yearned from sorrow, even though his only reason for living was universal joy."[109]

Sambikin is a surgeon obsessed with longevity. He would not be out of place among Bogdanov's blood transfusion enthusiasts. Dissecting the baser strata, his concern is with a more physiological layer of being than the social being of Bozhko. "His mind lived in a terror of responsibility for the entire senseless fate of physical substance."[110] In a troubling scene, he operates on the brain of a sick child, but leaves a little of the infection in him, as removing it would require paring his little body down even to its toenails. It is the molecular that irks him.

Like many of Platonov's more conscious comrades, he can see around the corners of the dream that protects us from material life, and adopts an experimental attitude to it. "Sambikin began to ponder the life of matter—the life of his own self; it was as if he were a laboratory animal, the part of the world he had been allocated so that he could investigate the entirety of everything, in all its obscurity."[111] But where Bozhko lights upon the totality and not the particular; Sambikin loses himself in the molecular.

Sambikin extends true but partial metaphors out of his labors. This is how one can read his "dialectical psychology," which holds that what is distinctive about our species-being is that we obsess about the gap between two kinds of thought isolated from the world, which for animals are separate, yet intimately related to their world. He locates them in the brain and the spinal cord; cognition and sensation; reflection and labor; molar and molecular—as if dualism were an evolutionary error.

Unhappiness is a body where cognition and sensation are out of joint. "But then our two consciousnesses couple together again, we once again become human beings in the embrace of our 'two-edged' thought, and nature, organized according to the principle of an impoverished singleness, grits her teeth and curls herself up to escape from the activity of these terrible dual structures which she never engendered . . ."[112] Sambikin is terrified of his "two passions eternally copulating." Unlike Bogdanov, Platonov is pessimistic about the feedback loop from cognition to sensation. The rift, he senses, may be inevitable. Both cognition and sensation are physiological, but that does not guarantee a smoothly functioning monism.

A possible name for one of those passions is *soul*. Sambikin the physiological materialist thinks he has located the soul in the intestine, in the gap between that part of the intestine that is digesting food and that part that is accumulating waste for excretion. He cuts open a cadaver to show it to his friend Sartorius: "This emptiness in the intestines sucks all humanity into itself and is the moving force of world history. This is the soul—have a sniff."[113]

Sartorius later decides, "If the passions of life were concentrated entirely in the darkness of the intestines, world history would not have been so long and fruitless."[114] Life, at least the life of our species-being, is also something else, dependent on, but not reducible to, want. Even Sambikin knows something of this. But to be human is to be limited, to not be up to the task of the shared life physiologically, at least not now. We are only the embryo of something. But it is unhappiness which shows the way forward, not happiness. The happy know not their own disingressions.

What Sambikin and Sartorius have in common is a "yearning for a definitive structuring of the world."[115] Sartorius is a famous engineer, and at first more immune to feelings for Moscow than Bozhko or Sambikin. Better to love atoms and dust! He is a little further along the way to becoming part of a baser, more molecular world. But he falls for her too. "If Moscow had squatted to pee, Sartorius would have begun to cry."[116] He sniffs her shoes. "He could have looked at the waste products of her body with the greatest of interest, since they too had not long ago formed part of a splendid person."[117] Sambikin's obsession with the intestine and the interiority of the soul here becomes reversed into an obsession with the body and the exteriority of life—and in Platonov the waste products of both body and soul can be sniffed!

Sartorius wants to marry Moscow but she is always exceeding what can be an "inalienable asset," and in any case Moscow refuses him, as she alone knows that the couple could be just a barrier to shared life rather than a step toward it. When they fuck it only gets worse. It does not dissipate his possessive desire. As Moscow insists, "it is impossible to unite through love" and "love cannot be communism."[118] It's an appetite, a *want*. It's like eating food, a necessity, but nothing sacred. Here Platonov pursues the death of God into what is still its last hold-out: romantic-cum-sexual desire.

Sartorius abandons the "high road of technology."[119] But he remains in a sense an experimental engineer, a human soul engineer, but in the reverse sense to that meant by Stalinist doctrine. "Sartorius could see that the world consisted primarily of destitute matter, which it was almost impossible to love but essential to understand."[120] The soul is that part of human matter that cannot be instrumental-ized, which has to be treated as the temperamental organ of an everyday practice. "Sartorius realized that love came into being as a result of the poverty of society, a universal poverty that had still not been eliminated and which meant people were unable to find any better, higher destiny and didn't know what to do with them-selves."[121] Love is a falling short of organization, or a compensation for its falling: the heart of a heartless, and Godless, world.

Sartorius buys a black-market passport and begins another life as someone else, and starts to forget being Sartorius.[122] This throws into shocking relief a moment when hearing Beethoven almost makes Sambikin recall some former life. What if everyone passed into someone else and forgot their former self? Sartorius goes out into the world to "research the entire extent of current life by trans-forming himself into other people."[123] And this might be Platonov's account of his own method, of locating fragments of lost labor, which in their sadder moments reveal the ungainly and partial synthesis so far achieved by our species-being, our fallings-short of dynamic equilibrium.

Sartorius at least gets as far as debunking the extorted reconcili-ation of contraries in a false totality supposedly ruled by communist will:

> Sartorius made a movement of his hand—thus, according to the universal theory of the world instigating an electro-magnetic oscilla-tion which must disturb even the most distant star. He smiled at such a pathetic and impoverished conception of the great world. No, the world was better and more mysterious than that: neither a movement of the hand nor the work of the human heart would disturb the stars—otherwise everything would have been shaken to pieces long ago by all this trembling piffle.[124]

Sartorius, become the worker Grunyakhin, can still say: "I'm an engineer, I can tell you: nature's something altogether more serious. You can't play games with nature." Even as nature toys with us.

All of Moscow's lovers and admirers are superstructural people, whose specialized intellectual labors grasp the world only partially. When Moscow herself commits her body to hard work it is below the surface, at the base of the base, as it were, working on the Moscow city subway. Her second "industrial accident," below rather than above the superstructure, is not self-inflicted, but inflicted by her selflessness. She hobbles toward the end of the book, worn and thin and on a wooden leg. Real labor is more mutilating than a technical or intellectual hack. The problem remains the separation of the two aspects of the labor point of view.

The last of Moscow's lovers and admirers is not one of the superstructural people but Komyagin, an ailing would-be artist eking out a marginal existence. His former wife still visits him. Moscow listens through the sewer pipe in the wall as they fuck. "Our love has grown into something better—into shared poverty . . ."[125] Komyagin, who reserves himself from the Soviet state and its great projects, is in some ways the character closest to communism with his "worn out love."

But there is something too enervated about Komyagin. Moscow rejects him too. "No, this was not the high road that led into the distance; the road of life did not pass through the poverty of love, or through the intestines, or through the zealous attempts of a Sartorius to comprehend precise trifles."[126] Moscow is not on a journey with a destination. There is no Hegelian overcoming and uplifting. There is no land or sky, or even horizon. As Bozhko, of all characters, realizes: "Mother history's made monsters of the lot of us!"[127]

Moscow's line is more a drift, a dérive, outside of the division of labor and its partial results, but one which touches on the fragments of what might have to be brought together in a shared life, a comradely life, the only life outside of death.[128] Bozhko's selfless communication, Sambikin's clinical regard of the material body, Sartorius' molecular precision, Komyagin's love shorn of self-involved desire—these are the traces Moscow finds in the city, after wandering high and low, and far and wide, within the city's perimeter, the stray leaves of the labor point of view. Where Voschev collects fragmentary objects, Moscow collects bits of subjectivity.

As Fredric Jameson has noted of Platonov, the molar and the molecular don't add up.[129] Something keeps falling out of the story, even at the scale of characters. Even big-hearted Moscow vents a Stalinist urge to have useless Komyagin erased from life. But in the end she knows that's no solution. The leap of faith comes down to earth, and in its self-regard, it burns itself up on its descent.

THE SOUL OF MAN UNDER COMMUNISM

At a time when Stalin declared the final victory of the socialist economy in industry and agriculture, Platonov managed at least a temporary escape to the Soviet far east. There the women still ground corn by hand, and Soviet power was still somewhat notional.[130] Unable to publish, Gorky got him attached to a writer's brigade expedition to Turkmenia in 1934, to which he was able to return for a few months the following year.

Soul, also known as *Dzhan*, is the novella that resulted. It is a détournement of "high Stalinist" adventure writing.[131] It is not about the mythic proletarian of the old Bolshevik imagination, but rather the cult of the Stalinist leader. It follows Chagataev from Moscow to the East, where he was born, and back again. He is of course an orphan, who found a father in Stalin, and whose return journey is to the country of his mother. *Soul* is, most astonishingly, an imagining of a kind of non-Stalin. It is also a restaging of the scenario of *Chevengur*, but with a surprising outcome.

Chagataev is from a homeless, wandering people called the Dzhan, made up of exiles and deserters of all nations. Their name means soul, their only possession, for they have less even than proletarians. And yet they outlive empires. "The beys thought that the soul meant only despair; but in the end it was their dzhan that was the death of them; they had too little dzhan of their own, too little capacity to feel, suffer, think and struggle. They had too little of the wealth of the poor"—rather like all ruling classes.[132]

The Dzhan play out a series of tactics. Cruelly oppressed by the Khan of Khiva, who tortures his subjects to make them fear him, the Dzhan walk right into his city and demand to be killed all at once. The Khan only manages to kill those Dzhan who feared death. The others walk about the bazaar unscathed, nonchalantly picking fruit from the stalls and eating freely without payment, before returning to the desert. It is not unlike Platonov's own strategy for enduring Stalinism.

As the child Chagataev says to his mother of living in the desert: "We can live without thinking anything and pretend we're not us."[133] But the desert is hard and poor, and the Dzhan exhaust themselves in it. The desert is an extreme version of Bartleby's, "I would prefer not to," a refusal of any and all engagement, but it comes at the price of extinguishing not only life and selfhood but also the soul, which requires a surplus of life for it to exist.

The Dzhan are the defeated in a spiritual class struggle. "The class struggle begins with the victory of the oppressors over the 'holy spirit' confined within the slave: blasphemy against the master's beliefs—against the master's soul, the master's god—goes unpardoned, while the slave's own soul is ground down in . . . destructive labor." And so the Dzhan nation chose to forget it had a soul. It was not tempted by anything and could live on next to nothing. "It pretends to be dead—otherwise those who are happy and strong will come and torment it again."[134]

Little Chagataev is sent off with the last of the food and with only a walking stick for company to find a new father for himself. The one he finds is Soviet power. He studies economics in Moscow, where he meets Vera, with whom he forms a relationship, but without "furious pleasure." Vera already has a child—Ksenya—and is pregnant again when she and Chagataev meet. Platonovian dissatisfactions trouble him: "Chagataev could not endure the strength of his own life," and "he could not understand why happiness seemed so improbable to everyone."[135]

Fortunately a mission intervenes: Soviet power sends him to find his lost nation. As the train heads east, he notices that the portraits of Stalin look less and less like the man they are supposed to represent.

"The artist tried to make Stalin's face resemble his own."[136] As perhaps does Platonov, who in *Soul* imagines a non-Stalin in his own image. Like Dvanov, Chagataev abandons the train and heads out on foot, beyond the reach of the locomotive of history, and even of the history of locomotives. Beyond the rails is a harsh landscape. The desert is not grand; nature isn't providence. It was not made for the human and is indifferent to us: "It was as if the world had been created for some brief, mocking game. But this game of make-believe had dragged on for a long time, for eternity, and nobody felt like laughing any more." And yet Chagataev sides, in this landscape, with the powers of life. He cares for "an entire, difficult world."[137]

He wanders the land of his childhood in search of his people. Most have gone their separate ways. Some are off working on irrigation projects around the Amu Darya River. Some still live in families, and have love for one another, but have neither hope nor food nor happiness. Chagataev finds his mother, and now "everything was here—mother and homeland, childhood and future."[138] But his mother moves about as if in a dream, and it is as if he wakes into this dream. His mother still believes in property, but hasn't the strength even for greed. The Dzhan are beyond thought and language.

Chagataev is not the first agent the state has sent out into this wilderness. He finds the skeleton of a Red Army soldier and adopts his helmet. He meets his immediate predecessor, Nur Mohammad, who gave up trying to bring the Dzhan to communism. "I can't resurrect the dead," he says.[139] Nur's policy is to keep burying the Dzhan until they're all gone, then return to the state and report "mission accomplished." Or so he says. Nur has something of the same cruelty as the Khan of Khiva: "If you torture people too long, they die. You should torture them a little, then let them play, then torture them again."[140] Plato has it in *The Laws* that we are all the playthings of the Gods.[141] Nur would have earthly power aspire to that Godly power, rather than to that of the things with which it plays.

The Dzhan lose a three-year-old child in the desert and barely notice. Here it is not communism but its absence that is responsible for the lost generation. One of the last born of the Dzhan is Aidym. Nur had intended to lead all the Dzhan into Afghanistan and sell them for slaves, but only Aidym is of any value now. Nur rapes her, but in this version of the story the children born of communism suffer yet don't die.

Chagataev, the good agent, the non-Stalin, bearer of the memory of the revolution, has to fight the bad agent, its betrayer. Chagataev is resolved that his nation, "more than anything, needed a different life, a life that didn't exist yet and which they could live without it being the death of them."[142] When he learns by telegram that his Vera, back in Moscow, has died in childbirth, he knows that the faith that was once an objective worldview has passed from this world, and there is nothing for it but to press on, if only to another iteration of this world.

Alone in the desert, Chagataev starts to tune in to the ambient chorus of the natural world, barely audible and indifferent to him: "All through the night he heard round him a vague humming, a diverse agitation, the troubled movement of a natural world that had faith in what it was doing and where it was going." But it offers nothing for the Dzhan. Their souls scatter and expire. Chagataev too succumbs. "He began to mutter words to himself, living his life as if it were superfluous to him."[143]

The Dzhan find sheep in the desert, but without a shepherd. The sheep watch impassively as one of their number is slaughtered, as if it were no concern of theirs. The Dzhan follow the sheep, while wild beasts follow the Dzhan in an endless routine of subsistence without direction or end. Life goes on by habit, inertia, while the sand grinds, grain against grain, in the wind. Sometimes the sheep stray, and like the tumbleweeds are blown off course, "and so the universal guiding force, of everything from plants to humans, is really the wind."[144] This is bare uneventful time, without accumulation or memory, genesis or goal:

> But what was the dream that nourished the consciousness of the nation, if the whole of this wandering nation was able to go on bearing its fate? The nation couldn't be living off truth; had it known the

truth about itself, it would have died at once from sorrow. But people live because they have been born, not because of mind or truth, and, while the heart goes on beating, it breaks up and grinds away their despair, losing its own substance as it destroys itself through work and endurance.[145]

In this closed loop of everyday, unexaminable life, the Dzhan forget themselves, but endure.

All except Chagataev, who is tormented by memories. "Stalin was alive and would bring about the universal happiness of the unhappy anyway, but it was a shame that the Dzhan nation, who had a greater need for life and happiness than any other nation of the Soviet Union, would by then be dead."[146] Or perhaps Chagataev, their non-Stalin, might have another idea, not one which introduces the surplus death of the universal into life, but rather one which both produces a surplus out of dead matter beyond subsistence, and which in turn introduces life into thought. The utopia of Chevengur starts with the universal of equality by which any violence can be justified, and which cannot support life. The Dzhan start with life, to which surplus is added, and out of which a comradeship might form, the only viable tektological formula.

Chagataev has to find a different way to lead, after the disenchantment with great men and their fatal plans, tempting though they are. He learns to lead *from* a situation rather than *to* a horizon. "It seemed to Chagataev that the whole of humanity, were it here before him, would be looking at him with this same expectancy, ready to delude itself with hopes, endure disillusion, and busy itself once again with diverse, inescapable life."[147] Having endured disillusion with the universal, there's nothing for it but designs for life, low theories, and everyday praxis from the labor point of view.

Chagataev is the expendable, rather than conquering, vanguard. He is not Stalin, to whom a people belong like slaves. "He felt as if he belonged to others, as if he were the last possession of those who have no possessions, about to be squandered to no purpose, and he was seized by the greatest, most vital fury of his life."[148] The last possession of bare life lies in someone else's memory of it. Chagataev both remembers the Dzhan as they are and loves them as they might be, in advance and forever.

Chagataev designs a viable life with his people. Aidym becomes the president of their soviet. They no longer have to strain their memories to remember themselves. It is hardly utopia. The Dzhan still prefer oblivion to communism. They have forgotten the aim of life, like zombie-Bartlebys. They forgot their own wants, since nothing had ever come of them. They live only through inertia. They may have no soul left to lose. "Had everything there been so worn away by suffering that even imagination, the intelligence of the poor, had entirely died?"[149]

Praxis starts and ends with the struggle for life; everything else is just useless duplicity or dangerous theology. Chagataev helps them find food. "He knew that this was very important, since only a minority of people living on the earth dine every day and the majority do not." The nation are still not convinced life is an advantage, but they now grasp that life at base upon which soul depends, and without the fetishism which makes soul appear as autonomous or even causative. They know that the soul, like the body, has to eat. "They ate without greed, taking care of the food in their mouths, with a consciousness of the food's necessity and meek thoughtfulness, as if seeing in their imagination the faces and souls of all those who had labored hard to procure the food and give it to them."[150]

His mother dies, leaving Chagataev orphaned now from both the state and his own family. In *Soul* it is the past that falls away, as it should, not the future. But the Dzhan go their separate ways. Dreams separate us, *even when they are dreams of communism*. Or rather: communisms, since in Platonov, actual communisms are never a stage in a molar narrative, but are at best proliferating situations in which comradely love prevails, if just for a time. Like all people, the Dzhan can find how best to live for themselves. Chagataev is surprised not to be of any use to his nation any more. As Aidym says, "We want something different now, a different kind of grief, a more interesting grief."[151] The Dzhan want a grief adequate to the tragedy of the totality.

The role of Chagataev as non-Stalin can only be negative, a vanguard that dissolves itself in acts. Yet Chagataev wants to gather the nation back, and goes in search of them. In a market town he meets Khanom and experiences love—one of the few such instances in Platonov. "And then Chagataev put both his arms around Khanom, as if he had seen in her an image of what had never been realized in him and never would be realized in him but would remain alive after him—in the form of a different, higher human being, on an earth grown kinder than it had been for Chagataev."[152] Sexual love can now generate an image of a future evolution. Perhaps the memory of the future can be kept there, rather than buried deep in some base crypt.

Chagataev writes a report to the capital, which is perhaps like the one Serbinov writes from Chevengur, except that this one is about the happiness of the shared life of the Dzhan, and also their still-pressing material need. In *Chevengur*, the documenting of one or several communisms is the end of them. The troops arrive on horseback in answer to Serbinov's report. In response to the report of *Soul*, trucks arrive not with guns but with provisions, a great gift from elsewhere.[153] Comradely love and the production of a material surplus, like clay and top soil, rest on one another but are separate achievements. Chagataev takes Aidym to Moscow, and the Dzhan elect Khanom president of the soviet. Chagataev reunites with Ksenya. The text ends with them holding hands.

SOCIALIST TRAGEDY

None of Platonov's great series of (anti)novellas were published in his lifetime, although some of his very fine stories were. Somehow he survived the 1930s. He became a war correspondent, and after the war published versions of traditional folk tales. His last story appeared in a children's magazine, and recounts the fortunes of a speck of grain and a speck of gunpowder. Even this molecular fable attracted censure.[154]

While without doubt one of the great writers of the Soviet experience, he can be read also in other registers. The critical misalignment of the non-living, the living, and the organizational diagram is no less a problem of our own time. One can't help suspecting that the Carbon Liberation Front would have come as no surprise to him. He was already thinking about the problem of labor and nature as a problem calling for new kinds of writing outside of socialist realism. The challenge of writing in and against capitalist realism calls for another Platonov, or perhaps rather for a new kind of proletkult.

I want to conclude these meditations on Platonov with two of his (non)essays, fragments that point toward a Platonovian practice for our time. One is on "Socialist Tragedy" (1934), and the other is on "The Factory of Literature" (1926). The former defines the problem, and the latter the method, for Platonov's heretical Marxist practice.

Platonov's Marxism is an ascetic one, based on the experience of sub-proletarian everyday life. Nature is not abundant—and just as well. If nature was abundant then it would have been plundered and squandered by history already. Or perhaps nature would have destroyed itself by now, even without human agency. "The dialectic is probably an expression of miserliness, of the daunting harshness of nature's construction, and it is only thanks to this that the historical development of humankind became possible." Otherwise it would all be over, "as when a child plays with sweets that have melted in his hand before he has even time to eat them."[155]

Technology plays a decisive role in the struggle within and against nature. Technology for Platonov is not just machines and such, but, as in Bogdanov, a method, or even a design, of organization. Included in a technology is its technicians, and even their ideology. This ideology is not superstructural. It is internal to technology's organization, one of its elements. The technology, technician, and ideology assemblage, or apparatus, organizes itself and its objects in particular ways, and is prone to breakage, decay, and misdirection. Platonov pays particular attention to the technician's part within this as a kind of love for the machine.

"The situation between technology and nature is a tragic one." Technology offers leverage on the world, but always from a particular vantage point. Nature can always surround or surmount it. The "dialectic" of nature always eludes the apparatus of labor and technology. Nature is the enemy of our species-being.[156] Technology can only soften it. There's no end to the struggle in and against it. The unruliness of nature never goes away, not least because it is part of the technical anyway, an unsleeping rust.

In both Bogdanov and Platonov, in complimentary but different ways, we find the resources to think again about labor's relation to nature as primary. Capitalism keeps capturing our attention. Communism fascinates some once again, as an understandable but hardly helpful nostalgia. Meanwhile, the two most useful categories to think with, and think of—labor and nature—receive hardly any love. This is where Bogdanov and Platonov come, like Dvanov and Kopenkin, to the rescue.

Every increase in productive forces comes at some cost, somewhere. As Platonov says in a prescient pair of lines: "The ancient life on the 'surface' of nature could still obtain what it needed from the waste and excretions of elemental forces and substances. But we are making our way inside the world, and in response it is pressing down upon us with equivalent force." The mining of the earth for its properties undermines at the same time this very labor. It is Bogdanov's biregulator in a more pessimistic mode. There's no enclosure that can keep nature out. It is as true of Stalin's grand projects as of our time's gated communities.

Language is a thing, and like other things it can be appropriated and shared by labor. But while it belongs to the class of things, no thing has special access to the objects beyond their ken. The world of things keeps coming to light through a range of practices, and sometimes in difficult and intractable forms. Hence the vital significance of Platonov's experience of electrical and hydrological engineering, through which the molecular thing enters his field of perception and also his writing. The intractability of things gives rise to a special kind of tragedy.[157]

Sadness is the mood by which the divorce between the sensation of the world and the idea of it is felt and thought. This rift can be ignored, and thought can go its own way, leaping fatally into the void. Or, grief can be shared. The *comrades* are the ones with which we share life's task of shoring up its impossible relation to a recalcitrant world. All we can share are the same travails, and we are only comrades when we might all share all of them. An injury to one is an injury to all.

We live on in spite of the impossibility of living, as if by habit. Everyday life is a kind of inertia. Molecular matter yields a surplus on which life fuels; life in turn can yield another surplus, for that other life of the soul. But there's no transitive relation between these superstructures and their base, between topsoil and clay. It's hard to actually know anything about the infrastructure and nature from the experience of its surplus. We are nature's orphans, or perhaps just its clones. We know it as cause but not so much what or how it causes, and even our own actions are included back in its causative effect on us, unilaterally, without a two-way exchange or shadings of difference.[158]

That surplus that is soul can dream of a higher, universal idea, but those ideas are always singular and inflected by private desires. They can't be generalized. Only (non-intellectual) labor and (non-romantic) love are shared—Platonov adds love to Bogdanov's labor—and in both cases not without their limitations. An idea is always a folly, but a necessary folly. The idea is a sort of impossible crystal, dead and inert, without which boredom and grief weather us. But the idea on its own is only the concept of death, as if it could be outside of the entropy, inertia, and forgetfulness of life in time. Ideas are there as material for experiment and substitution.

Better to live then on a *secondary idea*, which mediates between the idea and labor, keeping the dead ideal from direct contact with life, where either the idea of death will live and kill life, or life itself will kill the deathly idea, but leave only boring emptiness. The secondary idea should be practical, attaching itself to the problem of life and inert matter, rather than life and soul. The secondary idea is usually a design problem, and hence, in principle, soluble.

There is only one hope, and it is in eternal life, but this endless life has nothing to do with spirit or even the idea. It isn't universal. It exists only in the sensation of shared existence. Living things are each other's comrades, even in their struggles against each other. Our species-being is lost from shared life when we make a fetish of a particular idea, a particular love, or a particular labor, as Bogdanov might say. Platonov shows the deadly consequences of fetishes of this type.

Comradely life, devoted to its secondary ideas, is a homeless, rootless nation, in which each labors for another who labors for another. It is a life done with the death-image of the absolute outside and beyond itself. Comrades are orphans by choice. It is not the parent who has abandoned them, it is they who drift away from the spirit of the paternal idea, and who accept the poor truth that nature is no mother but at best a "step-mother nature"—or even no kin at all. Let's have done with these Oedipal substitutions.

When drawn into the practice of everyday life, ideas dissolve into their constituent parts, the bits of language, which are articulated in new and surprising forms. This is détournement at work, the molecular labor of making and remaking sense in given situations. The people make meaning, but not with the means of their own making. The proletariat might one day substitute for its various fetishisms an objective worldview, a tektology that might organize base and superstructure. The "relative autonomy of the superstructures" is actually one of the fetishes to be overcome.[159]

THE FACTORY OF LITERATURE

While it is of considerable antiquarian interest, Platonov's "The Factory of Literature" also lends itself to a reading as a method of constructing text that anticipates not only détournement, but several critical forms of twenty-first-century cultural production that are usually seen as separate or even antithetical. Here is a bold precedent for the "uncreative" writing methods of Kathy Acker, Vanessa Place, and Kenneth Goldsmith. It is also based in part in a kind of "cultural analytics" of big data of the kind advocated by Lev Manovich. And it touches on the kind of "networked book" advanced by Kathleen Fitzpatrick and Bob Stein.[160] Even so,

Platonov's version might have as yet unexplored affordances. Where socialist realism would subordinate the labor of writing to the mythic templates of the party, Platonov, as usual, reversed the procedure. He built a prose from the bottom up. It might yet work as a procedure in and against capitalist realism as well.

Platonov describes a sort of fieldwork version of the "convolutes" Walter Benjamin constructed for his *Arcades Project*. Platonov:

> I bought a leather notepad and divided it into seven sections with the following headings: 1. Work, 2. Love, 3. Everyday Life, 4. Personality traits, 5. Discussion with oneself, 6. Unexpected thoughts and findings and 7. Miscellaneous and special . . . I include into this journal everything that I find interesting and everything that can be a readymade component for literary work, including excerpts from newspapers, separate phrases from the same source, pieces from different popular and not popular books, real dialogues from different sources, and I write my own ideas, themes and pieces. I am trying to live my life in a way that I notice everything that is valuable for the notepad.[161]

One could see this as a sort of tagging exercise, sampling language and adding *metadata* to it of seven kinds. But that's just the start. Now comes the hard part: "I flip through the notepad in the evenings and I focus on one specific note and I start working on that theme, also taking into account the next notes and sketches. I focus on dialogues, description of streets and other miracles that I slightly alter, depending on my goals and my capacity to connect these pieces by personal cement."

As with Platonov's contemporary, the filmmaker Dziga Vertov, the emphasis moves from making the elements of the work to the editing:

> You end up with an essay where your contribution is only 5–10% but it's all about my edits and ambitions. Editing is what brings us closer to the author since it is a very intimate spiritual individual corrector, that illustrates the presence of a real and passionate hand

and personal passion, as well as the ambition and goal of a real person. Borrowed from people, I give it back to them having thought it through . . . The result is, or is supposed to be, truly fascinating because thousands of people worked on it and contributed their individual and collective reviews of the world.[162]

Like détournement, it's a matter of borrowing and correcting ready-made elements. In Platonov, the metaphorical substitution runs from prepared ingredients in food preparation to text preparation:

> What exactly are ready-made ingredients? Myths, historical and modern facts and events, everyday activities and an ambitious or better destiny—all of these which are proclaimed by thousands of mouths and hundreds of dry and anonymous official papers will be ready-made components for writers, since all of these are made unintentionally, genuinely, for free and by chance and you cannot write better than that: this is a 100% equivalent of life that is enriched by a virgin soul.

Like Kathy Acker, Platonov experiments with mixing "real" and "fake" biographical elements:

> You write all kinds of things and improve . . . Your friends will ask you where this is coming from. You smirk and I say that it comes from people themselves. A lot of writers do a better job in telling the story than writing it. I decided to experiment once and included my friend's speech into my essay. He read it and got excited but didn't remember since I edited it a bit. He still doesn't get it that work that actually produces big results just requires manual dexterity.[163]

Writing is work for Platonov, a kind of labor, not the "life of the mind." On the contrary it is more mineral than spiritual:

> Art is organically an essential part of life, just like sweating is part of a human body and motion is part of wind. However, in passing

within the subsoil of a body, in geological layers in areas with narrow coverage of human collective structures, art is not always visible and publicly accessible. It is about making it visible and bringing it out of the geological layers onto the surface of everyday life.

Like Bogdanov, he is aware, however, that language has a peculiar kind of materiality: "Words are just social materials and they are very manageable and reversible."

Given how malleable words are, it is striking how the labor of transforming them is still caught up in petit-bourgeois ideas of the craftsman producer, as if each writer could make a motor car by hand: "They still make cars by themselves forgetting that there is Ford and Citroën . . . comparing the knowledge and intellect circulating in the world of builders with circles of writers—the comparison is not in favor of latter."[164]

One division of labor that might advance the production of literature would be a kind of critic-engineer, whose job is not to anatomize forms, but to actually produce them: "the critics' job and main mission is to develop new methods for writing that simplify and improve the writers work . . . Critics need to become constructors of 'machines' that produce literature, and the artist will work on the machines." A second division of labor, once such a form exists, is between the inductive and editing labor processes. The literary component is not the making of the words, but the editing of that product: "But literature is a social phenomenon and therefore it needs to be developed by social collective force only under the leadership and editing drive of one person— the writer."

The factory of literature works up the raw material of speech and text into prefabricated elements, being careful not to edit out in advance what is "nutritious" in it:

In every national republic or area there must be at least seven literary factories. Maybe the story can be divided into sections and each factory works on one section. So these literary factories are primary workshops where ready-made ingredients are processed. And then this material gets delivered to national literary factories that are the most experienced ones, where actual writers work . . . However, it is not required that the literary factory have excellent editing skills—that unique capacity to add something to the ready-made ingredients and make an essay out of it.

Here we can see how much Platonov reverses the procedure of socialist realism. His imaginary factory hews close to the popular speech act, selecting and organizing those acts. Even the language from above is to be read back through the feedback loop of what speech from below makes of it:

The national literary factories need to have all the qualities listed above plus education. The material that is received from this unit gets sorted into different notepads, getting it cleaned of unoriginal thoughts and ideas that are not valuable for literature . . . The national literary factory is a laboratory that controls the quality. They don't need to add their own input to these pieces. For their own ideas there is another space called "accidental thoughts."

Platonov imagines not only a whole discourse network and division of labor, but also distribution of the rewards. "Honorarium should be the following: 50% – the writer, 5% – critic, 5% – national literary factories, 40% – literary factories, for each piece published by this unit. The pieces are published under the writer's name and with the insignia of the literary factory." The unpaid, precarious labor of today's internet is in this model at least not entirely unacknowledged and unrewarded.

To the extent that anyone built anything like this, in the Soviet Union it was the secret police, and in our time the National Security Agency. But the difference is that while those textual factories attribute statements to individuals to make them culpable, Platonov's version does the reverse. The circulation of language produces its effects—heretical or orthodox—in its speakers, not the other way around. "This isn't hierarchy . . . The most important benefit of the factory is of course the division of labor and the fact that it covers lots of human lives, masses and territories, thousands of eyes." But eyes that aren't looking for suspects. Platonov's factory is anonymous.[165]

Of course the Factory of Literature is a fantasy, a utopia, or perhaps a meta-utopia, a means of making not only actual but virtual worlds out of language. It is not a communist horizon but a non-Euclidian space of possibility, of n-dimensions, folds, forkings, and joining paths. And while it may be the case that the twenty-first century has the technology to realize it, what was actually built is quite the opposite. Still, it remains just one of a whole menagerie of living forms, possible but not actual, with which to shape what Anne Balsamo calls the *technological imagination*, but one that integrates a unique form of workers' inquiry, or in the era of the social factory, of mass observation.[166]

In everyday life, language acquires a necessarily partial adhesion to whatever loves and labors it is made to work with. This is why the personae of Platonov's texts matter. Each embodies a given practice and the fetishisms specific to that situation. Comradely life becomes possible when the rule of the universal over such situations is abandoned. Such situations cannot even be grouped in sets, for there is no ruling idea even of their separation and ordering.

In *Foundation Pit*, Voschev gathered up lost things, forgotten things, wasted things, things that deviated from the fantasy realism of the times. Voschev gleans them and keeps them in a bag, as an inventory and offering, as a gift to another time. Perhaps it is now time to look for such gifts from times past. Here in the overdeveloped world, it is as if, in the dream of the seven fat decades, we forgot about the seven lean decades. We lived in and looked only to the superstructures, assuming the base was too basic and vulgar for our refined minds. The Carbon Liberation Front changes all such calculations.

The great patrons of the critical thought of our time are still speaking mostly of useless things. Their words are dead to us. We find ourselves orphaned from those other queer ancestors who, like Platonov, might speak to our most vulgar problems. Fortunately, it is still possible to cobble together a kind of mad Golem that can speak to this era of metabolic rift in something like the accent of the overdeveloped world, who can rail against capitalist realist certainties with a quite other kind of realism, one which limns close to what's there to be actually sensed.

PART II
Science and Utopia

3

Cyborg Donna Haraway: Techno-science Worlds and Beings

California! Über alles!

—The Dead Kennedys

THE CALIFORNIA IDEOLOGY

If Part I of *Molecular Red* is set in a slightly mythical early twentieth-century Soviet Union, Part II spirits us off to an even more mythical late twentieth-century California. This story too can begin as a story about water, and metabolic rift. This western edge of American Empire is a coastal plain backed by a vast mountain range, the waters of which have been routed through a hydraulic engineering project about as vast as that which drained the Aral Sea.

The centerpiece of this infrastructure, which would have staggered the imagination of Platonov, was built on the ruins of the Sacramento-San Joaquin Delta, the largest estuary in the western hemisphere. The State Water Project and the Central Valley Project pump water falling on the Sierra Mountains through here on its way from northern to southern California, mostly for agriculture, but also providing a small though crucial part of the water supply for the great southern cities. Not to mention the golf courses of

California, which between them use more water than the city of Los Angeles. The water can travel 500 miles, and the whole exercise uses 5 percent of the state's electricity. It is perhaps a ruin still in slow-motion progress, plagued by drought and rising sea levels.[1]

But for now it hydrates the fresh skin of that familiar California landscape of suburbs and gulags, malls and freeways. Like its water infrastructure, that landscape was built after the Pacific War and on Pacific trade, but also in large measure on military industries. This is where capitalist realism's "California Ideology" was born. It is a feral cross between cyber-culture and counter-culture, where the disruptive power of "tech" is supposed to power the freeing of any and every resource for commodification. Part II of *Molecular Red* is about some Californians who have been critical of the California Ideology, but who did not seek any refuge from it in returning to the worn clichés of a bourgeois liberal humanism.[2]

As we shall see, there's no haven to be found in any of those romantic longings for something outside of the combined powers of strategic command, commodified vectors, and technological refashioning that undergird the California Ideology. It is no longer the case that art or literature or the imagination or the body or desire or the human or nature or the absolute or even the communist horizon could be the ethical or cultural or political avatar of the thing-in-itself, the *locus solus* outside the machine of the military-entertainment complex. It has no outside, and it is accelerating.

Even California's majestic, ancient Sierra Nevada mountains no longer stand as mute witness to the human vanity below. They too are changing as the climate changes, and irrevocably.[3] In the era of the Carbon Liberation Front, there is no way to return to a lost ecology, where that is understood as a cyclical, healing and soothing natural orderliness. The California coast, that most westerly edge of this new world, is no longer the terminus of manifest destiny.

California's *latent destiny* is now that of which we must speak. Manifest destiny had a spatial horizon, the ever-westward advance of a civilization that took that very colonizing momentum as proof of its own virtue. Latent destiny has a more temporal horizon. It is an undoing of that time in which the future was like the present, only *more of it*. Latent destiny is a temporary temporality populated by spectacles of disintegration, of glyph and .gif glimpses of new futures that refute old pasts. The going is getting weird.

Packing an intellectual knapsack for clambering around the sierras of this new kind of unstable 'cene is a challenging task in itself. My wager is on the utility of a group of writers who could be thought of as coming from the same bag as Bogdanov and Platonov. They might equip us with a latter-day empirio-monism, tektology, and labor point of view, and even a utopian fiction for the times. Part II of *Molecular Red* is the prep list for the trek out of theories-past toward the Anthropocene present.

Given the advanced stage of the division of intellectual labor, there's nobody in late twentieth-century California who attempted to write theoretically about as many topics as Bogdanov, let alone in fiction as well. The writer who comes closest is Donna Haraway. Certainly, the History of Consciousness Program at the University of California (Santa Cruz), where she taught, is the closest thing in the United States to a tektological research program. Haraway and her colleagues and students performed both critical and constructive work on the way metaphorical substitutions leap between scientific, technical, social scientific, and humanistic knowledge production.

But it seems fittingly Bogdanovite to approach the creation of a latter-day tektology as a collaborative and collective project, rather than focus on Haraway's work as a solo act—great though it is. Hence our itinerary visits with one of her sources (Paul Feyerabend), then Haraway's own work, then that of a colleague (Karan Barad), followed by one of Haraway's students (Paul Edwards). Their respective labors allow us to update in turn Bogdanov's empirio-monism, his tektology, the labor point of view, and his attempt to think at the scale of the molecular and of the biosphere. I approach these writers as if they were what Haraway calls *messmates*. I call the composite that arises out of their breaking bread together Cyborg Haraway, as it is a sort of text-machine of indeterminate type that makes itself through critical thinking in and about the various sciences.

I will firstly try to reconstruct for the era of the Carbon Liberation Front something like the Machist-Marxism of Bogdanov, but retooled for the times, and built out of a détournement of some writings by Paul Feyerabend. The aim here is a minimalist theory that hews close to sensation and to the techniques that produce it. As we shall see when we get to Paul Edwards, a knowledge of the Anthropocene comes from scientific labors in fields such as climate science. Thus, having a grip on this era *at all* relies on having some relation to scientific knowledge in relatively new and distinctive fields. Thus the traditional indifference, disdain, or lordly sense of superiority of humanistic knowledge to the sciences will no longer suffice. Unlikely as it may seem to those who know his work, it is via Feyerabend that I think one might revive a Machist-Marxist, empirio-critical approach to the sciences that is critical and constructive, collaborative and comradely.

The Anthropocene calls upon all the labors of our species-being. But what in these times is labor? Can a concept of labor include scientific labor, reproductive labor, affective labor, precarious labor, even non-labor? What prevents twenty-first century labor from acting collectively by and for itself? Is it not just another kind of fetish to try to think the worker as something apart from the mesh of flesh and tech that is the composite material of twenty-first-century organization? Here we touch on the central node of this chapter, a reading of Donna Haraway, who advances some new versions of what fetishism might mean, such as corporeal fetishism and code fetishism, via which to diagnose impediments to a twenty-first-century tektology. Here too I revisit Haraway's most famous text, "A Manifesto for Cyborgs," as a prescient document which points toward new languages, ironic and utopian, for articulating a latter-day worker's point of view.

Thinking about labor today, not least scientific labor, calls for a close attention to something that does not quite rise to the level of a concept in Bogdanov—the *apparatus*. The highly specialized and differentiated kinds of labor of the twenty-first century, particularly in the sciences, give off fascinating and diverse substitutional chains of metaphor, image, and diagram through which to construct basic metaphors for worldviews of far more generality than Bogdanov could ever have imagined, but also a host of new dangers. Here the physicist and feminist science studies professor Karan Barad can help us grasp what it means to think through the apparatus and the sensations of modern physics, to construct a worldview whose experimental bases really are molecular, if not sub-atomic.

Bogdanov's Socialist Academy did not come to pass, but it is curious how his tektology does anticipate some things about how scientific labor came to be organized. There is no better example of this than climate science. Here we look at the work of Haraway's former graduate student Paul Edwards, whose work on climate science pays close attention to how it is organized both as a technical infrastructure and as a culture. In the spirit of Bogdanov, a genuinely Marxist approach to the sciences has to pay close attention to the leading *practical* sciences, understood through their means of production.

Those are the component and interactive parts of Cyborg Haraway. This is a strictly amateur, non-professional reading where the sciences are concerned, looking for images, metaphors, and diagrams that might suggest augmented worldviews, but where such use is yet to be experimentally verified. Let's reorient critical thought to a kind of comradely practice, where each kind of labor or science produces its own specific worldview, extending via substitution from its particular encounters and sensations, and where none claims to be the master discourse with authority over them all. It is a low theory approach, moving between scientific knowledges, not a high theory flying high as a drone above to adjudicate, legislate, or police them.

Having assembled a Cyborg Haraway remake of empirio-monism and tektology, the last chapter of *Molecular Red* asks whether there is a role then for the speculative fiction of Bogdanov's *Red Star*, and his anti-theological insistence that writing respond to yearnings and desires for a horizon of the absolute with popular fictions rather than specialized philosophies. It proposes the writings of Kim Stanley Robinson as an equivalent to Bogdanov's utopian writing in the era of the Carbon Liberation Front.

The special virtue of Robinson's post-Bogdanovite science fiction is that it is no longer about just one worldview, but about the negotiation between worldviews that result from different kinds of labor, scientific, technical, political, and cultural. For perhaps we need a more plural conception of utopian possibility to match the plurality of sensations and the worldviews of the times. Rather than the endless competition between different visions of changing life, the challenge might be rather to organize between them. Here a utopian, or perhaps *meta-utopian* mode of writing might point the way forward.

Early twenty-first-century critical thought is expressing the desire for another life in two main ways. One is a revival of a kind of revolutionary subjectivity, a psychoanalytic Leninist sublime. The other is a kind of speculative absolute, a theory purified of any merely human phenomenal dimension and set free in a hyperchaotic or vitalist cosmos.[4] The former radicalizes the category of subject; the latter absolutizes the category of object. What tends to get evacuated in both cases is the bit in the middle, the media between object and subject (or whatever contemporary avatars of those ancient concepts is in vogue). The situation which mediates between and enables the cut that delineates object from subject is where we find sensation, apparatus, and the labor point of view.

This is where we build a contemporary empirio-monism, tektology, and that component of a proletkult that might take the form of a meta-utopian fiction, all of which in their lowly way is where we might start to grapple with the Anthropocene. After working through Robinson's conceptual personae and their narrative arcs as myths for a new proletkult, we can then turn, by way of conclusion, to thinking how labor and nature, science and utopia, might forge organizational forms for the Anthropocene. But first, let's turn to that most unlikely Californian—Paul Feyerabend.

FROM MACH TO FEYERABEND

The "Machist" strand of thought fell silent among the competing leftist theories of the late twentieth century.[5] But Mach himself had at least one first-rate champion in science studies. "The nineteenth century produced one philosopher who was not prepared to accept the status quo, who was not content to criticize science from the safe distance of a special subject either, but who proceeded to suggest concrete means for its change. The nineteenth century produced Ernst Mach."[6] The twentieth century produced Paul Feyerabend.

While he was once offered a job by Bertolt Brecht, Feyerabend was always remote from, not to mention contemptuous of, Marxism. Feyerabend: "Is it surprising that I dislike reformers like Brecht who turn the theater, one of the last strongholds of magic, into a sociological laboratory?"[7] His was more of a dadaist soul. The challenge is to think forward from Feyerabend's revival of Mach to what a more contemporary strain of Machist Marxist thought, one adequate to the twenty-first century, might become. Perhaps even one with a little, but not too much, magic. The question of whether Feyerabend's Mach is the actual Mach-in-himself, or only one refracted through Feyerabend's own lens, need not detain us. Nor do I claim to give all that complete or accurate a resemblance of Feyerabend.

The Mach who colors Feyerabend's world is the philosopher-scientist, running theories through practices and vice versa. He grants science autonomy from any logical construction or idealized reconstruction. Science is as science does; a knowledge without foundation. The scientist is not someone with access to a special portal to the real, and the knowledge he (yes he for now, we shall come back to that) creates can be connected to other kinds of knowledge practice, and other kinds of knowledge practitioners.[8]

Feyerabend's thought anticipates more of a democratic than a proletarian knowledge. He had a keen sense of science as an alibi for colonial power, but his sense of how class and capital work in knowledge production is rudimentary. The quality of his work is elsewhere. He wanted to demystify science, to open the possibility of critique to science as a whole. He wanted a way to move across the divisions of labor within not only science but knowledge more generally. There is no unthinking border between science and folk knowledge, sentience and sapience.

Not many people other than Mach could dilate with such verve about "the awful Newton," who is not a scientific hero to Feyerabend, but rather someone who set the pattern for science as a mode of authority, as a *discipline* in its creeping senses.[9] But at least the scientific revolution of the seventeenth century involved a close collaboration of science and philosophy. Things really went wrong when philosophy became separate, and started to produce its own problems, or when it specialized in codifying science without a reciprocal relation to it (particularly with Kant). By defining the limits of the reasoning subject, philosophy claims to ground science by specifying the conditions under which the phenomenal object of knowledge correlates with a thinking subject.[10]

Recall that Bogdanov read these symptoms in slightly different terms. Idealist philosophy practiced a mode of substitution that privileged the experiences of intellectual labor. Its problems were the problems of overcoming the organization of the subjective element, rather than more "objective" ones. Curiously, Feyerabend, like Bogdanov, had a preference for sticking closer to those philosophers for whom the organizing of perceptions of the objective world were closer to hand. They land on one of the same figures in such a counter-history of Western thought: Ernst Mach.

With the benefit of a little more hindsight, Feyerabend is clearer than Bogdanov that Mach's influence has not always been beneficial. Feyerabend defends Mach's practice, not his theory. Reifying his theory, as Mach himself and certainly Bogdanov sometimes do, could only lead thought astray. What matters is that Mach connected philosophy-as-practice back to science-as-practice. As a scientist he was able to treat all of science's components—its theories, methods, apparatus, and results—as available for critical suspension. Science works on the play between all of these elements.[11]

Most of us are inclined to agree that there is a real world beyond our minds, even if the really-real aspects of it may be hidden from us. The problem with such—broadly—realist approaches to either science or philosophy is that they fix a boundary between object and subject in advance. Some object, whether apparent or hidden, is real. Some subject, perhaps aided by some special method, apprehends it. This diagram can be a complicated one, with all kinds of faculties and forms, but something remains unthought in assuming in advance that there is *this* object and *this* subject.

Particularly troubling for such realisms are *mediating* phenomena. Something has to go on at the boundary between the object world and subjective cognition. Such phenomena trouble the structure of the concepts which cluster and encrust a prior decision, separating object and subject at some arbitrary point. To use a language very foreign to Feyerabend, such mediating phenomena might even *deconstruct* the givenness of object and subject.[12]

An alternative starting point might be to take the mediation, the stuff between the object and subject, to be what at first glance or grasp is most real. But it is only a starting hypothesis, not a first philosophy: start by treating phenomena as in some sense that which is real. Mach called these phenomena *sensations*, but they are not reducible to subjective sense impressions, contrary to what Lenin and many other critics of Mach assume.[13]

Rather than posit in advance that there are objects behind the sensations which a subject apprehends, Mach asks a prior question: what are these sensations that end up being parceled out into the subjective and objective? What is the activity that chunks sensation into an index of some object, on the one hand, and as traces via which a subject might come to assert its own separateness, on the other? Inquiry might begin then with the apparent reality of sensations, and an attempt to assay the most simple and regular connections between elements of sensations.

This treatment of phenomena as real is a tactic for Feyerabend rather than a dogma. It does not preclude the possibility of touching on a real, external, even alien world. It is simply a matter of wanting to tack close to practices where the existence of such things can actually be established. Mach used this *tactical monism of sensation* against the physics and philosophy of his time, which insisted too strongly on a version of a metaphysical real that could not be assayed and tested, and was likely to be a barrier to further knowledge. In Bogdanovian terms, metaphysics was then a resistance to overcome in organizing inquiry.

Sensations are not an absolute. Sensations are to be parsed into elements and connections. Hence the title of Mach's book, *The Analysis of Sensations*, where Mach adopts a realism, the realism of sensations—and then applies it.[14] He introduces the working rule that sciences should contain only those concepts that can be connected to sensations. Hence his objection to metaphysical ideas, such as Newton's, of absolute space and time. These are ways of describing a noumenal world, beyond phenomena, beyond sensation, but which are merely philosophical and cannot be tested. Feyerabend:

> Mach develops the outlines of a knowledge without foundations. He introduces cosmological hypotheses as temporary measuring sticks of criticism. The cosmological hypothesis he appeals to most frequently assumes that all our knowledge is related to sensations. Using this hypothesis he criticizes physical theories such as . . . Newtonian mechanics. The cosmological criticism is strengthened by a more specific examination and by the suggestion of alternatives. In this way Mach achieves unity between science and philosophy that has been lost as the result of the dominance of Newton's physics and his philosophy.[15]

But Mach's would-be inheritors, such as the logical positivists of the Vienna circle, lost this unity again. For them, sensation primacy becomes a dogma. They mistook the tactic of deploying specific hypotheses in particular circumstances for a generalizable method. In Bogdanov's terms, what they lacked was the point of view of scientific and technical labor which still imbues Mach's whole approach. Science is not an object of philosophical contemplation to Mach. It is something at which certain people, including himself, have to work.

It is not for philosophy to extract from past science its universal principles, with a view to imposing them on the future. Feyerabend is a dissenter from that moment when the critique of actual science was replaced with either its logical construction or idealized reconstruction. Such procedures relied on a selective reading of scientific results or on scientists' self-reporting, after the fact, of their methods. His main object of attack was his own teacher, Sir Karl Popper, but the various epistemological edicts which dog Western Marxism all through the twentieth century attracted his ire in a passing fashion as well.[16]

The one thing a Marxist theory of knowledge could not be in that long dark century was "positivist," and Mach was held loosely to be—at best—an example of such. But Mach's writings on physics show an approach to knowledge that is not dogmatically positivist. What he calls "instinctive" principles play a large role, and not least because they may be in productive conflict with particular empirical facts. Sometimes the facts have to adapt to the principles. Facts sometimes need to be extracted from the rather particular circumstances in which they are produced. The natural sciences are not then always inductive. Abstraction and imagination are key practices. Mach: "grasping nature by imagination must precede understanding so that our concepts may have a lively and intuitive content."[17] Ideas do not follow facts; ideas and facts adapt to each other.

Mach did not think that the psychological domain of thoughts, feelings, desires, could know itself by itself, but he did think that research which traces the physical connections could bring thought closer to knowledge of itself. His methods are hybrid methods: knowledge of the physical world should take account of psychological factors; knowledge of psychology should take account of physical factors. These mixed methods have a critical function, of bracketing off the fixed assumptions of the division of subject from object, mind from matter, body from soul, not to mention certain divisions of intellectual labor. In the sciences it has the merit of putting under critical pressure the faith in an absolute external world. In humanistic knowledge, it has the reciprocal merit of critical leverage on the assumption that the reasoning subject alone is the guarantor of knowledge.

Mach did take his distance from a kind of naive faith in a real external world, which Feyerabend finds even in amazingly talented scientists such as Planck and Einstein. This faith is a kind of supplement or double of the positivist elements in their accounts of their method. If one imagines in a positivist fashion that knowledge starts inductively, with disorganized impressions, then among those impressions must be, in no matter how distorted or indirect a fashion, impressions of a noumenal world that is absolutely real.

Mach has no such faith. His "instinct" works in particular historical situations, with results from this or that particular apparatus. Rather than attribute theoretical leaps to "creativity," to some humanist derivative of divine inspiration, he asks a more immediately "realist" kind of question: what concrete situations produce such instinctive substitutions? One could call this détournement, or tektology. Feyerabend thinks it's a species of dada collage method.[18] Perhaps all of these are ways of thinking an historical, and in a sense materialist, approach to the production of novelty in the domain of knowledge. Novelty comes from instinct, which mediates between previously separate domains of inquiry.

Curiously, the apparent lack of immediate foundation for an instinct in specific experiments, conducted in known ways, is what lends it a certain strange authority. Instincts appear independent of our actions and beliefs, even if they are the product of determinate historical circumstances. They usually appear to negate particular assumptions. They emerge more often in situations where the researcher has some contact with a wide range of scientific, technical, and labor processes, and is able to intuit something that cuts across their specificity. This is what Bogdanov, rather than Feyerabend, would stress about Mach: that instinct might be a matter of the speculative substitution of an idea from an adjacent work in progress to the one at hand.

Mach famously held out against the theory of the atom, and this often counts against him in retrospective accounts of the outbreak of revolutionary philosophy-physics around the turn of the century.

Feyerabend defends him on this: "There is no need to discredit Mach for his unwavering opposition to atoms. For the mechanical atom of the nineteenth century has indeed disappeared from the scene."[19] This atomism was not so much a physics as a metaphysics. This atom was a noumenal rather than phenomenal thing, an absolute thing-in-itself rather than a theory about particular sensations.

Rather than reject atomic theory outright, Mach made it a provisional substitution. To be useful, atomic theory had to become phenomenal rather than noumenal. This is exactly what Einstein achieved: a reformulation of physics in ways that would meet Mach's objections. Whatever Mach himself may have thought, Einstein's special theory of relativity is "Machist," not in corresponding to some dogmatic theory of knowledge, but in the sense that in this case Einstein works the way Mach works, for example by suspending belief in an absolute noumenal time.[20] In the subsequent debates about quantum mechanics, Niels Bohr will deploy Machist tactics against Einstein.

For Feyerabend, there is no royal road to science. Incorrect ideas can lead to good experiments, theories can succeed even when they don't account for significant facts. As he notoriously put it: "anything goes."[21] Or so the actual history of science would appear to a rationalist, including those Marxists, who, like Lukács and Althusser, think there are special methods, and that the philosophers are their guardians. Feyerabend makes a useful counterpoint to those versions of Western Marxism that were obsessed with coming up with a correct exposition of dialectical materialist method, and which thought that philosophy had some privileged, legislative role in adjudicating what that method ought to be.

Let's think Marxism then as a heterogeneous collection of rhetorics, theories, methods, results. It is a labyrinthine archive of conceptual personae whose hidden riches may well lie in unexplored aisles. In the absence of a secret police, it no longer has an orthodoxy, regardless of how orthodox some in that archive might have wanted to consider themselves. Haraway: "I want to know how to help build ongoing stories rather than histories that end. In that sense, my kinships are about keeping the lineages going, even while defamiliarizing their members and turning lines into webs, trees into esplanades, and pedigrees into affinity groups."[22]

This would queer a certain precious heirloom from the Marxological cupboard. Lukács:

> Let us assume for the sake of argument that recent research had disproved once and for all every one of Marx's individual theses. Even if this were to be proved, every serious "orthodox" Marxist would still be able to accept all such modern findings without reservation and hence dismiss all of Marx's theses in toto—without having to renounce his orthodoxy for a single moment. Orthodox Marxism, therefore, does not imply the uncritical acceptance of the results of Marx's investigations. It is not the "belief" in this or that thesis, nor the exegesis of a "sacred" book. On the contrary, orthodoxy refers exclusively to method. It is the scientific conviction that dialectical materialism is the road to truth and that its methods can be expanded and deepened only along the lines laid down by its founders.[23]

In relation to dogmatic insistence on the truth of Marx's results, this venerable passage might still seem like progress, but in place of it is a dogmatic privileging of method. Gone is the putting to work of all of the elements against each other, of facts and theories, intuitions and substitutions. In Bogdanov's terms, it is knowledge as authority; it is philosophy as high theory. Philosophy rules! It is not a comradely effort at collaboration through experimental substitution between particular efforts.

It is not often noticed that Lukács elaborates this theory-dominant approach in opposition not just to the positivism of the "vulgar Marxists," but also against the "Machists," whose thought-crime is different: a comradely equality of different modes of inquiry. The problem with the Machists, says Lukács, is that for them reality is "impenetrable, fatalistic and immutable."[24] They concede too much to nature's resistance, to the objectivity of particular sciences, and they do not recognize that science is merely a "weapon of the bourgeoisie." They refuse the philosopher's top-down causality of the totality, and limit themselves to the bottom-up procedure of working collaboratively from the particular sciences and labors. Lukács sees the Machists as a product of the decline of bourgeois self-confidence that its thought adequately described the world, although unlike Bogdanov, the Lukács of the 1920s does not seem to know very much about actual sciences.

Feyerabend had a strong dislike for philosophy as a totalizing and controlling kind of discourse. He much preferred it when it was connected to what Platonov called secondary ideas, or rather practices, which have to encounter the resistance of the world's materiality. Thought had no value to him without the struggle of life. He detested the attitude of both philosopher-kings and philosopher-commissars, as any genuine radical must. Feyerabend:

> To me this attitude is alien, incomprehensible and slightly sinister. True, I, too, once admired the phenomenon from afar; I hoped to enter the castles from whence it spread and to participate in the wars of enlightenment the learned knights had started all over the world. Eventually I noticed the more pedestrian aspects of the matter: the fact, that is, that the knights—the professors—serve masters who pay them and tell them what to do: they are not free minds in search of harmony and happiness for all, they are civil servants . . . and their mania for order is not the result of a balanced inquiry, or of closeness to humanity, it is a professional disease. So while I made full use of the sizeable salaries I got for doing very little, I was careful to protect the poor humans (and, in Berkeley, dogs, cats, raccoons, even a monkey now and then) who came to my lectures from the disease.

Thus spake the philosopher in the land of the lotus-eaters. Feyerabend is useful for keeping critical thought once again from getting lost in the misty domains of the speculative realisms or the void, vibrating, or vitalist materialisms of high theory. He isn't much help for bringing it closer to what actually became of the metabolic control of molecular processes on the planet, and their ever widening rift. If Feyerabend can help us reanimate the corpus of Mach for the twenty-first century, then who can help us do the same for Marx? Here we turn to a very different kind of Californian thinker and writer, with whom Feyerabend shares a fondness for dogs and primates, if nothing else.

FROM MARX TO HARAWAY

It is hard to imagine a landscape more remote from Russia in the early twentieth century than the West Coast of the United States in the late twentieth century. In place of scarcity, a bright abundance. Some central nodes to the military industrial complex were born and grew there, particularly in the aerospace industry, not to mention the Air Force's own private think-tank, the RAND corporation. And as California prospered, so did its finest universities, such as Stanford and Caltech and Berkeley, not to mention Berkeley's rivals at the peak of the public University of California system. Pump enough Pentagon money into this cluster of institutions and the result is Silicon Valley.[25]

It is hard to imagine an organization of knowledge and labor more remote from what Bogdanov was proposing at the Socialist University after the Bolsheviks came to power, or even from that extensive and effective apparatus that the Soviet Union actually constructed after Stalin died.[26] But in its own terms, the Californian military-industrial complex worked. It is not too much of an exaggeration to say that the dominant forms of power, economy, even of human life, owe their existence to what Donna Haraway calls the *techno-science* that issued from a handful of research universities in the Cold War years. It was not pure serendipity that brought Paul Feyerabend to Berkeley to teach the philosophy of science in the midst of an astonishing flowering of both pure and applied science. The term techno-science highlights how implicated science is and was in particular moments in the history of technology.

Feyerabend's grasp of this part of the picture was never strong. Perhaps he was fatally hampered by his endemic hatred of all things Marxist. Perhaps the new world would not reveal its workings to someone so touched by the old. More useful in this regard is the work of Donna Haraway. Born in the 1940s, trained as a biologist, radicalized during the Vietnam War years, and lodging at the University of California at Santa Cruz in 1980, Haraway is, on her own admission, a product of both Cold War techno-science and the struggle in and against its imperial consequences. Haraway: "I have a body and mind as much constructed by the post-Second World War arms race and cold war as by the women's movements."[27]

If for Bogdanov the catalyst that diverted him from the life sciences was the labor movement, for Haraway it was feminism. Haraway: "Feminists re-appropriate science in order to discover and to define what is 'natural' for ourselves. A human past and future would be placed in our hands. This avowedly interested approach to science promises to take seriously the rules of scientific discourse without worshipping the fetish of scientific objectivity."[28]

There is an interesting tension here, even a productive one. With some startling exceptions such as Shulamith Firestone's *Dialectic of Sex*, most strands of Western Marxism taken up by critical thinkers in the United States in the postwar period were allergic to techno-science.[29] Even among radical social scientists of this period, knowledge of, and commitment to, some version of natural science as a mode of inquiry was rare, and where it existed it was not often combined with such a strong commitment to a thoroughgoing critique of the existing form of science.[30]

Haraway's is a very different intellectual formation to the one that grew out of the influence of Herbert Marcuse, who taught at the other end of California to Haraway, in San Diego, from 1965 until he was forced to retire in 1970.[31] While there are détourne-ments of Lukács and Marcuse in Haraway, they are very much applied to understanding two immediate phenomena: new kinds of techno-science, and the rising social movement of feminism. What formed at the juncture was feminist science studies.[32]

Science? Technology? Goddess preserve us! There are plenty of feminisms that try to take their stand against techno-science from without, as if it had some prior and given claim to speak for nature. Haraway: "Feminist theory has repeatedly replicated this 'naturalizing' structure of discourse in its own oppositional constructions."[33] A useful attribute of feminist science studies is that it tends not to make the assumption that there is something inherently radical about philosophy, or culture, or play or poetry over and against the scientific and technical. It does not take sides in advance within the existing intellectual division of labor. It is, among other things, a practical critique of that division of intellectual labor. "Destabilizing the positions in a discursive field and disrupting categories for identification might be a more powerful feminist strategy than 'speaking as a woman.'"[34]

It retains a sort of double discomfort, asking critical questions in a scientific zone, and speaking knowledgeably about actual sciences in a humanities zone. This is irritating, and usefully so. Feminist science studies persistently recasts the objectivity claims of the sciences, and does so, to make it worse, without dismissing the scientific endeavor. It is so much harder to dismiss a critic who takes a knowledge practice seriously, who wants not to abandon objectivity, but wants a stronger one, grounded in making a more extensive series of mediating links in the production of knowledge available for scrutiny.[35]

This is irritating in another way as well. Haraway: "Marx insisted that one must not leap too fast, or one will end up in a fantastic utopia, impotent and ignorant. Abundance . . . is essential to the full discovery and historical possibility of human nature. It matters whether we make ourselves in plenty or unfulfilled need, including need for genuine knowledge and meaning."[36] This is what Platonov knew from daily experience. Surplus feeds the body which feeds the soul. There can be no retreat into the superstructures when there is no food, shelter or safety. The production and reproduction of our species-being, whatever it may be, has to be a central concern of any critical knowledge. Given the rising inequality, poverty, and hunger in twenty-first-century California, to which the state has responded by mirroring its great universities with a series of equally great prisons, questions of material need that were so palpable to Platonov return at the heart of the empire.[37]

Haraway's California is that part that is still a land of surplus, where some more complex questions about food arise other than its insufficiency. Haraway tells two archetypal California stories about food. On arriving in Santa Cruz in 1980, she is plunged into a debate about what to do with the placenta after a "natural" childbirth. Should it be eaten? How should it be cooked? Who should eat it? Can vegans eat human placenta? Maybe vegans ought to be obliged to eat it: not only was no animal killed in its making, one was brought into the world of the living. In the second story, a religious studies professor prepares a meal for the department party, the centerpiece of which is a feral pig he shot with an arrow. Complex debates ensue about ritual, ethics, impossible ecologies, and so on.[38]

Both stories are like metonymic fragments of Marx's metabolic rift. Molecules—in this case proteins—lack enclosing loops back through any sort of dynamic equilibrium. Haraway eschews any easy answers on either of these questions, and makes a wry nod to "the contradictory, thick quality of what we mean when we say 'California.'"[39] They are all the same real questions. If for Platonov the question of a surplus to feed body and soul was a matter of quantity, in California the uneven conquest of quantity reveals the qualitative problems. Here in a contemporary, ramified form, is Bogdanov's tragedy of the totality, a vast yet molecular process that only reveals its contours when something goes wrong, when there is a metabolic rift, of which there are now many, from feral pigs to feral carbon.

What is of interest in feminist science studies that is in some ways reminiscent of Bogdanov is a commitment to studying the reality of the process of the production and reproduction of knowledge. There is some progress to be made by weaving Bogdanov back into the fabric of critical approaches to scientific and technical knowledge, of which feminist science studies is now a leading exemplar. This is not, let me hasten to add, an attempt to subsume feminist science studies under the head of the Great Man who precedes it; quite the opposite. It is that there may be modest contributions Bogdanov can make to supplement Haraway and her messmates.

Haraway has on occasion described herself as an illegitimate daughter of Marx, and "something of an unreconstructed and dogged Marxist." She remains attentive to how relations congeal into apparently natural things. "Property is the kind of relationality that poses as the thing-in-itself, the commodity, the thing outside relationship, the thing that can be exhaustively measured, mapped, owned, appropriated, disposed."[40] As we shall see, this becomes in her work a useful starting point for understanding how distinctly twenty-first-century modes of property and technology are organized.

Unlike many other Marxists, Haraway insists on including nonhuman actors in what would be an otherwise relentlessly human category of that-which-labors. "The actors are not all 'us.'"[41] Techno-science explodes the already wobbly partition between object and subject, nature and culture, apparatus and labor. Marx may have shown how the thing is full of labor, but the category of chimerical objects, those mash-ups of flesh-tech, has much expanded, even if there is still a tendency for the fetish of the thing to obscure the relations of its making. Hence the world can now appear as a vast accumulation not just of commodities or spectacles but of "big data" or "selfish genes."

Marx was already well aware of capital's "unnatural" acts, causing something to reproduce in new ways, on its own terms. He even puts the figure of the vampire to work.[42] Capital is a vampire, sucking life out of labor to make and remake its own undead carcass. Bogdanov nods to this vampire figure of capital too, but for Haraway it's a more polymorphous figure. The vampire is both threat and promise: blood-sucking capital but also the marginal other of "impure" sexual and racial mixing. Like Bogdanov, Haraway is always showing how the metaphors embedded in knowledge do their work, but she is also interested in what other work they might do.

Haraway tries to keep in view the relations of production that the fetish of the commodity obscures. "I believe wealth is created by collective practice, figured by Marx as labor, but needing a messier metaphoric descriptive repertoire."[43] There is a fetishism of labor itself—man-with-hammer—that needs attending to as well. If, like Bogdanov, one takes the labor point of view to be what is central to Marx's work, then what, in the age of techno-science, might now constitute such a point of view?

If Marx proceeded through a critique of the dismal science of political economy, Haraway works through a rather more lively if no less difficult science—biology. "I have always read biology in a double way—as about the way the world works biologically, but also about the way the world works metaphorically."[44] One of the many functions of biology is to "discursively reproduce the species," defining the limits of what can be said about the potentials of the human, about our species-being. Is there a "human race," or are some races not fully human? And if all races are human, what might the human become?

Haraway tries to untangle the matrix of figures of nature, nation, sex, race, and blood that both impinge on biological science but which are also centrally produced and modified in biology. It is not that biology is reducible to culture and politics, rather, "the material-semiotic tissues are inextricably intermeshed."[45] Haraway expands the object of Marxian critique from political economy to the life sciences, which are no less implicated in the production of the infrastructural givens of the contemporary commodified world. This adds an essential dimension, if critique is going to grasp— such a primate metaphor!—Marx's no less full-bodied metaphor of metabolic rift, and flesh it out.

Here the job might be to refract Haraway through Bogdanov, to show that there have been three basic metaphors of the causality of the human in the modern period: race, population, and gene. Each has its dissenters, critics, and utopian or dystopian writers.[46] Each has its genuine scientists caught up in substitutions drawn from social organization which color and overshoot the process of producing evidence. Each also has its ideologues and moral entrepreneurs.

Race causality held that accumulated cultural differences are somehow carried in the blood. Even among progressives, the very category of race could create a fear of race mixing. Haraway: "The evolution of language, the progress of technology, the perfection of the body, and the advance of social forms seemed to be aspects of the same fundamental human science. That science was constitutively physiological and hierarchical, organismic and wholist, progressivist and developmental."[47]

Bogdanov's intervention within this regime is a queer one. He seemed to accept that blood carries differences, but advocated the *sharing* of blood to overcome them.[48] Rather than be prey to the vampire of capital, labor shares among its own, as if the brotherhood of man could be made physically so through blood exchanges. There's a will to sameness at work here which is a usefully perverse read on the obsessions of the era, but which remain of their era.

A more common response was the welter of attempts to categorize and characterize the races, arranged in some sort of hierarchy. Differences of culture or power become expressions of an order of nature. Haraway: "No wonder universal nature has been a less than appealing entity for those who were not its creators and its beneficiaries."[49] To which one might add that the temptation to overcome a supposed biological destiny of race, by severing the social from biological being altogether, is and remains a powerful temptation. It has the unfortunate side-effect of cutting critical thought off from thinking biology as a techno-science with powerful and perhaps increasing abilities to create new unequal relations for the production and reproduction of life.

While popular racialism lives on, the substituting of racial for other kinds of difference did not survive in biological science. In the postwar years, after the debacle of racialized Nazi biology, and in the wake of new research methods, the basic metaphor of *population causality* arose in its place. A population is a semi-permeable group within a species. There may be as much variation within a population as between. Each may nevertheless be a pool which contain adaptations that are more or less successful.

Populations are not types in a hierarchy; nor are they sets. Each is constantly in flux in changing environments, rather like Bogdanovite ingressions. The metaphysical shift is from a hierarchy of self-same types, where miscegenation at the boundary produces less viable instances, toward a different way of figuring difference and similarity. Populations are internally differentiated but formally equivalent in relation to each other.

Population became a central figure in the modern synthesis, which brought together naturalists, geneticists, and experimentalists in a new kind of biological science and culture. Haraway: "This was a scientific humanism that emphasized flexibility, progress, cooperation, and universalism."[50] It broke with the language of race and blood. It stressed the flexible and plastic nature of the human condition, and its capacity to change through education. The human can be socially self-constructing. Actual differences in power, such as the colonial relation, are elided by what ought to be: the "family of man."

The organizational challenges of postwar capitalism put on the agenda the question of the limits to the adaptive nature of the human. Primate studies became a way of conducting experiments and building theories aimed at the adaptation of the human to the rising complexity of technics and organization. Primate researchers focused on two linked topics: sex and dominance. The male primate fights with other males for access to reproduction. Researchers substituted Freud into the animal realm and back again. Alongside interest in observing primates in their "natural" setting were experiments on the primate as an embodiment of drives to sex and power, designed to see how adaptable its species-being was to the office politics of living in cages and pressing levers for food.

The primate was an experimental subject who could yield insights into techniques for regulating sexuality and power in the modern world for human primates too. Rather than repressing desire or the will to power, technologies and therapies could help the human primate adapt. It's a small step from the study of primate behaviors to the hormones that supposedly regulate them, and then on to the construction of a techno-science of intervening in the hormonal regulation of primate sexuality—particularly that of humans. The contraceptive pill is here the great techno-science success story.

Population causality naturalized the patriarchal family. Its origin myth is that of man the hunter. It is man who is assumed to be the maker of tools, the inventor of elaborated social organization and hence of language. It is man who is curious, who explores, while woman stays home yanking yams from the dirt with babies on her teats. This figure was supplemented rather belatedly by woman the inventor of basket-weaving, in some cases as a result of the work of feminist researchers.

Haraway has paid particularly close attention to the role of field studies of natural primate populations in legitimating some elements of the family of man story. The figures of the headman, the sexual division of labor, woman as burdened by children, all pass back and forth from science to culture as substituted figures. Through a study of the basic metaphor of biological economy, Haraway hones her critique of the foundations of postwar American liberalism.

Liberalism's finest hour was its efforts to overcome, in both science and culture, the benighted effects of the category of race. Haraway wants to push on from that self-congratulatory ethos. "I believe that this capacity of reproducing the Same, in culpable innocence of its historical, power-charged specificity, characterizes not just me but people formed like me, who are liberal, scientific, and progressive . . ."[51] The problem with the liberal family of man is that "what's not collected in a reproductive family story does not finally count as human. For all the . . . emphasis on difference, this is the grammar of indifference, or the multiplication of sameness."[52] Tautology reigns: that which survives is functional; that which is functional survives.

The liberal family of man gave way to the neoliberal "selfish gene" of sociobiology, and the basic metaphor of *gene causality*. The population regime took as its units of thought individual bodies and their social groups. Now the gene becomes the controlling code which uses both bodies and groups for its own ends. The causal metaphor is still functional, but the unit to which it applies is now molecular: the gene that survives is functional because the function of the gene is to survive. Haraway: "Sociobiology is narratively a hyper-functionalism and a hyper-liberalism."[53] Genes are logos in the market of life. "My genes, my self, my investment, my future. It's much more strictly capitalist."[54]

Such a science is the product not only of a certain naturalizing of the exchange economy, but also of powerful technologies which produce the gene itself as an artifact in a database. Haraway: "something peculiar happened to the stable, family-loving, Mendelian gene when it passed into a database . . ."[55] The gene becomes one of the units of currency of the era of "big data." Genomics and informatics merge. The gene can exist in a variety of media, from software to wetware, and some in between. Nature starts to yield not the authoritarian causality of race hierarchies or patriarchal families, but the exchange causality of property in a purified form.

The genetic database is at once about the genes of specific individuals, but also sub-units of that code, and at the other extreme, about our species-being. The design of such a database shapes what can be compared, what kinds of labor can most easily be performed, but meanwhile the gene becomes a thing separated from a totality and accorded its own agency.[56] Meanwhile sub-disciplines of biological science, such as genetics or population biology, start to fork off and coalesce around much more differentiated apparatus, practices, and objects of knowledge.

The construction of the gene as an object of techno-science is just one component in an important shift in the practices of substitution between organizational levels. Haraway:

> Nineteenth-century scientists materially constituted the organism as a laboring system, structured by a hierarchical division of labor, and an energetic system fueled by sugars and obeying the laws of thermodynamics. For us, the living world has become a command, control, communication, intelligence system . . . in an environment that demands strategies of flexible accumulation. Artificial life programs, as well as carbon-based life programs, work that way. These issues are about metaphor and representation, but they are about much more than that.[57]

Ideology, as Bogdanov well knew, is productive. The shift from thinking organization as energy systems alone—as Bogdanov himself does—to thinking in terms of a combination of energy and information systems, enables not only new kinds of science, technology, and power, but also opens up a space for their critique.

Interestingly, some of the new modes of substitution producing both ideology and knowledge might no longer be metaphorical so much as algorithmic. Haraway sees in genetic code and computer code a new kind of fetishism that is partly, but not entirely, legible to the old Marxist and Freudian versions.[58] One might call it the fetish of the program, a new kind of *code causality*, of which gene causality is but one instance. It is not entirely reducible to either authoritarian or exchange causality, although it has features of both. It is certainly not the comradely causal universe that Bogdanov and Platonov imagined.

By way of illustration, Haraway points to an issue of *Mammalian Genome*, which offered its readers a representation of the contents of the chromosomes of a mouse under the headline, "the Complete Mouse (some assembly required)."[59] Code becomes the master layer in the stacked protocols by which an organization is managed. In genetics, code becomes the part via which a whole can be reductively understood. In place of messy flesh, the clean execution of command and control, although as we shall see there are code-based sciences where such a reduction is not easily made.

Commodity fetishism occurs when relations between people take on the features of relations between things. The formula for the fetish Lukács offers is caught in a prior distinction between object and subject, even if this distinction appears in a more sophisticated form. Collective labor is what hides behind the commodity. But perhaps it is not so easy to separate labor and thing. So Haraway, like Bogdanov, wants to broaden the fetish concept a little. "Curiously, fetishes—themselves 'substitutes', that is, tropes of a special kind—produce a particular 'mistake'; fetishes obscure the constitutive tropic nature of themselves and of worlds."[60] A fetish is a naturalizing of the very thing whose "nature" needs calling into question, but while it may be limiting, it may nevertheless be peculiarly productive: "There are amazingly creative aspects to commodity fetishism."[61]

Gene technology is implicated in commodity fetishism, but maybe also in "another and obliquely related flavor of reification that transmutes material, contingent, human and nonhuman liveliness into maps of life itself and then mistakes the map and its reified entities for the bumptious, nonliteral world."[62] Haraway's détournement of the fetish repurposes it. Rather than the *commodity* fetish, she asks about the *corporeal* fetish. How do bodies appear as autonomous things against a background of invisible nonbodies? In commodity fetishism, the apparent world of things, governed by the code of exchange value, obscures social relations among people and the production of use value. In corporeal fetishism, the apparent world of bodies, governed by the code of the gene, obscures the tangle of both human and nonhuman processes that produce life.

In corporeal fetishism, the gene becomes a source of value as a kind of thing-itself, or perhaps code-itself. "So the fetishist sees the gene itself in all the gels, blots, and printouts in the lab, and 'forgets' the natural-technical processes that produce the gene and genome as consensus objects in the real world."[63] An abstraction replaces the concrete; the map becomes the territory. "Gene fetishists 'forget' that the gene and gene maps are ways of enclosing the commons of the body—of corporealizing—in specific ways, which, among other things, often put commodity fetishism into the program of biology at the end of the Second Millennium."[64]

Just as the commodity fetish makes all things property to be exchanged, so too the corporeal fetish makes all of life a thing to be commodified through ownership of its code. "Genomics 'globalizes' in specific ways. Species-being is materially and semiotically produced in gene-mapping practices, just as particular kinds of space and humanity were the fruit of earlier material-semiotic enclosures."[65] Private property produces the split between commodities and the labor that makes it; intellectual property produces the split between the gene and the organism that makes it.

What was once biology's commons of research materials becomes increasingly commodified. Haraway takes the Human Genome Diversity Project as a case study in agency in the age of the gene. It was supposed to gather samples from populations at risk of losing their more or less distinctive characteristics. Indigenous communities were not involved in formulating the project, which at best sought their permission, not collaboration. Many indigenous peoples are strongly against the results of such work leading to patents.

The "mutation" of the private property form into strictly controlled "intellectual property" makes whole new classes of things available for commodification. "Like the stigmata of gender and race, which signify asymmetrical, regularly reproduced processes that give some human beings rights in other human beings that they do not have in themselves, the copyright, patent and trademark are specific, asymmetrical, congealed processes—which must be constantly revivified in law and commerce as well as in science."[66] Intellectual property grounds a new kind of class power.

A patent defines what is nature and what is not. An artifact of "nature" cannot be patented. For that to happen, nature has to be mixed with labor. Patent is a site of struggle over what counts as subject and what as object. Haraway's famous example is DuPont's OncoMouse, the first patented mammal, specifically engineered for the study of breast cancer. All sorts of organisms are now integrated into a strange techno-nature meant to support human life, or at least those parts of it that can be commodified. Not only mice but dogs and all sorts of other beings are our "companions" within techno-science. In place of the liberal-humanist family, quite another kind: "the technoscientific family is a cyborg nuclear unit," now that "life is a system to be managed."[67]

What kind of critical agency is possible in the world of OncoMouse? Do lab rats belong to the working class? Should battery hens be unionized? Should one have the right to share in the surplus produced by one's cells, even when those cells are not in one's body? Consider the case of Henrietta Lacks, an African-American tobacco worker who died of cervical cancer. Cells taken from her body, without her knowledge or consent, were cultured and used in all kinds of research long after her death, from the polio vaccine to AIDS treatments and gene mapping. Those cells proved not only useful for research but profitable for medical business, while her descendants could not even afford health insurance.[68] How is one to think the molecular agencies of such a story?

For Haraway this is a question of "how to queer the modest witness."[69] There is a certain historical structure of feeling that might characterize the ideal of the scientist: the modest witness. Driving women out of forms of knowledge and power is not unconnected to the rise of science.[70] How could the "man of science," who refrains from public contests of valor and power, resist becoming a feminized figure? By proposing a new structure of feeling: the noble woman is modest of body; the good scientist will be modest of mind.

How can this figure be retrieved? Not by returning to a feminine modesty, but rather by imagining a feminist one. "My modest witness is about telling the truth—giving reliable testimony—while eschewing the addictive narcotic of transcendental foundations." It is about reconnecting the making of observations to the scene of their making. There's a limit to how far an observation can be abstracted from the situation that produces it. A thorough witnessing sees also the means by which it sees what it sees, and knows what it knows. "The modest witness is the one who can be engaged in situated knowledges."[71]

Perhaps these gestures made to establish science as a whole way of life were tactical rather than essential. Perhaps there are other tactics by which the struggle for objectivity can be waged by others, even by those whom this structure of feeling once excluded. That might be exactly the reason to work in and against it: "The point is to make a difference in the world, to cast our lot for some ways of life and not others. To do that, one must be in the action, one must be finite and dirty, not transcendent and clean."[72]

The figure which Haraway famously proposed as a point of view is the *cyborg*. "Like any important technology, a cyborg is simultaneously a myth and a tool . . ."[73] It is not the labor point of view, as if labor existed independently of the apparatus with which it is entangled. It is not women's point of view, as if one could speak of it as a universal subjective perspective, existing prior to the social and technical relations in which it meshes. Cyborgs are affinities rather than identities, hybrids of human and other organics, information systems, ergonomic laboring, producing and desiring. Cyborgs are monsters, or rather *demonstrations*, in the double sense of to show and to warn, of possible worlds. "As monsters, can we demonstrate another order of signification? Cyborgs for earthly survival!"[74]

In moving on from proletkult to "cyborgkult," the point of view expands somewhat from the makers to the makings of the molecular. In place of the "God-trick" of speaking as if one had access to a portal to the absolute, the cyborg is a kind of ironic myth, a heretical counter-story to the human as pre-given. "Blasphemy protects one from the moral majority within, while still insisting on the need for community."[75] Like the Marxist-feminist critic inside the research university, the cyborg is always an insider and outsider to techno-science, which after all is pretty much the case now for all of us. "I think the way I work is to take my own polluted inheritance—cyborg is one of them—and try to rework it."[76]

The cyborg isn't an innocent figure. "The main trouble with cyborgs, of course, is that they are the illegitimate offspring of militarism and patriarchal capitalism, not to mention state socialism. But illegitimate offspring are often exceedingly unfaithful to their origins. Their fathers, after all, are inessential."[77] Cyborgs are a kind of orphan, in a more troubling sense in that parentage is not lost or forgotten but never quite existed, even though "the cyborg . . . doesn't have a mother, but it does have a matrix."[78]

The cyborg is a contemporary kind of Platonovian conceptual persona, although it is not so much that which is *beneath* the proletarian, as that which is *between* the worker and her apparatus. Or rather, between three kinds of boundaries: between the organism and the machine, the animal and the human, the physical and the nonphysical. Indeed, looking back now on Platonov's orphans, Chicklin and his shovel, or the terrifying hammerer-bear, many of them are indeed already proto-cyborgs in the making, in the age of steam engines rather than difference engines. Haraway: "Too many people, forgetting the discipline of love and rage, have read the 'Manifesto [for Cyborgs]' as the ramblings of a blissed-out, technobunny, fembot."[79] Surely this stems from the persistence of the ideological pull of the figure of nature, and an inability to think and feel through the emerging forces of production as anything other than poisoned product of techno-science. Haraway:

> From *One Dimensional Man* (Marcuse 1964) . . . the analytic resources developed by progressives have insisted on the necessary domination of technics and recalled us to an imagined organic body to integrate our resistance . . . But a slightly perverse shift of perspective might better enable us to contest for meanings, as well as for other forms of power and pleasure in technologically medi-ated societies.[80]

Perhaps it would be possible to sense a web of human and nonhu-man agents, more a mechanically and digitally reproducible compound eye than a single labor point of view.

Perhaps this point of view could be broader than that of labor, and not separate, out in advance, production from reproduction. Perhaps it could also include something a bit distinct from either, a kind of activity that neither produces nor reproduces, but proposes other means of doing either, or neither, or both. Could it even include the hacker class as a distinctive point of view not entirely reducible to labor? One might start here with Bogdanov's notion of organization, rather than production, as a "basic" level of analysis, but look aslant at its unquestioned functionalism.

There is no real traction to be gained from trying to base a critique on nature versus culture, or the human versus the machine, nor is there leverage in play versus labor. In an era where there is money to be made from all sorts of effort people put in to volun-tarily creating and sharing information, labor itself becomes an unstable category. Haraway: "We are living through a movement

from an organic, industrial society to a polymorphous, information system—from all work to all play, a deadly game."[81]

Information is more than a powerful metaphor extended via
substitution into an explanatory causality for the world, or even for
the cosmos. It becomes a powerful means of organizing worlds.
Haraway: "Communications science and modern biologies are
constructed by a common move—the translation of the world into
a problem of coding, a search for a common language in which all
resistance to instrumental control disappears and all heterogeneity
can be submitted to disassembly, reassembly, investment, and
exchange."[82] It's a matter of seeing this, as Bogdanov would, as at
once an actuality, as an ensemble of real phenomena, and yet also
as historical, as the product of certain kinds of labor, or more
specifically of techno-science as a central way that power works in
this stage of the commodity economy—whatever it might be.

It was prescient of Haraway to notice, and early on, that "the
new communications technologies are fundamental to the eradica-
tion of 'public life' for everyone."[83] The reduction of a wide range
of processes, and not just labor, to a thing, or in this case to code,
supports a vast extension of private property relations. Bogdanov
was rare among Marxists of his time in thinking that commodification may have a long course to run before a transformation into
other modes of production might be possible, but not even he
imagined anything like this.

The monstrous omens Haraway detected in the late twentieth
century came to pass:

A major social and political danger is the formation of a strongly
bimodal social structure, with the masses of women and men of all
ethnic groups, but especially people of color, confined to a home-
work economy, illiteracy of several varieties, and general redundancy
and impotence, controlled by high-tech repressive apparatuses rang-
ing from entertainment to surveillance and disappearance . . . The
only way to characterize the informatics of domination is as a massive
intensification of insecurity and cultural impoverishment, with
common failure of subsistence networks for the most vulnerable.[84]

And so it came to pass, only it came to be called *precarity*. Creating any kind of knowledge and power in and against something as pervasive and effective as the world built by postwar techno-science is a difficult task. It may seem easier simply to vacate the field, to try to turn back the clock, or appeal to something outside of it. But this would be to remain stuck in the stage of romantic refusal. Just as Marx fused the romantic fiction that another world was possible with a resolve to understand from the inside the powers of capital itself, so too Haraway begins what can only be a collaborative project for a new international[85]—one not just of laboring men, but of all the stuttering cyborgs stuck in reified relations not of their making.

While Marx was rather diffident about the utopian side of socialist culture as a counter to capitalism, these days it sometimes seems to be about all we have. And so Haraway proposes as theorists for cyborgs some late twentieth-century analogs of Charles Fourier and Flora Tristan.[86] If the critical cyborg is made in part from encounters with both science and feminism, its other liaison is literary: Joanna Russ, Samuel Delany, John Varley, James Tiptree Jr., Octavia Butler—to which list we shall shortly add Kim Stanley Robinson.[87] As Bogdanov and Platonov knew well, the alternative to trying to work the God-trick in our favor is some version of that mythical Marx who loved us always and forever, in the form of queer encodings in the language of the times of what another time could be.

God is dead, and so too is the Goddess. The disenchanting corrosion of all that is solid into the molecular abrades more than one way. If there is no thing-in-itself, no scientific-realist absolute, then there's no prior and originary subject for a social movement, either. We are always and already insiders:

Feminisms and Marxisms have run aground on Western epistemological imperatives to construct a revolutionary subject from the perspective of a hierarchy of oppressions and/or a latent position of moral superiority, innocence, and greater closeness to nature. With no available original dream of a common language or original symbiosis promising protection from hostile "masculine" separation, but written into the play of a text that has no finally privileged reading or salvation history, to recognize "oneself" as fully implicated in the world, frees us of the need to root politics in identification, vanguard parties, purity, and mothering. Stripped of identity, the bastard race teaches about the power of the margins.[88]

This is part of the terrifying force of Platonov's insistence on the figure of the orphan. There's no mother nature, no father science, no way back (or forward) to integrity. To be orphaned is not to be alienated, in the sense of the parting of a thing from a former "organic" whole. Tektology is all about constructing temporary shelter in the world, but it is something that has to be made, now and for a future, rather than an inheritance or entitlement to be retrieved.

There is work to be done, however, to bring Bogdanov and Platonov fully into the present, as comrades on the cyborg reading list. What needs reworking is the struggle of labor in and against nature. Haraway:

Humanistic Marxism was polluted at the source by its structuring ontological theory of the domination of nature in the self-construction of man and by its closely related impotence to historicize anything women did that didn't qualify for a wage. But Marxism was still a promising resource in the form of epistemological feminist mental hygiene that sought our own doctrines of objective vision. Marxist starting points offered tools to get to our versions of standpoint theories, insistent embodiment, a rich tradition of critiques of hegemony without disempowering positivisms and relativisms, and nuanced theories of mediation.[89]

The cyborg point of view is shaped in part by social movements around labor, race, gender, sexuality, and indigenous rights. The cyborg point of view is also shaped in part by the sciences, by struggles to produce objective knowledge of the world, complete with substitutions transposed into it from the dominant forms of organization. Part of the operation of a twenty-first-century tektology is to beam the former through the latter and vice versa, in a speculative play and comradely labor of working toward a knowledge adequate to the tragedy of the totality from the bottom up.

The cyborg point of view has at least one other component: the point of view of the apparatus itself, of the electrons in our circuits, the pharmaceuticals in our bloodstreams, the machines that mesh with our flesh. The machinic enters the frame not as the good or the bad other, but as an intimate stranger. The apparatus, like sensation, is liminal and indeterminate—an in-between. It is an *inhuman* thing, neither object nor subject. One of its special qualities as such may, however, be to generate data about a *nonhuman* world. The apparatus renders *to* the human a world that isn't *for* the human.[90] An apparatus is that which demonstrates some aspect of a monstrous, alien world. An apparatus yield aspects, particular monstrosities, which never add up to that consistent and absolute world that remains the God, or Goddess, of all realists. An apparatus affords the real, material and historical form of mediation.

If critical theory is to grasp what techno-science has made of us in the twenty-first century, then at least a passing understanding of biological science might be an asset, for this is an era in which life itself has been disaggregated and brought under forms of molecular control. What makes that control possible is a whole series of technologies based on sciences whose object is not just on the molecular but even the sub-atomic level. Rather than assert a claim to contemplate these transformations as if from the outside, what might actually be more useful is a way of accounting from the inside for the apparatus that produces us as cyborg beings in an Anthropocene time on a planet experiencing vast metabolic rifts. With that aim in mind, I turn now to the work of Karen Barad on the apparatus, and then using concepts extracted from that study, I move on to the work of Paul Edwards on the science of climate change.

FROM BOGDANOV TO BARAD

Bogdanov wrote at a time when the science of physics was undergoing a profound revolution. This was not the least reason he avoided any attempt to define nature by means of materialist philosophy alone. If such a theory of matter has any content it will be rendered obsolete by further discoveries, and if it cannot be rendered obsolete then it is a metaphysical add-on that the practice of knowledge can do without. Better, he thought, to stay close to the materiality of the process of the production of knowledge about "matter," whatever that might now mean. What "matter" might be changes, even the means of knowing what it might be changes, but what is constant is that matter is known through the combined efforts of labor and apparatus. As the apparatus for the production of such knowledge has extended on the one hand to the subatomic scale and on the other to planetary and even cosmic scales, all kinds of new metaphors await for substitutional play, not to mention new kinds of causation.

Of particular interest here is the work of Karen Barad. A colleague of Haraway's at the University of California Santa Cruz, Barad has a PhD in physics, and has worked as a physics professor, but her book *Meeting the Universe Halfway* is more an attempt to extract a feminist theory of scientific practice from particle physics. It could, as we shall see, actually be a work of tektology. Barad and Bogdanov practice kinds of politics of knowledge that overlap. Their situations are very different. Regardless of its quality, Russian science of the early twentieth century did not come close to the power and extent of the American science of today. A critical thought for the times needs at least a passing acquaintance with the techno-science that makes these times.

Born in the 1950s, Barad, like Haraway, grew up in the heyday of American scientific and technical leadership and power. In the physical sciences, that leadership really accelerated in the 1940s. The development of the atom bomb is the best known instance, but it is worth noting that during World War II the United States committed even more resources to the development of radar.[91]

That research built the theoretical foundations and technical infrastructure for postwar electronics and computing, which in turn influenced many other fields of scientific research. If one attempted to untangle the sticky ball of the postwar American military, economic, and technical complex, then physics would be a consistent thread running through it.

American postwar techno-science grew so far and so fast it even drew women into its operations to meet its "manpower" needs. Thousands of women trained in technical and scientific fields. If they succeeded in these fields it was against tremendous odds. Sharon Traweek, in her classic ethnography of particle physics in the 1970s, refers to an image from a standard textbook of the time, which illustrates for the aspiring physics undergrad what they are to look for and what they are to ignore as distractions. Among the things to ignore is the body of a woman.[92] On this account, physics as big science was a machine for producing, among other things, certain kinds of white guys. Not surprisingly then, another strand one can pick out of the sticky ball of postwar American power, a very tiny strand but a strong one, is feminist science studies. The conditions were right for producing a cadre who understood one or another science very well, but who also understood only too well that they were enmeshed in a field of gender and other relations of power that called for systematic critique and action.

I want to concentrate in this chapter on some interesting resonances Barad's work has with Bogdanov's analogical thought. At first, this might seem like a stretch. Barad is leery of the legitimation of power and exploitation by reference to analogies from the natural world. And yet her writing makes tactical use of analogies, as we shall see—just different ones, even queer ones. Interestingly, Barad tries to draw useful tropes and images directly out of the practices of scientific labor. Perhaps it's a matter then of a kind of tektology, of a poetics of producing alternate analogies to the dominant ones, but also a critique of the limits of analogical transposition.

This applies in particular to Barad's "over-arching trope"—*diffraction*—that she borrows from Haraway.[93] Diffraction patterns occur in everyday life. The Marxist philosopher Henri Lefebvre tells the story of swimming seaward one day and getting caught too far from the beach when the weather turned. The imaginary order, his body's power against the world, is suddenly rent, and all is plunged into surviving the wavy real. As he strokes shoreward, his strength waning, he finds a pattern in the chaos of the water, a rhythm and a form in the peaks and troughs of the waves. He is in a diffraction pattern, waves interweaving with waves, their forms passing through each other, as if occupying the same positions. Some peaks are specially high, where two waves coincide; some are reduced, where a peak coincides with a trough. As he swims Lefebvre finds the rhythm. Waves are not things existing in a void; they are forms passing through fields.[94]

Diffraction is also a key phenomenon in physics. For example, Lefebvre's contemporary, the Marxist scientist J. D. Bernal, kicked off his long career with studies of the diffraction of X-rays passing through crystals to find their structure.[95] X-ray crystallography does not produce images that reflect the form of the crystal. Rather, the X-rays pass through the crystal lattice, which blocks and bends their path toward an X-ray sensitive plate. Bernal had to measure and interpret the two-dimensional diffraction pattern to find the three-dimensional structure of the crystal. As a kind of evidence, a diffraction is more like an index than an icon, more a trace of an event than a mimesis of a thing.[96] X-ray crystallography, in this instance, is a record of an event that happened within its apparatus.

Diffraction is not about how one thing is an imaginary reflection or double of another. It does not take as given what is object and what is subject, or what is nature and what is culture. It is about their joint production. Diffraction is about how things pass through and produce differential patterns. Barad: "Diffraction attends to the relational nature of difference."[97] Barad goes on to claim for her own approach that "calling a method 'diffractive' in analogy with the physical phenomenon of diffraction does not imply that the method itself is analogical."[98]

Actually, it might, but there might be different ways to produce analogies. One way is representationalist, which tries to get one domain to resemble another via the analogy. Nature is like culture, or culture is like nature. Diffraction, on the other hand, is a non-representational analogy. Diffraction, at its best, does not look for the way science is just a mirror of culture, as the social constructivists might. Nor does it take science to be a mirror of nature, as scientific realists might. Rather, it's a question of taking apparently separate things, passing them through each other and seeing how they interact, how they might in part be mutually produced by each other, yet not alike.

Barad aspires to "respectful engagements with different disciplinary practices."[99] Her diffractive tektology passes an image or figure from one domain of practice through the apparatus of another, not to produce similarity, but to produce a pattern of refracted differences. It is an experimental procedure for language, another orphan practice to put alongside Bogdanovite tektology, Platonovian détournement, Feyerabendian dada or Haraway's irony.

Diffraction is only partly about the passing of a form from one domain into another. It is also about the testing of the pattern of that transposition. Descriptions of nature are always caught up in substitutions, but there might be a way to work it so that assumptions from the dominant organizational forms are filtered out a bit, and some patterns from the labor of working in and against apparently natural materials come more to the fore. It's a practice of diffracting one body—or are they waves?—of knowledge through another.

Barad: "*interpretive* questions about quantum theory plagued me as a graduate student in theoretical particle physics."[100] Even in Bogdanov's time, advances in physics seemed to rule out certain kinds of metaphysics. For example, devotees of dialectical materialism applied interpretive contortions to bring it into line with both experimental results and theories in modern physics, but it was just one of a series of positions that physics called into question. Any kind of strong realism—which assumes that it can describe in advance the constants of a real world with which every genuine experimental result should be consistent—was in trouble.

What can one say of the real when different experiments produce reliable results which are not consistent with the same metaphysics of what that real, independent world actually is? For example: Is matter made of waves or particles? It can't exactly be both. Particles are localized in space and time, whereas waves can extend. Waves can overlap, like the waves of water that produced the polyrhythm of peaks and troughs through which Lefebvre swam to save his life. The problem for physics in the early twentieth century was that there were reliable experimental results that showed *both* wave and particle behavior.

One solution to this sort of problem is Werner Heisenberg's uncertainty principle.[101] This in essence says that there is a lower limit to the certainty with which a behavior in an experiment can be observed. The experiment will influence the observation. This saves the honor of realism at the expense of a closer examination of what actually transpires in experimental labor. A metaphysical real world is still assumed, entire and complete in all its primary qualities. It's just that this noumenal world of things-in-themselves is always just out of reach of the phenomenal world of experimental confirmation.

Here Barad prefers to follow Niels Bohr, who had a subtly different approach. He notes more accurately that wave behavior and particle behavior are observed in different and particular—he would say complimentary—kinds of experiments using different apparatuses, and mutually exclusive ones. Both are "real" phenomena—sensations in the Machian language—but each is the product of a different apparatus. Bohr's challenge is to Newtonian assumptions: that the world is composed of objects with individual and determinate boundaries that can be represented by abstract values independently of any particular apparatus.

At first sight this would appear to wreak havoc with any notion of *objectivity*. Now, it needs to be said that objectivity is a category with a history.[102] There was a time when it meant something like the word of a gentleman as a modest witness. As science got bigger and the act of recording results became industrialized, what was objective no longer took the discriminating powers of the gentleman to observe, but was more a matter of a worker checking a dial and writing down the number on the log sheet. Curiously, in both these versions of objectivity, the labor of making something objective does not really figure. In the first case, because gentlemen don't work; in the second case, because while workers work, that is all they do. The work is just there to prove or disprove what really matters, which to a wide variety of theories of knowledge, including even some supposedly Marxist ones, would be the conceptual problematic of knowledge alone.

Whether objectivity rests on a gentleman's honor or a worker's labor, in both cases it is supposed to be a mirror of nature. What makes a statement objective is that it reflects nature without being unduly influenced by what is around it, either because of the moral probity of the gentleman scientist, or because of the rote work of the lab assistant. This is an image of objectivity which derives, not so much from Newton's actual practice, as what was said about it after the fact. In Newtonian epistemology, the object and observer are both physically separate and conceptually separate. What emerges is Newton's strict causal determinism. Given the position and momentum of a particle, its trajectory can be determined both in past and future time, irrespective of who or where the observer is.

Bohr does not abandon objectivity so much as pay closer attention to how it is produced. Bohr's objectivity is about being accountable to a materialization of which the scientific worker is a part. Objectivity means producing a certain kind of *cut* in the world, over and over again, and getting comparable results. But the results are always the product of a particular apparatus, which makes this cut in the world in a particular way. What is measured is not the world, it is rather the phenomena produced in this particular apparatus. Actually, this approach is more, rather than less, "realist." It's a realism of the experimental medium itself.

If you want to measure the position of a particle, you need a fixed point of reference. If you want to measure the momentum of a particle, you need something movable, which can absorb that momentum and measure its force. These are different kinds of apparatus, one producing position-sensation, the other momen-tum-sensation. They are determined by mutually exclusive apparatuses. We can't subtract the practice of measuring from the phenomena measured. But the larger consequence is that there is no good way of discriminating between the apparatus and its object. No inherent subject/object distinction exists. There is an object-apparatus-phenomena-observer *situation*. The experiment itself produces the cuts which make these appear to be separate things.

For Heisenberg, *uncertainty* was a problem of knowledge, an epistemological problem. For Bohr, *indeterminacy* is something a bit more. In a move from the Mach field manual, he sheers off the assumption of a noumenal world. There is nothing behind or hidden, there is only the apparatus and the phenomena that happens there. The crucial question is how the apparatus produces the particular cut that makes a phenomena appear as an object for a subject. It is not about uncertainty, but about what can be said to simultaneously exist. A particular apparatus makes a particular cut, making particular sensations appear. These are not random or a mere whim. Empirio-critical thinkers, including Mach and Bogdanov, still imagined they could distinguish the objective from subjective belief. The advance of Bohr and Barad is to insist that what objectivity really comes down to is repeating the situation of the experiment and communicating the result.

One can be a realist about the object of knowledge or about the process of knowledge, but it is very hard to be both at the same time. To be a realist about the object of knowledge requires putting oneself in a quasi-Godlike position, outside of the process. To be a realist about the process of knowledge requires bracketing off the idea of the noumenal object and engaging closely with practices and their particular points of view. Mach, Bogdanov, Bohr, and Barad, despite their many differences, can be read as this second kind of realist. They all break in one way or another with the image of knowledge as a representation of the world, with nature as an object of contemplation. Theirs is a realism of the means of produc-tion of knowledge. It might even be a realist *media theory*, where the media in question are scientific ones.

Barad's version overlaps with some standard accounts, including that of Feyerabend, in seeing Bohr as this kind of realist.[103] As Barad says, for Bohr:

there aren't little things wandering aimlessly in the void that possess the complete set of properties that Newtonian physics assumes (e.g. position and momentum); rather, there is something fundamental about the nature of measurement interactions such that, given a particular measuring apparatus, certain properties *become determinate*, while others are specifically excluded. Which properties become determinate is not governed by the desires or will of the experimenter but rather by the specificity of the experimental apparatus.[104]

The key category Bohr advances, which is only implicit in Bogdanov, is *apparatus*. "As Bohr says, there is no inherently determinate Cartesian cut. The boundary between the 'object of observation' and the 'agencies of observation' is indeterminate in the absence of a specific physical arrangement of the apparatus . . . The apparatus enacts a cut delineating the object from the agencies of observation."[105] This is an elegant solution to the problem of how the object of knowledge is supposed to correlate with the subject of knowledge. In place of that binary, Mach offered a monism based on sensation, Bogdanov on labor, and now Barad on apparatus. Mach draws attention to the making of knowledge, Bogdanov to its relations of production, and Barad to its forces of production.

Any particular apparatus makes a particular cut. The real is not observation-independent nature nor does it collapse back into the cultural. The real is a phenomena that the apparatus produces. An apparatus is not an idea; it is techne, a media.

Apparatuses are not Kantian conceptual frameworks; they are physical arrangements. And phenomena do not refer merely to perceptions of the human mind; rather, phenomena are real physical entities or beings (although not fixed or separately delineated things). Hence I would conclude that Bohr's framework is consistent with a particular notion of realism, which is not parasitic on subject-object, culture-nature, and word-world distinctions.[106]

Like Bogdanov, Barad escapes the Kantian correlation, where objects may only appear to subjects. Here rather is a realism of the sensation and the work of the apparatus that produces it. Only where Bogdanov stresses the work, Barad stresses its techniques. These we can think of as complimentary aspects of the techno-science cyborg. And where Haraway stresses the connected and undecidable "nature" of the human and inhuman cyborg ensemble, Barad stresses that aspect of the cyborg apparatus that makes the cut, producing the appearance of a subject distinct from its object.

Even if one acknowledges that the apparatus produces the cut that makes the observer-subject, it is tempting to put data on the side of the apparatus and the concept on the side of the subject. But for Barad, no such neat assumption can be made. "Apparatuses are the conditions of possibility for determinate boundaries and properties of objects and meanings of embodied concepts within the phenomenon. Indeed, this embodiment of concepts as part of the apparatus is ultimately what secures the possibility of objective knowledge, as defined in terms of Bohr's epistemic criteria of reproducibility and communicability."[107] That the apparatus is a kind of media that can reproduce not just a result but also its concept is what makes not just the data but also the concept part of objective knowledge.

Barad: "Apparatuses produce differences that matter."[108] So far so good. But for Barad, Bohr reifies the apparatus, freezing it in space and time, as if it too did not have a history, as if it was not the product of labor. He limits the apparatus to the laboratory. He cuts the apparatus itself off in advance. How is the cut that makes the apparatus (which in turn makes other cuts) itself produced? Barad: "Apparatuses are neither neutral probes of the natural world nor social structures that deterministically impose some particular outcome."[109] The apparatus has its own history. It is part of a larger mode of production and organization, but it does not necessarily reflect it. Rather, Barad steers our attention to how the specific apparatus might rather refract the larger world of productive forces and relations.

The apparatus is the condition of possibility of the meaning of concepts as well as of measurements of phenomena. Knowing, measuring, theorizing, and observing are all material practices of interacting with a part of the world. Bohr and Barad dispense with Heisenberg's metaphysical postulate of a noumenal world of objects with properties and parallel concepts with meanings, as if these could exist without an apparatus and without labor. Thinking, experimenting, and labor are engagements with a world of which they are just parts.

The challenge is to abandon a realism of the object of knowledge, the idea of the real as a separate world, while holding on to a realism of the process, the sensation, or the phenomena, that the apparatus produces. "The phenomena that are produced are not the consequences of human will or intentionality or the effects of the operations of Culture, Language, or Power."[110] Phenomena are real, but their specific reality does not warrant too firm an assertion of a reality in general of which they would then be representative examples.

Here Barad has something to offer beyond Bogdanov. Her primary metaphor of refraction steers away from the analogical excesses of tektology, drawing attention to the apparatus that makes a refractive field of differences rather than a reflective doubling of labor into a picture of the world. Analogy has its place in Barad, but her thinking is more metonymic than metaphoric, in that it is more interested in the apparatus as that which produces a part of the real than in labor as a metaphor for the production of the real as a whole, as is sometimes to be found in Bogdanov.

Things don't necessarily exist as separate or separable prior to the cut made in the world by the apparatus, which yields the phenomenon of something separate and knowable as an object of knowledge to a subject. It is the apparatus that produces the phenomena, here of waves, there of particles. There is thus a bit less one can claim about the causal order of the real. The deterministic universe, separate from the observer and relentless in its cause-effect sequences, can't be said to be there.

Another way to approach this might be to ask: What counts as *agency*? What can be said to act? Agency is not something that humans or even nonhumans "have." It is not something that some possess and some do not. It's an effect of a situation, often a situation that includes an apparatus. For an agent to appear, there's a prior cut. The agent appears separate as an effect of a kind of "exteriority-within-phenomena."[111]

Barad abandons an approach in which agents interact, as if the agents always existed before the actions. She speaks instead of *intra-actions*. "Intra-actions always entail particular exclusions, and exclusions foreclose the possibility of determinism, providing the condition of an open future. But neither is anything and everything possible at any given moment. Indeed, intra-actions iteratively reconfigure what is possible and what is impossible—possibilities do not sit still."[112] Agency is, then:

> a matter of intra-acting; it is an enactment, not something that someone or something has. It cannot be designated as an attribute of subjects or objects (as they do not pre-exist as such). It is not an attribute whatsoever. Agency is "doing" or "being" in its intra-activity. It is the enactment of iterative changes to particular practices—iterative reconfigurations of topological manifolds of spacetimematter relations.[113]

Such might be the beginnings of a basic metaphor for comradely cyborg labors for our time.

The objectivity of the labors of producing knowledge is not waved away on this account. Rather, the work of constructing a particular determinate cut within a particular apparatus, but in such a way as to be repeatable and communicable, is the basis, the infrastructure, for a certain kind of knowledge, a science. "The condition of possibility for objectivity is therefore not absolute exteriority but agential separability—exteriority within phenomena."[114] Strangely enough, "intra-actions enact agential separability—the condition of exteriority-within-phenomena."[115] There is no a priori object, or subject, or correlation between them. "Knowing is not about seeing from above or outside or even seeing from a prosthetically enhanced human body. Knowing is a matter of intra-acting."[116]

As in *Hamlet*, where a king can go through the guts of a worm; as in Platonov, where peasants, burdocks, water, and steam engines are comrades, so too in Barad: the category of possible agent does not decide in advance what is an active and what is a passive partner. Barad calls this an *agential realism*, but one might also say a queer realism. And as in any attempt to write about the materiality of process, the effort puts some pressure on the material of writing itself, on language, leading to sentences such as: "Intra-actions are non-arbitrary, nondeterministic causal enactments through which matter-in-the-process-of-becoming is iteratively enfolded into its ongoing differential materialization."[117]

The apparatus has entered critical theory mostly as a way of accounting for the production of bodies. From Michel Foucault to Judith Butler, there's a line of thought whose substitutions are architectural, and which pay close attention to the building of worlds that productively shape bodies, which in turn generate resistance against that shaping, and sometimes come to perform themselves even against that shaping apparatus. This framing of the subject via the meat-space of its making can go further, however.

Barad: "Theories that focus exclusively on the materialization of human bodies miss the crucial point that the very practices by which the differential boundaries of the human and the nonhuman are drawn are always already implicated in particular materializations."[118] There's a fetishistic quality, then, to such procedures, which show in detail the moments of the human emerging out of the mesh of power apparatuses, but pay less attention to the reciprocal creation of those very apparatuses as apparently inert and resistible things.

Butler and Foucault might point toward a sort of post-humanities, but one still a bit too tied to the point at which the human appears out of the apparatus.[119] However, "apparatuses are not merely about us."[120] Barad's writing might point instead to a kind of critical rewriting of what might instead be thought of as the *inhumanities*. The *inhuman* would here be the apparatus, the cuts it makes, the phenomena it records and communicates, that produce sensations from a *nonhuman* world. The inhuman mediates the nonhuman to the human. This preserves the queer, *alien* quality of what can be produced by an apparatus—particle physics for example—without saying too much about the nonhuman in advance.

Marx grasped the inhuman quality of machine production as the pushing to the periphery of the human worker's labor. The machine came to have its means of both power and control, and the worker becomes a monitor of these systems. What Marx did not anticipate was the pushing of the human to the periphery of not just the industrial apparatus but the scientific one as well. In the late Marx at least, species-being is entirely enmeshed in the processes that produce it rather than being a pre-given essence. But the human is orphaned not just from laboring but from knowing. Thinking this process cannot stop with the peripheral production of the laboring or knowing body, but has to press further into the techno-science that produces many such cuts, between objects and other objects, just as much as between the object and subject, even when thought in the more sophisticated form of the cut between apparatus and body in Foucault and Butler.

In the early twenty-first century certain philosophies became popular which dispensed with the subject of knowledge as the necessary correlate of the object and opened up a speculative relation to it rather than a critical one. Having grown bored with the subject being all and the object nothing, now the object is all and the subject nothing. But this is just a reversal of a certain kind of fetishism, in which the whole of collective labor and apparatus which produces the cut between object and subject is elided and a purely contemplative realism asserted in its place. To the contrary, our journey through Marx, Mach, Bogdanov, Platonov, Feyerabend, Haraway, and Barad is among other things one that restores to the center of attention the realism of labor, practice, apparatus, and as we shall see even in science—*infrastructure*.

The subject of knowledge is as much a production of the apparatus as the object with which it apparently correlates. But this is neither a dogmatic nor a speculative realism, both of which concern themselves with an object of knowledge that is metaphysical in nature. Such realisms are not comradely, as each insists on philosophy's unique power to legislate at the portals of the absolute. What appears most likely to be productive of new knowledge is a phenomenal or agental realism that inquires closely into the means of its own production.

Both Marx and Platonov have moments of a kind of schizophrenic vision, where subjects and objects appear to dissolve completely into their constituent processes, not just of production and reproduction but also of disruption and disorder. In Marx it's the metabolic rift he glimpses in volume three of *Capital*, of the molecular out of joint. In Platonov it is Dvanov's delirious merging with the objects of everyday life. It's the vision Bogdanov tries to temporally stabilize and orient from the labor point of view.

In Barad, we likewise glimpse the queer world of particle physics, that inhuman view of a nonhuman world that is so far below the threshold of human perception that we struggle for language to describe it.[121] Barad nevertheless offers certain concepts that help push the game of substitution in a new direction, and that might help in particular with Marx's vision of the metabolic rift. The apparatus and its cuts, and the intra-actions that the apparatus both effects and stabilizes, might help us with thinking what might be the central discipline of the inhumanities: climate science, to which we turn next.

We started Part II of *Molecular Red* with Feyerabend's reading of Mach, which would have us stay close to the realism of sensations, but is not entirely without its playful and creative use of substitution. Then Haraway helped us put that in the context of thinking our cyborgian point of view, in which we are at one and the same time a product of techno-science and yet inclined to think ourselves separate from it. There we learned not to make a fetish of either the thing or the body but to inquire as to the molecular relations in which such nodes emerge. Barad then extends the cyborg's agency deep into the inquiry as to the physical composition of things. It's time then to jump to a much larger scale—a planetary scale—and examine not just the apparatus but the whole infrastructure of apparatuses via which we come to know our climate as potentially unstable and as destabilized by metabolic rifts opened up by the collective laboring cyborg that is our species-being, itself shaped by the commodity form and techno-science.

CLIMATE SCIENCE AS TEKTOLOGY

Platonov worked on four kinds of infrastructure: the railways, electricity, irrigation, and the rather more subtle but pervasive one of standards, when he worked on weights and measures. He gives a vivid description of the struggle to build up infrastructure in "The Motherland of Electricity." Set in 1921, his story tells of a young engineer, "haunted by the task of the struggle against ruin," who is summoned to a remote village by a rather poetic communiqué from the secretary of the village soviet.[122] The land is parched, the peasants are starving. So the engineer concocts a scheme to build some infrastructure to help them.

There are few resources: searching through the loot expropriated from the landlord, the poet secretary and his new comrade the engineer find some Picasso paintings, but no pumps. There are irrigation channels but no way to move the water. The young engineer persuades an old peasant to give up the alcohol he makes in his still. The alcohol will run the one engine in the village, an old motorcycle. The engineer then persuades the local mechanic to take some scrap metal and make a paddlewheel. This replaces the back wheel of the bike, and now pumps water through the old irrigation channels.

The engineer succeeds—at least for a moment—in building an infrastructure out of available parts in which the technologies—such as they are—interlock. In this case the social practices that might go with this system don't quite take. The still explodes, killing the old peasant. He was using his own stomach as the apparatus to test the proof of the liquor, and fell asleep on the job.

Often in Platonov the infrastructure fails to live up to the super-structure of the revolution. Nevertheless, he thought a key piece of it should be a *knowledge infrastructure*. In his plan for a literary factory, he imagined a distributed network of specialized text-filtering centers with central nodes for the final synthesis of literary works. This, like Bogdanov's Socialist Academy, did not come to pass. The knowledge infrastructures that did get built around the planetary west, such as California's great research universities, inti-mately intra-act with commodification, military strategy, and digital technology.[123] This aggregate apparatus, all these cyborg knowings and inhuman doings, have the queer quality of both reproducing the world as commodity and strategy, and yet also of generating intimations of a nonhuman world.

A quite surprising knowledge infrastructure that did get built is the one through which scientists came to know about climate. What distinguishes climate science from particle physics or even genetics is that the data has to come from the whole of the big, bad, outside world. In climate science, it is not possible to build an apparatus that makes a cut, separating and delineating the object of study in its totality. Atmosphere is all around. You are sucking it in right now. The study of climate called into being a whole infra-structure of discrete apparatuses, of distinctive cuts. Climate science thus poses some fairly novel problems as to what a science is or should be, and not least what a comradely, cooperative science could be.

Our guide to climate science is *A Vast Machine*, by Paul Edwards, who was a graduate student with Haraway before becoming a noted historian of science. *A Vast Machine* takes its title from a remark by John Ruskin, who in 1839 imagined a panoptic system for knowing simultaneously the state of the weather on the entire surface of the planet.[124] Ruskin prefigures in some respects what actually came to pass—the building up, bit by bit, often from existing parts, first of partial systems, then a network, and by the twenty-first century an entire infrastructure for gathering weather data.

In some other respects, perfect weather surveillance turned out to be as impossible as the perfect surveillance of elementary particles. What Edwards calls *friction*, for which Bogdanov's term *resistance* could well substitute, stands in the way of a perfect knowledge of real weather. There is data resistance, which impedes the gathering of weather data readings. There is metadata resistance, which is a limit to what is known about the circumstances relevant to particular weather readings. There is computational resistance, which limits the accuracy of the calculation of future weather states from weather data. Edwards also gives many examples of kinds of cultural and political, or in Bogdanov's terms organizational, resistance that had to be overcome to produce a global knowledge of global climate.

Even with the advanced technology of the twenty-first century, human meteorologists are not entirely obsolete as components in weather forecasting cyborgs. Interpreting the data sometimes needs a little human experience. Predicting future weather is hard. Predicting *past* weather isn't much easier. Climate is the history of weather. The resistances which make predicting weather hard make the rather different science of understanding climate even harder. Weather is a complex system. Small variations can have rather large consequences. Even when the resistance that results from gathering data, knowing about the gathering of the data, and processing the data is small, that small variation can produce rather significant differences in the prediction of both past and future climate, even in today's advanced climate modeling computation systems.

Despite the differences in the results that climate modeling scientists get from their efforts, there is an overwhelming consensus around certain propositions that could at this point be called facts. Average temperatures around the world are rising. One of the causes of that trend is increases in the levels of atmospheric carbon. The cause of that increase is collective human labor.[125] In short, climate science holds that what I am calling the Carbon Liberation Front is real. As in any established science, there is plenty of controversy, but debates occur within this consensus.

The scientific recognition that collective human labor is causing climate change could well be one of those great discontinuities in perspective such as the heliocentric universe of Copernicus and

Galileo, the evolution of species in Darwin and Wallace, and what Althusser rather problematically calls Marx's opening up of the "continent of history."[126] In the Anthropocene, some neutral, pre-given planetary nature is no longer available as a fiction of the real. We fucked it up.

Labor in and against nature is an intra-action which produces a second nature, a constructed, material world, the ant-heap of so-called civilization. Perhaps it even produces a third nature, a networked, communicative world, a digital pheromone trail of signals, signs, and symbols, a global interactive spectacle.[127] Nature always appears in the rear-view mirror, as a reflection of that which recedes from this juggernaut of an SUV in which we rattle on into the future. Or perhaps nature is just the movie that's playing on the screen now embedded in the dashboard, while the SUV idles in a ditch, no longer going anywhere, just waiting for the wave of travail it left behind to catch up with it. Here comes the Carbon Liberation Front, and the slo-mo replay of the molecular products of metabolic rift catching up with the vehicle which tore across the world, excreting it.[128]

Edwards doesn't spend much time on the concept of the Anthropocene as discontinuity, but it would surely have interested Bogdanov. It is an historical moment when one true worldview is superseded by one of greater generality. Mother Nature as passive resister to he who acts no longer holds as a basic metaphor. Resistance has to be rethought a bit, perhaps along the lines of Platonov, as a labor that presses on an earth pressing back. But certainly there can be no resort to the figures of Gaia any more than to Prometheus.[129] The Gods cannot save us; the Goddess cannot save us. As Haraway insists, the engendering habits of thought about nature have to become an object of critique as a whole, rather than merely reversing the poles and celebrating a divine feminine nature. Our cyborgian selves are at last forced to face, with sober senses, our un-kind relations with the real.

Having something to say about climate science is surely a central test for any viable critical theory in the Anthropocene. Climate science understands the planet as a system with a history. It is the coming together of three separate kinds of knowledge: weather forecasting, the empirical study of climate, and theoretical meteorology. Bringing those three fields together required the growth of an extensive infrastructure of observation, communication, processing, and modeling. This infrastructure is a vastly more elaborate form of exactly the same sort of thing Platonov was working on in the countryside. It is embedded, extensive, standardized, modular, and—as he knew all too well—visible when it fails.

Infrastructure connects diverse structures, such as the liquor still, the motor bike, and the irrigation ditch. Science, like irrigation, requires an infrastructure, and any Marxist theory of knowledge rightly begins with some study of that infrastructure. In *A Vast Machine*, Edwards is not offering a Marxist theory of knowledge, although as a former grad student of Haraway's, he is attentive to both machines and metaphors. Edwards usefully provides the tools with which to start building one. Such a theory starts and ends not with math or method but with the infrastructure by which a science is made.

Climate science differs from bench science in the extent of its dependence on cooperative labor and communication for the production of data. Its history is one of various bits of infrastructure slowly accreting and linking. Colonial occupations provided some of the first opportunities for recording data from very different climates. The US Navy early on started keeping detailed meteorology. The first theories of global atmospheric circulation arose in part out of the global vectors of trade and empire and the still-partial sensation of a global space they produced.

Through war and peace, the various sciences of weather and climate oscillated between forms of scientific nationalism and internationalism. Imperial power brought with it attempts at universal standards, a universal time, Morse code, and the vector of telegraphic communication, which moves information faster than weapons or commodities, although as yet not much faster than weather itself. Attempts at international cooperation on weather collapsed during both world wars. Yet war made weather an even higher priority. Meteorology aids accurate ballistics, not to mention the timing of troop movements and air sorties. Just as the ship had once become a mobile weather station, so too did aircraft, adding a third dimension to data-space.

As a field, climatology started off as descriptive and empirical.[130] The notion that clearing forests could cause local changes in climate had already occurred to David Hume, and it would appear that early on Marx and Engels had grasped something of the same perspective:

> The first premise of all human history is, of course, the existence of living human individuals. Thus the first fact to be established is the physical organization of these individuals and their consequent relation to the rest of nature. Of course, we cannot here go either into the actual physical nature of man, or into the natural conditions in which man finds himself—geological, hydrographical, climatic and so on. The writing of history must always set out from these natural bases and their modification in the course of history through the action of men.[131]

But it was Eduard Brückner who in the 1880s came up with some plausible ideas about different causes of climate change. He thought German climate data showed periodic fluctuations around a thirty-five-year cycle, and he linked increasing desertification and drought to deforestation. Svante Arrhenius brought concepts from physics into climate thinking. He calculated that doubling atmospheric carbon dioxide would raise global temperatures by five or six degrees Celsius, but he was more interested in explaining periods of global cooling.

Thomas Chamberlin started combining gas physics theories with geological data, and arrived at both a concept of the carbon cycle and of the role of life in the carbon cycle. The idea that the carbon cycle was a driver of global climate changes fell out of favor until the 1930s, as other research with other apparatus seemed to show that the water vapor in the atmosphere had a stronger greenhouse effect than carbon dioxide. Bogdanov's interest in it in the 1910s and 1920s appears idiosyncratic. The idea that held favor was one linking climate change exclusively to variations in the earth's orbit and tilt.

The carbon cycle climate theory was revived by the steam engineer G. S. Callendar, who also grasped the role of fossil fuel combustion in the carbon cycle. More sensitive instruments now showed carbon absorbing heat in a wider spectrum than water vapor. Callendar calculated that temperatures were already rising. The Royal Society was unimpressed, and rightly so, given the poor state of theoretical climate science and unreliability of the data at the time.

A major advance on the theoretical side came when Vilhelm Bjerknes applied concepts from fluid dynamics and modeled weather with a system of seven equations. Here we have one of those non-metaphoric substitutions, more of the Haraway than the Bogdanov kind, where a logical and formal technique from one field becomes a diagram for another. There was a problem, however. There was no way to gather the data or compute it, or efficiently make the computations.

Edwards: "Data are things."[132] If we are to avoid a commodity or corporeal fetishism of such things, then critique has to inquire as to how data is produced. Data are the product of a whole series of labors, of observing, recording, collecting, transmitting, verifying, reconciling, storing, cataloguing, and retrieving. In each of these processes, human labor and the apparatus intra-act in all sorts of ways. The most utopian thing in Bogdanov's *Red Star* is that data and computation resistance have been overcome, but the overcoming of these resistances is not part of the back-story of *The Engineer Menni*. In climate science, we have just such a story of the labor of information, which overcomes resistances corresponding to neither Bogdanov's mental nor manual resistances to organization.

The exigencies of war were a great fillip to overcoming such resistances, and it leaves its traces. The image of a storm "front" is a substitution that derives from military forecasting. Speed was the essence of weather forecasting, and so the forecasters did not want too much data. The overcoming of communication resistance had outstripped the speed of the processing of data. The labor of processing data caught up with its transmission with the punch-card Holerith machines. In the United States, there was even a depression-era WPA project to put all past ship weather data onto punch cards for the study of climate.

World War Two was the weather war. Even the Western Marxist philosopher Jean-Paul Sartre found himself, in his brief military career, drafted into launching weather balloons and recording wind velocity data for the artillery.[133] Military aircraft discovered the jet streams, and, finally, theories about how upper level weather controls ground weather could be confirmed. Weather data captured from the Germans was treated as an intelligence find and several tons of records were carefully shipped back to the United States. It was an era when computing resistance was falling, but data resistance was still high. Too much manual processing was still involved. The human labor took the form of a series of analog-digital conversions: recording an observation from an instrument in a log book, then transcribing those numbers for communication by telegraph, then writing them back into tables by hand, and so on.

The Normandy invasion confirmed the military value of forecasting. It was launched under cover of appalling weather conditions, based on a meteorological prediction that the weather would clear once the Allied forces had crossed the English Channel. It could be said that the weather was not a chance circumstance in this instance but had been fully *weaponized*. Postwar weather data infrastructure was a vast improvement on its prewar state, but as in Platonov, it had been cobbled together from different kinds of parts. For example, teletype automated part of the data transmission, but shortwave and microwave transmission vectors were used in some situations as well.

The wartime development of computing made numerical weather prediction a possibility for the first time. John Von Neumann grasped how computers could be used for weather data. Like the hydrogen bomb, weather is basically a matter of fluid dynamics. Via a kind of tektological redeployment of the algorithm, what worked in one field might work in another. Jule Charney used the ENIAC computer for forecasting experiments, although it took more than twenty-four hours to compile a twenty-four-hour weather forecast. This was the beginning of a shift from analog to digital forecasting. As in other fields, early results led to optimism about computing power, which took a long time to pay off.

What particularly appealed to military taskmasters was the prospect of controlling the weather. The Normandy invasion weaponized the weather that just happened to occur through accurate prediction. What would appear a next logical step would be to command it. But before it could be controlled, it had to be measured and modeled. Not for the first or last time, a fairly remote military objective fueled a whole range of research. The postwar period is one of the growth over time of model sophistication, model resolution, and computing speed, in part fueled by military funding and imperatives, but in the process creating something else. Edwards: "In the 1960s and 1970s, this data-driven, regionally oriented, descriptive field would be transformed into a theory-driven, globally oriented discipline increasingly focused on forecasting the future."[134]

Something quite strange happens when computing power reaches the point that it can handle the complexity of a climate model: "If you can simulate the climate, you can do experiments."[135] The computer itself becomes the laboratory. And over time, more and more processes can be integrated into the model, starting from a—relatively—simple thermodynamic engine which transports air from the equator to the poles, and eventually including a comprehensive model of how the atmosphere and the oceans process solar energy, of the effects of clouds, ocean currents and turbulence, of the albedo effect of different surfaces, and so on.

Climate models become earth system models that include the entire carbon cycle. Such an apparatus still can't predict the actual weather too far in advance. Weather is complex, so predictive models aren't accurate past a week or two. No model yet reproduces all features of recorded climate, but they do simulate its general patterns. The computer becomes the apparatus for a kind of infinite forecast, predicting both past and future climates of simulated planet Earths.

What made all this possible was supercomputing infrastructure. "No fields other than nuclear weapons research and high-energy physics have ever demanded so much calculating capacity."[136] Climate science is one of the few fields that has influenced the development path of supercomputing. The first Cray supercomputer (model 1) shipped to a client was a prototype that went to Los Alamos in 1977 for weapons work, but the next (model 3) was for climate research.

In this regime of code-causality, modeling problems remain. There is a trade-off between the resolution and the complexity of a climate model: should it have more finely grained detail and only a few processes, or more processes but less fine detail? Then there is the problem of rounding-off error. To how many decimal points should a result be calculated? Tiny errors accumulate and effect the outcome. Even when starting with the same data, small differences in computer code can result in different simulation outcomes when modeling the same climate on different machines. The simulated Earths of climate science all differ a bit from each other—although all of them heat up.

Meanwhile, on the actual Earth, connecting up the weather data-gathering practices of the planet turns out to be an interesting precursor to the creation of the internet. Overcoming geopolitical resistances to get agreements on standards, and getting them implemented, took patience and persistence. Cold War geopolitics and decolonization movements favored a kind of infrastructural globalism. The superpowers sought global information in all sorts of areas, of which weather was just one, and preferably from some direct technical means, rather than relayed via allies. Former colonies attempting to establish themselves as sovereign states wanted to participate in global information sharing, but were not in a position to make major infrastructural commitments. Global weather data came to rely on two standard kinds of Cold War apparatus: the computer and the satellite.[137]

The Cold War saw an escalation of the "techno-politics of altitude."[138] When the Soviets shot down Gary Powers's U2 spy plane in 1960, the Americans claimed it was doing weather research, which may even have been slightly true. Climate science inter-sected with the Cold War in one particularly eerie way: the "atmospheric" testing of nuclear weapons also turned out to be a nuclear testing of the atmosphere. Tracking radioactive fallout was a boon to the development of three-dimensional models of global circulation patterns, and also to atmospheric chemistry.

The United States and the Soviet Union each launched their own weather satellite systems, but superpower rivalry generated a subsidiary counter-discourse of peace, cooperation, and scientific progress. Weather was an area in which to realize all three. "The project enrolled scientists and weather forecasters in the competi-tive goals of the superpowers while simultaneously enrolling the superpowers . . . in scientific cooperation."[139] The Soviet Union shared weather data from the vast territory it controlled, although it withheld the locations of certain weather stations, which of course were likely military installations.

With some sort of infrastructure cobbled together, it was feasi-ble by the late 1970s to execute something called the Global Weather Experiment, which is possibly one of the largest scientific experiments ever conducted, and the first to attempt to produce a fully global data set about planetary weather. It also led to regular meetings of climate modelers from around the world. Climate emerges as a global object of a global knowledge practice, but over-coming geopolitical resistances hardly resolves the other kinds of resistance.

A key part of Edwards's presentation of the genesis of climate science is his insistence on what Barad might recognize as a kind of intra-action. The data and the models co-produce each other. It's not that there is data and then a model of that data. At a certain point in its evolution, the model acquires the capacity to create a certain quality of the data set itself. "Adding the third dimension, computer model grids became an ideal Earth: the world in a machine. Data from the real atmosphere had to first pass through this abstract grid-space, which transformed them into new data calculated for the model's demands."[140] Interpolation algorithms adjust data to what the model predicts it to read.

To test how a model fits the world, climate science does not compare model to data, but model to another model, to a *model of the data*. "Simulating data to test simulation models; using one model's output to measure another one's quality: welcome to the mirror world of computational science."[141] The mutual adjustment of model grid-points and observational records is a kind of data assimilation. Data and models intra-act. Sometimes models with simulated data predict better than ones with actual observations. Such might be some of the peculiarities of trying to produce knowledge in the era of code-causality.

Part of the difficulty for climate science is that the difference between "raw data" and analysis is much wider than in a lot of fields, due to the kind of data gathered.[142] The apparatus is an inside-out cyborg, as it were. In a bench science, the apparatus effects a cut from the world, producing a situation where an event can happen that can be contained and repeated. In climate science, there are thousands upon thousands of instruments, each of which is an apparatus that makes a particular and local cut, measuring the value for temperature, or humidity, or barometric pressure. What is between and beyond these cuts remains indeterminate. The data have to be gathered "in the wild," and will always fall short of being perfect records due to the instabilities inherent in the placing of the apparatus within the situation it records, rather than having an apparatus produce the situation then record it. The theory-laden nature of data is pushed to extremes in this science.

Climate science is not a *reductionist* science; it is a *reproductionist* science. "Reproductionism seeks to simulate a phenomenon, regardless of scale, using whatever combination of theory, data, and 'semi-empirical' parameters may be required. It's a 'whatever works' approach . . ."[143] From a rationalist perspective, this looks like Feyerabend's "anything goes." From a naive positivist perspective, it starts to look like it's "not science." But it makes sense from the point of view Mach practiced, at least as Feyerabend understands it, which sticks close to the sensations that the apparatus produces, which toggles between data, model, and theory, and which uses conceptual, even critical tools to understand how each element in the practice of producing this knowledge, in and against the world, proceeds.

Models emerge as a relatively new category of knowledge production, when the basic metaphor becomes one of code-causality. Models are mediators between the apparatus, the data, and the theory. They are a distinct kind of technology, embodied in code and the machines that run it. As Feyerabend might expect, there's no purity in either the data or the theory. The scientist's chief job is trying to control for *artifacts*. How is the apparatus itself turning up as an artifact in the results as a kind of index of its own determinate form? An unwanted refraction may show up in an image made with a compound lens as lens flare. Digital devices produce quite different and strange artifacts of their own.[144]

The vast panoptic machine Ruskin imagined did not come to pass, even in the era of big data. More data seems always to mean more data resistance. There are limits to observability. The apparatus produces the data it's designed to produce, and has value precisely in its determinate quality, in the cut that makes it. Edwards: "You will never get perfect knowledge of initial conditions."[145] Any particular model will always diverge from observations, in part because of the determinate quality of those very observations.

The problem with climate data is that most of it is actually weather data. It was collected for the purposes of short-run prediction, not long-run modeling. There is no consistent metadata attached to the data. There are not always records of what instruments were used, or if there were changes in the conditions of their use, nor are there always calibrations of a new instrument against the one it replaces. Perhaps the instrumentation was moved further up the hill, or a gauge was replaced by one from another manufacturer. Artifacts in the data set can result from all sorts of such little changes.

For instance, there appears to be a sudden drop in sea temperature of .03 degrees in 1945, but it might be caused by a switch from data gathered by American ships that measure engine intake water to British ones that drop a bucket over the side. Edwards: "Historically, climate scientists have often found themselves stuck with damaged goods—leftovers from a much larger forecasting enterprise that ignored consistency and reliability in its constant drive to move forward with newer, better technology."[146] Ironically, this is a situation where the constant revolutionizing of the means of production introduces resistances of its own.

The methodological response in climate science is in a curious way an historical materialist one: "If you want global data, you have to make them. You do that by inverting the infrastructure, recovering metadata, and using models and algorithms to blend and smooth out diverse, heterogeneous data that are unevenly distributed in space and time."[147] Inverting the infrastructure might be thought of as a way of working past a fetishism. The fetish is not so much of the commodity or the corporeal kind, but a kind of *communicative fetishism*, where what is communicated is severed from how it is communicated. Climate science requires a theory and a method of studying the means of production of its own data—a media theory.

This makes climate science vulnerable to attack by those with an interest in preserving a carbon-fueled commodity economy, or those with an emotional investment in maintaining the everyday life it appears to sustain. Techniques pioneered for the defense of tobacco, acid rain, and ozone depletion now appear in attacks on climate science. Edwards: "During the George W. Bush administration (2001–2008), even as the scientific consensus grew even stronger, political appointees carried the manufacture of controversy to the point of criminal corruption."[148]

Crucially, both the social constructivist and Heideggerian critiques of science now shift in their effects to the right, by undermining confidence in the methods of climate science and the consensus reached on climate change. Hence the need for progressive forces to think tactically about where and when the critique of science is prudent. Perhaps returning to something like the classical Marxist and Bogdanovite open-mindedness toward the sciences might be appropriate, rather than the Heidegger-inflected critique of Marcuse and others, which sees all science and technology as embedded in the same Western metaphysics.

Here we arrive at something of a crisis point for what one might call the *romantic left*.[149] This current wants a totalizing critique of technology more than of capital, that would ground its rejection of techno-modernity on a claim to something prior to or outside of it: on being, on nature, on poetry, on the body, on the human, or on communism as event or leap. But the problem is that the attendant closing of thought to science and technology now plays into the hands of climate denial. That the Carbon Liberation Front is changing the climate is a knowledge that can only be created via a techno-scientific apparatus so extensive that it is now an entire planetary infrastructure. To reject techno-science altogether is to reject the means of knowing about metabolic rift. We are cyborgs, making a cyborg planet with cyborg weather, a crazed, unstable disingression, whose information and energy systems are out of joint. It's a de-natured nature without ecology.

Climate science has no need for Marxist theory, but Marxist theory has need of climate science. Its project has to move on, from the critique of political economy to the critique of its Darwinian descendants in biology, to the critique of climate science as a knowledge which shapes the most general worldview of the Anthropocene. It may sound like hubris to name an entire epoch the Anthropocene, as this seems at odds with the decentering and demoting of the human that was a significant achievement of ecological thought. But the Anthropocene draws attention to androgenic climate change as an unintended consequence of collective human labor.

The Anthropocene calls attention not to the psychic unconscious or the political unconscious but to the *infrastructural unconscious*. What labor builds is a disingression. Moreover, viewed via the Anthropocene, human action remains quite modest and minor, it's just that in fluid systems a small action can have disproportionately large effects. Bogdanov had glimpsed something of this in his law of the minimum.

Bogdanov is an unacknowledged precursor to today's reproductionist sciences. While his grasp of the actual science, even for his own time, was limited and idiosyncratic, he understood that critique has to advance from political economy to other sciences that shape the horizon of organizational possibilities. Rather than retreat to the high ground of philosophical method, he plunged on into a practice of comradely sharing among different knowledge practices.

For Bogdanov, there is no Marxist philosophy as such, only the labor point of view. Philosophy was not to legislate on method for other kinds of knowledge, and in this Bogdanov is not of a piece with the grand search for a method that stretches through Western Marxism from Lukács and Korsch to Sartre and Althusser. Those philosopher-kings imagined philosophy as the master discourse, which thought the *way* the party ought to think, and hence *what* the party ought to think. Bogdanov, by contrast, proposes a comradely organization of all kinds of knowledge and practice, not subordinated to a center or a theory. And hence Bogdanov belongs to a different practice of knowledge to those inheritors of Western Marxism like Slavoj Žižek or Alain Badiou, for whom philosophy is no longer a precursor to the thought of Lenin's party, but rather where Lenin's party is a precursor to the thought of philosophy.

Still, as Bogdanov knew only too well, language always extends a little too far. It extends its metaphorical chains to girdle whole worlds, real or imagined. As Haraway insists, there is a positive role in metaphorical extension, as it can open up lines along which new forms of experiment or labor might develop. But as Barad would have it, such extensions need not be thought of in terms of resemblances. The refracting powers of language might have their uses in producing language that can work between the sites of the division of labor. Taking Barad's refractive studies of the apparatus and applying them to Edwards's on climate science, we can see how a vast, inhuman apparatus producing a quite nonhuman view of the world is paradoxically the condition of possibility for thinking the problem of the metabolic rifts produced by human-cyborgian labor.

So far I have made the case for a revised empirio-monism, to shear off the metaphysical extrusions of a pre-Anthropocene era. I have made a case for a revised tektology in which a humanist style of thought might collaborate with the sciences without futile attempts to legislate for them, and yet without accepting a naive scientific realism either. I have advocated a more nuanced version of the labor point of view, which understands labor's imbrication in the apparatus. What remains then of Bogdanov's orphan legacy is to rethink what might become of proletkult. Here, rather than follow Platonov, I return to Bogdanov's foray into utopian science fiction.

One version of what might constitute a popular, affective way of writing low theory that is close to the experience of the technical and scientific labor of our times might be science fiction. There's no finer exponent of it than Kim Stanley Robinson, to whom we turn next. Robinson is very much a Californian writer, who grew up in the shadow of its booming aerospace industries, but also had time for the Sierra Mountains nature writing of Kenneth Rexroth. He is even, in part at least, a writer shaped by California Marxism. He studied at the University of California (San Diego) after Herbert Marcuse's tumultuous time there, but was shaped by his influence, not to mention that of Fredric Jameson, under whose direction he went on to produce a doctoral thesis on another great Californian writer, Philip K. Dick.[150] Not of least interest in Robinson's work is the way these influences are woven together into a forward-looking fictional world.

4

Kim Stanley Robinson: The Necessity of Creation

Alternative futures branch like dendrites away from the present moment, shifting chaotically, shifting this way and that by attractors dimly perceived. Probable outcomes emerge from those less likely.
—Kim Stanley Robinson

RETURN TO *RED MARS*

"Arkady Bogdanov was a portrait in red: hair, beard, skin"—and red politics, although it will turn out that there is another kind entirely.[1] He is a descendant of Alexander Bogdanov, and he is on his way to Mars, together with ninety-nine other scientists and technicians. Or one hundred others, it will turn out, when the stowaway surfaces. This First Hundred (and one) are the collective protagonist of Kim Stanley Robinson's famous *Mars Trilogy*: *Red Mars*, *Green Mars* and *Blue Mars*, published in the early 1990s.

If Bogdanov's 1908 novel is a détournement of pop science fiction, then Robinson's *Red Mars*, is a détournement of the *robinsonade*, a version of Defoe's *Robinson Crusoe* story. If we were to pick just one book as the precursor to capitalist realism, *Crusoe* might well be it. What makes it so characteristic of the genre is that it lacks any transcendent leap toward the heavens or the future. It is as horizontal as a pipeline. It is about making something of this world, not transcending it in favor of another. It makes adventure into the calculus of arbitrage, of the canny knack of buying cheap and selling dear.

In *Robinson Crusoe*, the shipwrecked Robinson does not depend on God or Fortune for help, he helps himself. He sets himself to work, as if he were both boss and laborer. There's no spontaneous bravery, no tests of honor, no looking very far upwards or very far forwards. Robinson's labors are nothing if not *efficient*. What is useful is beautiful on the island of capitalist realist thought, and what is both beautiful and useful is without waste. There is no room for Platonov's fallen leaf. The world is nothing but a set of potential tools and resources.

Defoe organizes the bourgeois worldview with a forward-slanting grammar in which time is segmented and arranged serially. Robinson confronts this, does that, attains this benefit. Here's a characteristic sentence: "Having mastered this difficulty, and employed a world of time about it, I bestirred myself to see, if possible, how to supply two wants." Moretti: "Past gerund; past tense; infinitive: wonderful three part sequence."[2] It's the "grammar of growth." Bourgeois prose is a rule-based but open-ended style.

This grammar creates a whole new visibility for *things*. In Defoe, things can be useful in themselves. They are connectable only sideways, in networks of other things. With this you get that, with that you make this, and so on. Things are described in detail. Everything appears as a potential resource or obstacle to accumulation. What is lost is the totality. The world dissolves into these particulars. The capitalist realist self sees a world of particular things as if they were there to be the raw materials of the work of accumulation, for it knows no other kind of work.

In *Red Mars*, Robinson bends the robinsonade to other purposes. There is neither heaven nor horizon, but the practical question of how various ideologies overcome the friction of collaborative labor. It is not a story of an individual's acquisition and conquest. It's a story about collective labors. The problem here is the invention of forms of organization and belief for a post-bourgeois world.

Robinson's ambition is the invention of a grammar that might come after that of capitalist realism.

In *Red Star*, Bogdanov's voyager to Mars is a single representative of the most technically skilled and class-conscious workers, out to see the utopian society of labor as an already existing form. In *Red Mars*, on the long and dangerous voyage from Earth to Mars, and in the early days of their arrival, the First Hundred debate just exactly what it is they have been sent to organize on the "New World" of Mars. Several positions emerge, each an unstable mix of political, cultural, and technical predispositions. As in Platonov, characters each bear out a certain concept of what praxis could be. Over the course of the three books, which are in effect one big novel, these positions will evolve, clash, collaborate, and out of their matrix form the structure not just of a new polity but of a new economy, culture, and even nature.

The leaders of this joint Russian-American expedition are Maya Toitovna and Frank Chalmers, experienced space and science bureaucrats. Frank and Maya are different kinds of leaders, one cynical the other more emotive. They quickly find their authority doubled, and troubled, by more committed and charismatic potential leaders, Arkady Bogdanov and John Boone. Bogdanov and Boone *over-identify* with the political ideologies of their respective societies, Soviet and American, the Marxist and the liberal.[3] They actually believe! Chalmers and Toitovna find this especially dangerous to their more pragmatic authority.

These four could almost form a kind of "semiotic rectangle," an analytic tool used by both Fredric Jameson and Donna Haraway.[4] It's tempting to reach into the bag of tricks of formal textual analysis and run the *Mars Trilogy* through the mesh of such devices. The problem is that Robinson already includes such devices within the text itself. The character of Michel the psychiatrist is particularly fond of semiotic rectangles, for example. The usual "innocence" of the text in relation to the formal critical method no longer applies here—Robinson did, after all, study with Fredric Jameson. Perhaps that's why Robinson always seems to want his stories to exceed the formal properties of such a schema. Rather, his characters form loose networks of alliance and opposition, always making boundaries and linkages. The novel tracks one possible causal sequence in a space of possibilities. There's no single underlying design.

Complicating the four points of the semiotic rectangle of Maya and Frank, Arkady and John, are three outlier figures: Hiroko Ai, who runs the farm team; the geologist Ann Claybourne; and Saxifrage Russell, the physicist. Hiroko, Ann, and Sax are different versions of what scientific and technical knowledge might do and be. Hiroko's shades off into a frankly spiritual and cultish worship of living nature. Ann's is a contemplative realism, almost selfless and devoted to knowledge for itself. Sax sees science not as an end in itself but a means to an end—"terraforming" Mars.

Robinson did not coin the term "terraforming," but he surely gives it the richest expression of any writer.[5] While there is plenty in the *Mars Trilogy* on the technical issues in terraforming Mars, Robinson also uses it as a Brechtian estrangement device to open up a space for thinking about the organization of the Earth.[6] On Mars, questions of base and superstructure, nature and culture, economics and politics, can never be treated in isolation, as all "levels" have to be organized together. Maya: "We exist for Earth as a model or experiment. A thought experiment for humanity to learn from."[7] Perhaps Earth is now a Mars, estranged from its own ecology.

Of the First Hundred, Arkady Bogdanov has the most clearly revolutionary agenda, and one straight out of proletkult. He objects to the design for their first base, Underhill, "with work space separated from living quarters, as if work were not part of life. And the living quarters are taken up mostly with private rooms, with hierarchies expressed, in that leaders are assigned larger spaces . . . Our work will be more than making wages—it will be our art, our whole life . . . We are *scientists*! It is our job to think things *new*, to make them new!"[8]

There are many actually existing, contemporary or historical societies that for Robinson exude hints of utopian possibility: the Mondragon Co-ops, Yugoslav self-management, Red Bologna, the Israeli kibbutz, Sufi nomads, Swiss cantons, Minoan or Hopi matriarchies, Keralan matrilineal land tenure. One of the more surprising is the Antarctic science station. This he experienced first-hand in 1995 on the National Science Foundation's Artists and Writer's Program.[9]

Robinson imagines the first Mars station at Underhill as just like a scientific lab—and just as political. As Arkady would say, ignoring politics is like saying you don't want to deal with complex systems. Arkady: "Some of us here can accept transforming the entire physical reality of this planet, without doing a single thing to change ourselves or the way we live . . . We must terraform not only Mars, but ourselves."[10] Thus the most advanced forms of organization can be a template for the totality.

A field station like Underhill is not only an advanced social form, for Arkady it connects to a deep history:

> This arrangement resembles the prehistoric way to live, and it therefore feels right to us, because our brains recognize if from three million years of practicing it. In essence our brains grew to their current configuration in response to the realities of that life. So as a result people grow powerfully attached to that kind of life, when they get a chance to live it. It allows you to concentrate your attention on the *real work*, which means everything that is done to stay alive, or make things, or satisfy our curiosity, or play. That is utopia . . . especially for primitives and scientists, which is to say everybody. So a scientific research station is actually a little model of prehistoric utopia, carved out of the international money economy by clever primates who want to live well.[11]

Not everyone gets to live such a life, even at Underhill, and so the scientific life isn't really a utopia. Scientists carve out refuges for themselves from other forms of organization and power rather than work on expanding them. The crux of the "Bogdanov" position in the *Mars Trilogy* is making the near-utopian aspect of the most advanced forms of collaborative labor a general condition.

This Arkady Bogdanov, not unlike the real Alexander Bogdanov a century before him, is a kind of scapegoat to the revolution. Nearly all of the early leaders fall, in one way or another, and not least because they are too much the products of the old authoritarian organizational world. Mars has to transform its pioneers, or nurture new ones, on the way to another kind of life. A new structure of feeling has to come into existence, not after but before the new world. This is what Alexander Bogdanov thought was the mission of proletkult. Overcoming the logic of sacrifice is not the least of its agenda.[12]

John Boone, meanwhile, finds many of Arkady's ideas wrong, and even dangerous. John Boone is a charismatic, hard-partying Midwesterner. He is politically cautious, but acknowledges that "everything's changing on a technical level and the social level might as well follow."[13] His mission, at first, is to forget history and build a functioning society. But while dancing with the Sufis, he has his epiphany: "He stood, reeling; all of a sudden he understood that one didn't have to invent it all from scratch, that it was a matter of making something new by synthesis of all that was good in what came before."[14]

Bogdanovists are modernists who start over; Booneans are détourners of all of the best in received cultures. Boone practices his own style of détournement, copying and correcting, and tearing off enthusiastic speeches: "That's our gift and a great gift it is, the reason we have to keep giving all our lives to keep the cycle going, it's like in eco-economics where what you take from the system has to be balanced or exceeded to create the anti-entropic surge which characterizes all creative life . . ."[15] The crowd cheers, even if nobody quite understands what Boone is talking about.

Saxifrage Russell is a more phlegmatic kind of scientist, entranced by the this-ness, the "haecceity," of whatever he happens to be working on.[16] For Sax, the whole planet is a lab, and when John Boone asks him, "who is paying for all this?" Sax answers: "The sun." Sax quietly ignores the heavy involvement of metanational companies, for whom the whole Mars mission is a colonization and resource extraction enterprise. When John later uses this same answer to Arkady, the latter won't have it: "Wrong! It's not just the sun and some robots, it's human time, a lot of it. And those humans have to eat . . ."[17] Like Arkady, Sax sees science as a component of a larger praxis of world building, but for Arkady there's still more. There's the question of what kind of world and who it is for—the question of the labor component of the cyborg apparatus.

For Sax, science is creation. "We are the consciousness of the universe, and our job is to spread it around, to go look at things, to live wherever we can." Ann the geologist disagrees. "You want to do that because you think you can . . . It's bad faith, and it's not science . . . I think you value consciousness too high and rock too little . . . Being the consciousness of the universe does not mean turning it into a mirror image of us. It means rather fitting into it as it is."[18] But what does it mean, to "fit in," when the fitting changes what it is in? Is it not metaphorically more like a refraction?

Ann's is the most "flat" ontology of the First Hundred.[19] Human subjectivity has no privilege in her world, and neither does life. The real for her is this: "The primal planet, in all its sublime glory, red and rust, still as death; dead; altered through the years only by matter's chemical permutations, the immense slow life of geophysics. It was an old concept—abiologic life—but there it was, if one cared to see it, a kind of living, out there spinning, moving through the stars that burned . . ."[20] If the basic metaphor for Hiroko is that life is spirit, and for Sax that life is development, for Ann it is at best selection, the lifeless life of impacts and erosions of the geological eons.

Later, Robinson compares Ann's relation to Mars to that of a caravan of itinerant Arab miners: "They were not so much students of the land as lovers of it; they wanted something from it. Ann, on the other hand, asked for nothing but questions to be asked. There were so many different kinds of desire."[21] For the miners, nature is that which labor engages; for Ann, nature is that which appears to science only, shorn of any wider sense of praxis. Ann's worldview is not so entirely selfless, with its "concentration on the abstract, denial of the body and therefore of all its pain."[22] Nevertheless, it does speak to an absolute nonhuman outside to knowledge, an outside that even Sax will eventually have to acknowledge.

While also technically trained, Hiroko is more of a mystic. She believes in what Hildegard of Bingen called *viriditas*, or the greening power. This is the key to her *aerophany*, her landscape religion. Hiroko: "There's a constant pressure, pushing toward pattern. A tendency in matter to evolve into ever more complex forms. It's a kind of pattern gravity, a holy greening power we call viriditas, and it is the driving force of the cosmos . . ."[23] Arkady wants a kind of work beyond its alienation in wage labor; Hiroko wants work to be a kind of worship. As with Ann, Hiroko has a kind of ontology, but a vitalist and constructivist one, oriented to a practice that transforms its object.[24] In each case it's a substitution which starts with a kind of labor and imagines a universe after its basic metaphor.

There's a constant play in the *Mars Trilogy* between what is visible and what is hidden. Hiroko hides Coyote, the stowaway, and herself goes into hiding, with her followers, on Mars. She asks Michel the psychotherapist to go with them when they leave the Underhill base and set up a secret sanctuary: "We know you, we love you. We know we can use your help. We know you can use our help. We want to build just what you are yearning for, just what you have been missing here. But all in new forms. For we can never go back. We must go forward. We must find our own way. We start tonight. We want you to come with us." And Michel says, "I'll come."[25]

When Hiroko, the Green Persephone, surfaces again, her actions require some justifying: "We didn't mean to be selfish . . . We wanted to try it, to show by experiment how we can live here. Someone has to show what you mean when you talk about a different life . . . Someone has to live that life."[26] This is another tension in the *Mars Trilogy*: between political struggle and the enactment of another life directly, in the everyday, as experiments in self-organization that create new structures of feeling.

In the color scheme of the books, Hiroko stands for Green and Ann for Red. To estrange us a little from what we think these colors mean, the Greens are those who favor one or another kind of terraforming, to artificially make a biosphere for life. For the Greens, nature is synonymous with life. For the Reds, nature is prior to life, greater than life. "Ann was in love with death."[27] The Red Mars isn't really a living one, and the Green one is more like a garden or a work of art—culture. Neither are an *ecology*, if by that one means some ideal model of a homeostatic, self-correcting world. For the Greens, nature is that with which one works; for the Reds, it is that which one contemplates.

Part of the problem is working up an organizational language adequate to techno-science, or as Boone says to Nadia Chernishevsky the engineer: "Muscle and brain have extended out through an armature of robotics that is so large and powerful that it's difficult to conceptualize. Maybe impossible." Life is a tektological problem, lived against external constraints, but as Frank despairs, "they lived like monkeys still, while their new God powers lay around them in the weeds."[28]

It is like Platonov's tragedy of nature and technology in a different mode. The *potential* of technical power far outstrips organizational forms or concepts, which remain narrowly acquisitive and instrumental. They are on Mars to prepare the way for corporate resource extraction, after all. This is the driving tension of the *Mars Trilogy*. All of the experiences of Mars, through study, work, or worship, are fragments of a new ingression, but they have to link together, overcome their boundaries, and form a new boundary against the exploitative and militarized forms of life that sent them all there. But crucially in Robinson, not only is a potential politics (Arkady and John) counter-posed to an actual one (Frank and Maya), but a potential technics is counter-posed to the actual one of the metanationals (with the Sax character moving from the one to the other). The struggle for utopia is both technical and political, and so much else besides.

The first Martian revolution—there will be three—is in a sense against "feudalism," against a residual part of the social formation based on self-reproducing hierarchies. It is a revolution against a world where the ruling class, like the Khans of Kiva, is impoverished by its distance from any real work—in this case an inter-planetary distance. It arises out of the conflict that pits the First Hundred, leading the Martian working class, against the metanational corporations and their private armies. As Frank Chalmers says: "Colonialism had never died . . . it just changed names and hired local cops."[29] To the metanats, Mars has no independent existence. To the Martians, it's a place where the apparent naturalness of the old economic order is exposed as artifice, inequality, and fetishism.

The first revolution founders. Its vanguard is poorly coordinated, and relies too much on force, in a situation where the population in revolt is now heavily dependent on vulnerable infrastructure, which turns out to be egressive and fragile. The metanats and their goons need only shut down life support to bring refractory populations to heel. Bogdanov's law of the minimum applies here. The movement is forced underground. But perhaps this same techno-science can also support autonomous spaces outside the metanat order, where new kinds of everyday life and economic relation might arise.

The first revolution is perhaps their 1905 Russian Revolution, although as Frank says, "Historical analogy is the last refuge of people who can't grasp the current situation."[30] The first revolution results in a treaty of sorts, negotiated by Frank, the cynical and pragmatic politician. For Frank, "the weakness of businessmen was their belief that money was the point of the game."[31] Sax at this point still wants metanat investment, but Frank wants to contain it. As Frank says to Sax: "You're still trying to play at economics, but it isn't like physics, it's like politics."[32] Science and capital, it is clear to Frank but not yet to Sax, are not natural allies.

In defeat, Arkady and the Bogdanovists will hide in plain sight, to continue the revolution of everyday life: "Why then we will make a human life, Frank. We will work to support our needs, and do science, and perhaps terraform a bit more. We will sing and dance, and walk around in the sun, and work like maniacs for food and curiosity." They will create the counter-spectacle of an underground as a "totalizing fantasy,"[33] onto which everyone projects their wants. It is a matter of making extravagant proposals for another life with enough serious seduction to draw bored and disaffected labor into believing in it.[34]

Failure to spark a global revolution on Mars prompts a kind of theoretical introspection, not unlike the ones that happened after the failure of world proletarian revolution on early twentieth-century Earth, which resulted in the theoretical reflections of Western Marxism.[35] It is neatly captured in a dialogue between Frank Chalmers and his assistant:

> "How can people act against their own obvious material interests?" he demanded of Slusinki over his wristpad. "It's crazy! Marxists were materialists, how did they explain it?"
>
> "Ideology, sir."
>
> "But if the material world and our method of manipulating it determine everything else, how can ideology happen? Where did they say it comes from?"
>
> "Some of them defined ideology as an imaginary relationship to a real situation. They acknowledged that imagination was a powerful force in human life."
>
> "But then they weren't materialists at all!" He swore with disgust. "No wonder Marxism is dead."
>
> "Well, sir, actually a lot of people on Mars call themselves Marxists."[36]

Most Western Marxists thought ideology in its negative aspect, its misrecognition; Bogdanov was more interested in its affirmative aspect, in the way an ideology overcomes resistance to a given form of social labor.[37] From that point of view, what matters in this exchange is the form of the dialogue between Frank and Slusinki—master and servant—rather than the content, a Marxisant critique of ideology. The Martians do not yet have a form of communication that expresses the organizational style of their emergent social formation. The problem is not with the language or the theory, it's with the forms of organization and communication. The failure of this revolution does not call for the Western Marxist turn to the superstructures, but rather a

Bogdanovite turn to evolving new forms of organization, including a new infrastructure.

The Martians are not ready for their revolution. Still, even an unsuccessful struggle can create powerful structures of feeling, which may have future uses. "Arkady answered them all cheerfully. Again he felt that difference in the air, the sense they were all in a new space together, everyone facing the same problems, everyone equal, everyone (seeing a heating coil glowing under a coffee pot) incandescent with the electricity of freedom."[38] As Platonov says, we are comrades when we face the same dangers.

This moment of the fused group, united in action, might seed a memory for another time.[39] These moments in the *Mars Trilogy* are rather like the civil war section of Platonov's *Chevengur*: the new space and time, the new subjectivity it calls into being. But just as in Platonov, the disorganizing power works faster and more conclusively than any organizing power. The emphasis in Robinson is not on the moment of revolution as universal leap toward the communist horizon, but on the accumulation of minor, even molecular, elements of a new way of life and their negotiations with each other.

Civil war destruction and sabotage transform the Martian landscape. The First Hundred are on the run. Ann is distressed by the death of her dead world. "Here in the flesh she found it almost impossible to grasp. The landscape itself was now speaking a kind of glossolalia."[40] The civil war wrenches Ann from her strictly scientific relation to Mars. She becomes a contemplative realist of a more metaphysical sort, her antennae oriented to a great outdoors. "And it came to her that the pleasure and stability of dining rooms had always occurred against such a backdrop, against the catastrophic background of universal chaos."[41] Ann is alone with a chaotic, indifferent universe. A solitude which, paradoxically, draws others to her.

Anne's intuition of the absolute beyond the dining room window is beautifully described by the philosospher Quentin Meillassoux:

what we see there is a rather menacing power—something insensible, and capable of destroying both things and worlds, of bringing forth monstrous absurdities, yet also of never doing anything, of realizing every dream, but also every nightmare, of engendering random and frenetic transformations, or conversely, of producing a universe that remains motionless down to its ultimate recesses, like a cloud bearing the fiercest storms, then the eeriest bright spells, if only for an interval of disquieting calm.[42]

A hyper-chaos, in short, for Bogdanov is not thinkable, but for Ann is the very condition of possibility of knowing Mars at all, since it withdraws in advance any cosmic guarantee for any human project.

And yet it's the kind of thought that finds expression, and adherents, in moments not of cosmic but of social collapse. Struggling with the human, technical, and "natural" disasters of a failed revolution, Michel says to Nadia: "These are times that try men's souls." And Nadia answers: "Women, however, do fine."[43] As the arc of the *Trilogy* progresses, the gender balance of the human actants shifts. In the end it will be a victory over both property and patriarchy, but it's a victory still a long way off when the first volume concludes.

GREEN MARS: TEKTOLOGY AS REVOLUTION

Green Mars opens in Hiroko's world, a secret, green enclosure under the Martian polar ice cap. It opens too with a next generation character. Nirgal is a child of Hiroko's cyborg-matriarchal clan, as only Shulamith Firestone could imagine.[44] Nirgal is caught between not the Green and the Red, but the Green and the White:

Looking from the green side, when Hiroko confronted something mysterious, she loved it and it made her happy—it was viriditas, a holy power. Looking from the white side, when Sax confronted something mysterious, it was the Great Unexplainable, dangerous and awful. He was interested in the true, while Hiroko was interested in the real. Or perhaps it was the other way around—those words were tricky.[45]

Nirgal the "ectogene," raised in a matriarchy, outside of the nuclear family, still has to leave it to come into himself. He becomes a student of Coyote, a fellow wanderer. Nirgal is our guide to the Mars underground. Arkady is gone, but most hidden sanctuaries are Bogdanovist, except for Hiroko's, and those of the francophone utopians, readers of Foucault and Fourier.[46] He will also guide another character, a stock one in utopian writing: the visitor from something like our pre-utopian world.

Debord once said, "Yet the highest ambition of the integrated spectacle is still to turn secret agents into revolutionaries, and revolutionaries into secret agents."[47] On Mars, the character who is both is called Art. He can be read, among other things, as the stock character of the visitor from our world. Or as a stand-in for the commercial science-fiction publishing industry, of which the *Mars Trilogy* is a mature product, with its ambiguous role of both propagating and co-opting the radical imagination.

Art works for Praxis, a somewhat unusual metanational corporation, as a fixer and problem-solver. After "eighty continuous years of metastasizing," Praxis is one of the biggest companies, but the aristocratic elite who run it have a serious case of *noblesse oblige*.[48] Fort, its president, is enamored of the *full world economics* of Herman Daly: "We have been liquidating our natural capital as if it were disposable income . . . man made capital and natural capital are not substitutable."[49] The goal of Praxis is to get into the *bio-infrastructure* business, as natural resources have a theoretically infinite price, by acquiring them from distressed countries. As Fort says to Art: "We want you to acquire Mars."[50]

Art's intra-actions with the underground change him. Nirgal insinuates Art into the underground. He introduces Art to the principles of gift economy: "Get before you give, and give before you burn." Art is rather perplexed by Nirgal's explanations. "There's a money economy for the old buy and pay system, using units of hydrogen peroxide as the money. But most people try to do as much as they can by the nitrogen standard, which is the gift economy."[51]

The displacement of Red by White reveals also another "color" to the revolutionary flag, and another character: the legendary stowaway, Desmond the Coyote, late of Trinidad. Hiroko smuggled him to Mars. They were lovers once, but as Hiroko gathers around herself her matriarchal, polyandrous cult, the Coyote becomes a wanderer, moving between underground bases, teaching everyone the principles of eco-economics, with this double economy of gift and commodity. As Coyote says to Nirgal: "We are the primitives of an unknown civilization."[52] He teaches Nirgal the black arts of hiding in plain sight.

Coyote is not a great believer in revolutions. "It's not politics, but survival."[53] Rather like Platonov, he thinks revolutions are reactive, driven by fear and hunger more than universal ideals. He is not shy of illegality, just more of an anarchist than any of the other characters. He travels between the underground enclaves— Gramsci, Fourier, Mauss-Hyde, Bogdanov-Visniak, Fourier, Cole, Bellamy, Proudhon—as if on a caravan across the folds of the critical utopian archive.[54]

He is teaching and practicing a new kind of social relation. Coyote: "I'm saving people from their own ridiculous notion of economics, that's what I'm doing! A gift economy is all very well, but it isn't organized enough for our situation. There are critical items that everyone has to have, so people *have* to give, which is a contradiction, right?"[55] Coyote puts into practice the eco-economics worked out in theory by Vlad and Ursula. He bargains hard to give more than he gets, just short of *potlaching*, which is the problem of ever-increasing gifting.

Meanwhile, Ann is becoming a "bakehead," wandering too long on the surface of Mars alone. She survives a landslide, which she just watches and does nothing to avoid, her survival a matter of chance, a mere shake of the dice. "It had nothing to do with value or fitness; it was pure contingency. Punctuated equilibrium, without the equilibrium. Effects did not follow from causes . . . In the random flux of universal contingency, nothing mattered; and yet, and yet . . ."[56]

On her anabasis, she has a particularly intense vision of molecular red:

> the boulder field took on a weird beauty . . . The boulders were basalt rocks, which had been scoured by the winds on one exposed surface, until that surface had been scraped flat. Perhaps a million years for the first scraping. And then the underlying clays had been blown away, or a rare mars-quake had shaken the region, and the rock had shifted to a new position, exposing a different surface. And the process had begun again. A new facet would be slowly scraped flat by the ceaseless brushing of micron-sized abrasives, until once again the rock's equilibrium changed, or another rock bumped it, or else something else shifted it from its position. And then it would start again.[57]

While she perceives a molecular red world, she cannot see a project that would orient collective human labor within it. Ann has a vision of all the other leading protagonists and their orientation to a kind of tektology, in which organizing has an objective, or rather a criteria, but in each case a different one. Each wants a "net gain" in something, but not the same thing.[58] For Vlad and Ursula, the scientists who created the longevity treatment and then Martian eco-economics, it's a net gain in health. For Hiroko, beauty; for Nadia, goodness; for Maya, intensity; for Arkady, freedom; for Michel, understanding; for Frank, power; for John, happiness; for Sax, complexity. And for Ann? Nothing. She is the only character for whom a Meillassouxian nihilism is the ground tone.

Still, Ann's Redness remains a counterpoint for Sax's white hot passion for the techno-science of terraforming. "Terraforming isn't science," she insists.[59] As soon as science has a goal it loses its struggle for objectivity in advance. It loses the great outdoors. For Sax, favoring living over non-living systems is a value, a "holding action against entropy," and a struggle for a "net gain in information," to vary the formula once again.[60]

What makes all of these variations on the temporal signature of the Carbon Liberation Front is that they exclude in advance the narratives of capitalist realism and capitalist romance. Continuous growth, resolving its internal imbalance by projecting forward into an open world, is excluded. So too is a return to homeostasis, a closed loop balanced by some invisible hand or self-correcting order. Rather, progressive selection has to try to factor in all its own byproducts, but without the regulative ideal of a stable ecological model—that last avatar of God.[61]

Under Ann's influence, Sax starts to question his own reliance on secondary ideas alone, of applied science, terraforming, and so forth. For Sax, these secondary ideas keep at bay those deathly ideas of an absolute contingency that are so inimical to life, but to which Ann is in thrall. And yet, Ann claims, and not without justice, that Sax does not *know* Mars, at least not until his near death experiences. Sax will be put through trials. One of which, curiously, is a stroke that causes aphasia. He will lose language, just as Ann did, but far more severely. "You should hear the way he can say *bad results*."[62]

Language is a key aspect of Robinson's work. His novels are at once "realist" and have a heightened reflexivity about what realism in science fiction might entail. One aspect of this is a kind of détournement of scientific lexicons, not unlike Lautréamont's use of Buffon and other natural history texts in *Maldoror*. The *Mars Trilogy* books anticipate the search-engine age, as they bristle with terms that the reader can usefully look up. One can learn that a chasmoendolith, a life form that lives in the cracks in rocks, is different from a cryptoendolith, which gets into their internal cavities. There is even a fan-generated wiki.[63]

The Sax character himself becomes aware of the problem of language in relation to science, and even arrives at an understanding of language as universal ingression: "Analogies were mostly meaningless—a matter of phenotype rather than genotype (to use another analogy)." For Sax, culture is a "huge compendium of meaningless analogies . . . a kind of continuous conceptual drunkenness."[64] He thinks Michel's psychology is a mess of analogies. Freud thinks the mind is a steam engine: application of heat, pressure buildup, displacement, venting, and so on. Sax imagines the mind on the model of the more contemporary sciences that he knows, such as climatology.[65] The basic metaphors of causality are out of date.

For Sax, as for Bogdanov, language offers the most plastic medium of substitution but also the most dangerous, as most of its substitutions will not work at all in another medium. The problem is finding a method of *selection* from language into other practices. It's a problem for Sax, where it would not be for Ann, because of his attempt to find a praxis with a net gain. Organizing praxis calls for a theory of history, a language of goals and objectives, even if only a provisional one.[66] Praxis needs a conceptual space which relates knowable pasts to possible futures.

But it won't be a teleology. History has no plan. There is no horizon to orient toward, no line from present to future. "In that regard there was a similarity between history and evolution, both of them being matters of contingency and accident, as well as patterns of development. But the differences, particularly in time scales, were so gross as to make the similarity nothing more than analogy again . . . History *directing* evolution. It was a daunting thought."[67] The goal of science, external to it but orienting it, would ideally be a science of history. "He needed a science of history, but unfortunately there was no such thing. History is Lamarckian, as Arkady used to say."[68]

Or could be, or should be. If only we could acquire characteristics that have survival value and pass them on. We still tend to think that if we *stop* certain actions, an ecology will right itself and return to homeostasis. But perhaps that is not the case. Negative action might not be enough. It might take positive actions to create a new ingression. What if on the actual Earth, as on this fictional Mars, there is no ecology? What if there is only an unstable nature, a progressive selection, here on Earth too? What if it was a matter of continuous conscious adaptation through experimental variation via the détournement of existing forms?

The journey of the Sax character is one of finding a place along a continuum from rational, model-based science toward a more empirical and contingent one. He is representative of scientists as a class. "They were apolitical, supposedly, like civil servants—empiricists, who only wanted things managed in a rational scientific style, the greatest good for the greatest number, which ought to be fairly simple to arrange, if people were not so trapped in emotions, religions, governments, and other mass delusional systems of that sort."[69]

He is the godfather of terraforming, and still attracted to vast geo-engineering projects, particularly of the climate. The estrangement device here is that the problem on Mars is one of raising temperatures, rather than lowering them: "Sax moved on, a little smile fixed on his face. Twelve degrees! Now that was something!—over twenty percent of all the warming they needed, and all by the early and continuous deployment of a nicely designed gas cocktail. It was elegant, it truly was. There was something so comforting about simple physics."[70] Part of the project of *Green Mars* is to put this "accelerationist" glee in dialogue with tempering ideologies, without losing this sense of scale.

What brings Sax to an awareness of the problem with science in its complicity with the metanats is his encounter with what should be a kind of utopia—the scientific conference. But metanat-sponsored science becomes a war of competing corporate agendas. "Everyone knew what was going on, and no one liked it, and yet no one would admit it."[71] The aim of this science is nothing scientific. Sax does not abandon science for Hiroko's mysticism, or retreat into Ann's merely contemplative version of science. He starts to see that the passion of reason is the pull toward death, not just in Ann but in himself.

Sax embarks on a double project of bringing science to politics and politics to science. Fredric Jameson: "any first scientific reading of the *Mars Trilogy* must eventually develop into a second allegorical one, in which the hard SF content stands revealed as socio-political—that is to say, as utopian."[72] What is lacking from this reading is its dialectical complement. Any socio-political reading can also develop a secondary reading in which the utopian content intersects with its scientific—hard SF—determinants.

Actually it doesn't stop there. The *Mars Trilogy* stages encounters between otherwise *incommensurable* kinds of knowledge organization: science both pure and applied, engineering, design, politics, culture, religion, folklore, and so on.[73] It's not that there's a synthesis to be had. Rather, it's that each mode of knowing, and hence each layer of possible reading of the *Mars Trilogy* itself, can be usefully framed by another, which contains within it the positive, functional, working ideology of some component of the labor process as a whole. In this respect the *Mars Trilogy* is a work about tektology.

For Sax after his tribulations, as for Bogdanov after his, the useful framing knowledge comes from natural history. Sax makes his own observations in the field. Natural history is a real science, and "it had discovered, there among the contingency and disorder, some valid general principles of evolution—development, adaptation, complexification."[74] He does not abandon the modeling central to his original training in theoretical physics, but rather starts to take a more skeptical approach to it, to put cognition and sensation together more tentatively. All his field observations are of a wildly unstable nature, and like Bogdanov, he has already experienced the wild instability of political time. He comes to see scientific time as—at times—unhelpfully artificial.

"Here on Mars all kinds of hierarchies were destined to fall."[75] The problem of the *Mars Trilogy* is not unlike that of *Foundation Pit*, a problem of base and superstructure. Only here the superstructure already exists, at least *in potentia*. The scientific station is a working model of a superstructure. But it has to build its own base. It has to construct a nature that will support it.

The centerpiece of the middle volume is a conference of all the underground factions, hosted by the matriarchal Dorsa Brevia enclave. It is a negotiation between at least four kinds of vision for Mars. Coyote the anarchist has very little interest, and so the four parties are the Red, the Green, the White, and what one might call the multicultural question. How can a just society accommodate different ways of life? What are the limits to acceptable difference? Who gets to decide on the boundaries of exclusion?

Interestingly, Robinson seems to draw here on two preoccupations of late twentieth-century thought that often had little to do with each other: multiculturalism and civil society.[76] The former came out of the critique of colonialism, combined with American experiences of the politics of race, gender, and sexuality. The latter arose out of the experience of post-Soviet societies in transition. The Martians arrive, at their Dorsa Brevia convention, at a vision of a polyarchic society of federated city-states, bound by something like a new *Declaration of Independence*.

This Dorsa Brevia manifesto is a synthesis, in displaced form, not only of Terran civil society and multicultural thinking, but also of socialist and ecological economics. The land, air, and water are a commons. One of its key theses is: "The goal of Martian economics is not 'sustainable development' but a sustainable prosperity for its entire biosphere."[77]

How is the Dorsa Brevia manifesto to become a reality? Nirgal is out traveling, like Coyote but less hidden, and among those who are enacting Dorsa Brevia in their everyday lives. "They were agronomists, ecological engineers, construction workers, technicians, technocrats, city operators, service personnel."[78] These are the twenty-first-century equivalent of Bogdanov's class-conscious industrial workers.

Meanwhile, Maya divides her time between hydrology work for Praxis, the underground, and enjoying the new Martian theater and music. "Politics needed to coopt some of that erotic energy, or else it was only a matter of *ressentiment* and damage control."[79] Maya and the others from the First Hundred want to prevent "another October." They are like Mensheviks, educating and proselytizing, holding back, waiting for the right conjuncture, and not trying to force the pace of history. "It was frightening—as if history were a series of human wave assaults on misery failing time after time."[80] With Coyote, Maya fears the merely destructive leap.

They are waiting for the trigger, the spark, to restart the revolution. Back on Earth, the western Antarctic ice sheet collapses, causing sea levels to rise everywhere. Curiously, global warming is happening on this Earth, but Robinson does not make it the cause of the ice sheet falling into the sea. It is as if, in Bogdanovite style, one needs to pay attention not just to predictable challenges to organization. There is more than one metabolic rift, caused by all sorts of molecular liberation fronts, interacting in unpredictable ways.[81]

While the rising seas divert attention and resources on Earth, the Martians launch their revolution, and like most revolutions, it suspends habit as well as law. They can be understood via a kind of tektology. Nadia the engineer:

> Melting occurred when the thermal energy of particles was great enough to overcome inter-crystalline forces that held them in position. So if you considered the metanat order as the crystalline structure . . . But then it made a huge difference if the forces holding it together were interionic or intermolecular; interionic, sodium chloride, melted at 801C, methane, intermolecular, at -183C. What kind of forces, then? And how high the temperature?[82]

This time, the temperature is right.

BLUE MARS: AFTER UTOPIA

Like Bogdanov, Robinson finds that the interesting problems begin after the moment of revolution, not before it. Curiously it is Sax who grasps the power of the symbolic gesture. He destroys the soletta, which gathers and magnifies sunlight, as a concession to the Reds, to bring them back within the fold of a constitutional politics. The Greens will have to work harder to make up for the loss of their artificially augmented sun.

Cultural revolution, or "a new collective unconscious," plays a significant role in the transition to a new mode of production, much as Bogdanov thought it should.[83] It is not just that the Martians have new ideas, but that their new ideas organize new kinds of social relation. Michel: "On Mars it may be that the ego ideal is shifting back to the maternal. To the Dionysian again. Or to some kind of post-oedipal reintegration with nature, which we are still in the process of inventing. Some new complex that would not be subject to neurotic over-investment."[84] Or perhaps it is a twenty-first-century version of proletkult, an organic ideological product of self-organizing labor, learning from experience how to work with both objective and subjective resistances.

Turning the Dorsa Brevia manifesto into an actual constitution is no easy feat. It calls for another convention, and more rounds of furious politicking. Art: "It's kind of scary . . . Win a revolution and a bunch of lawyers pop out of the woodwork."[85] What Fourier called the cabalist passion has free reign here, and by some sort of "flocking algorithm" a new constitution emerges, and a first chair of the executive council: Nadia, because "she had the charisma of the sensible."[86]

The Martian post-revolutionary state manages to keep its radical commitment to the abolition of private property. The strongest advocate of this is Vlad Taneev, the co-inventor of the longevity treatment. Having seen extended life, his creation, denied to people on Earth by the commodification of medical science, he is passionate about overcoming the residues of feudal privilege. "That is what capitalism is—a version of feudalism in which capital replaces land, and business leaders replace kings . . . If democracy and self-rule are the fundamentals, then why should people give up these rights when they enter the workplace?"

Vlad reminds them that the Dorsa Brevia manifesto "says everyone's work is their own, and the worth of it cannot be taken away. It says that the various modes of production belong to those who created them, and to the common good of the future generations. It says that the world is something we all steward together."[87] While some think these ideas smack of old-fashioned socialism, Vlad insists that to defeat capitalism it is worth looking back to those social forms that capital itself defeated.

The centerpiece of *Blue Mars* is the return to Earth of Coyote, Michel, Nirgal, and others. Here Robinson works a double estrangement, showing Earth transformed by rising sea levels from the alien point of view of Martian revolutionaries. "We are the primitives of an unknown civilization," Nirgal tells the Terran crowds, détourning a line from Coyote's teachings.[88] Back in his homeland of Trinidad it is Coyote who is the hero, nicely displacing the First World characters among the First Hundred. Michel finds his native Provence both familiar and strange. The beaches are gone and will never return, but Arles is connected once more to the sea, and once again rivals Marseille as a port town.

Robinson's most striking image is of the Thames estuary, where a new inter-tidal civilization is being cobbled together. "And then the wind turned and poured over the tide, and all of the waves were suddenly rushing out to sea together. Among the long cakes of foam were floating objects of all kinds: boxes, furniture, roofs, entire houses, capsized boats, pieces of wood. Flotsam and jetsam . . . 'It's London,' Bly said, 'It's fucking London, washing out to sea.'"[89] Diving down around an abandoned, flooded village, "Nirgal swam slowly around the wedge-shaped building, looking in second story windows at offices, empty rooms, flats. Some furniture floated against the ceilings."[90]

The landscape of Mars is no less unstable: "The land was slumping in all its characteristic permafrost patterns: polygonal pebble ridges, concentric crater fill, pingos, solifluction ridges on the hillsides. In every depression an ice-choked pond or puddle. The land was melting."[91] Ann struggles with the concept of a *Red aerophany*, distinct from Hiroko's conflation of aerophany with viriditas. Is there a way to stand in relation to the unliving universe that does not privilege life? She wants to know how to live with an absolutely flat ontology in an age when ontology is dead.

Nadia finds herself enmeshed in one political crisis after another, but she and her factional backers insist that process is the most important thing about politics. Some of it is a cobbling together of many old ideas for limiting the concentration of power, such as electing representatives by lottery.[92] They resist the cult of personality that has developed around Jackie Boone and her party. Some of the new process involves new objectives, like legislating the height of the sea level, or rationing the heat each city can put into the atmosphere.

Nadia really wants to return to engineering, but there is no heavy machinery for her to drive any more. Most things are automated. She turns to the problem of making soil, but it turns out be as much a molecular art as a science:

> There were the macro-nutrients—carbon, oxygen, hydrogen, nitrogen, phosphorous, sulfur, potassium, calcium, and magnesium—there were the micro-nutrients, including iron, manganese, zinc, copper, molybdenum, boron, and chlorine. None of these nutrient cycles was closed, as there were losses due to leaching, erosion, harvesting, and outgassing; inputs were just as various, including absorption, weathering, microbial action, and application of fertilizers.[93]

Metabolic rifting and cleaving is no simple thing.

With the revolution won, Nirgal does not know what to do with himself. Jackie Boone has taken over the party of which he was once the charismatic center. "He wanted to settle into a full human life, to pick a place and stay there, to learn it completely, in all its seasons, to grow his food, make his house and his tools, become part of a community of friends."[94] For Nirgal as opposed to Jackie, politics was always a matter of everyday life rather than holding office or ruling a faction.

He is attracted to the teachings of some Zen gardeners, who "talked about ecopoesis, which for them was terraforming redefined, subtilized, localized. Transformed into something like Hiroko's aeroformation. No longer powered by heavy industrial global methods, but by the slow, steady, and intensely local process of working on individual patches of land."[95] He becomes an ecopoet. Like Thoreau, he tends his small corner of the world. But his plants are attacked by a viroid, which requires the most advanced science even to diagnose, and in the end a dust storm buries his whole world in a meter of mud. The world is not a garden.

As Sax says, "There's all kinds of invasions going on. Population surges, sudden die-offs. All over. Things in disequilibrium. Upsetting balances we didn't even know existed. Things we don't understand."[96] Sax has been cured of his earlier belief in mathematics as a kind of ontological reality, even if he is no less convinced of its modeling power. "Over and over Sax watched a thousand years of weather, altering variables in the models, and every time a completely different millennium flitted past. Fascinating."[97] In an expanding universe, order isn't order. It might just be the difference between actual and potential entropy. Humans mistake the difference for order. Sax is as committed to scientific methods as ever, but the sheer resistance of nature to method makes itself felt in him.

Sax does not abandon science. "It was surely one of the greatest achievements of the human spirit, a kind of stupendous pantheon of the mind, constantly a work in progress, like a symphonic epic poem of thousands of stanzas, being composed by them all in a giant ongoing conversation. The language of the poem was mathematics . . ."[98] Rather, he puts it in the perspective of labor's struggle in and against nature. "Science was a social construct, but it was also and most importantly its own space, conforming to reality only, that was its beauty."[99] There is something inhuman about science. Its modes of perception, modeling, and verifying are outside the parameters of the human sensorium, even though they are dependent on an apparatus that is itself the product of human labor. The objects of science are not dependent on human consciousness. And yet science happens in history, constrained by forms of social organization of a given type and of a given time. As such, existing social relations are a fetter upon science in its pursuit of the inhuman sensations of the nonhuman real.

Martian utopian science looks not unlike how Bogdanov imagined Soviet science could be organized. It's Sax's experience of the elite research lab or field station generalized:

> As he watched them Sax realized for the first time that the versatile, responsive, highly focused nature of science that he had been getting used to . . . was a feature of all the labs arranged as cooperative ventures . . . With the scientists in control of their own work, to a degree never seen in his youth on Earth, the work itself had an unprecedented rapidity and power.[100]

If *Blue Mars* is a realized utopia, then one of the tests of its utopian quality is the status of art within this world. Robinson offers several versions of what becomes of art. One is Harry Whitebrook, the genetic engineer, who invents whole classes of organism as if they were works of art. Another is Coyote's version of the early Situationist slogan: "Never work!" As he explains: "What I like to do . . . is to go to a sidewalk café and toss down some kava and watch all the faces. Go for a walk around the streets and look at people's faces."[101] Perhaps in effect the whole organization of the planet has become an artwork, although one heavily dependent on, and respectful of, scientific method.

History merges with natural history, which both Sax and Ann describe as "punctuated equilibrium without the equilibrium."[102] Sax: "See how beautiful it is—in its own way. In itself, the way it organizes itself. We say we manage it, but we don't. It's too complex. We just brought it here. After that it took off on its own. Now we try to push it this way and that, but the total biosphere . . . it's self organizing. There's nothing unnatural about it."[103]

But while natural history might be self-organizing, it is not homeostatic. There is no invisible hand at work in either natural or human affairs. One substitution that Robinson, like Bogdanov, resists, is to see nature as an *ecology*, as like a market, and markets as therefore also, by reverse-substitution, "natural." The emphasis is rather on the instability of the relations of the new Martian species to each other and their world, "all of them monsters together."[104] There may be patches of relative ecological stability, but they are local and temporary. To dispense with the invisible hand, and with homeostatic ecology as a basic metaphor, is to live once again after God is dead.

When his farm fails, Nirgal's new version of "Never work!" is running. He runs races around the entire planet, his victories full of "counter intuitive extravagance."[105] Out on a training run, he falls in with a nomadic feral co-op of hunters, gatherers, and farmers. Without the boundary lines and fences of private property, the landscape grows into a network of forms built as much as anything for wandering. It's like Constant Nieuwenhuys's utopian project

New Babylon, only on Mars rather than Earth. This is a world, as Sax says, of "so many different kinds of nomads."[106]

When Nirgal meets Zoya (or Zo) among the ferals, he does not know he is actually her father. She is a "wild" character, a thrill-seeker. She loves to fly with a bird suit. For Robinson, the question of what a utopian sport might be looms even larger than the question of a utopian art. For Zo, "this was the meaning of life, the purpose of the universe: pure joy, the sense of self gone . . . The best, cleanest use of human time."[107] Apart from a little diplomatic arm-twisting as her mother Jackie Boone's enforcer, Zo lives without dead time.

Alongside utopian art and sport, there's utopian sex, not unlike that in Fourier, with his emphasis on the combination of all the passions, on groups, and on tableaux. Here is Zo being *tabled* by friends of various sexes: "And then the whole group was on her, hands and mouths and genitals, a tongue in each ear, in her mouth, contact everywhere; after a while it was an undifferentiated mass of erotic sensation, total sexurround, Zo purring loudly."[108]

Blue Mars is not a closed world utopia. Zo meets the builders of a new life on the Jovian moons, "throwing themselves so energetically into a project that won't be completed until long after their death—it's an absurd gesture, a gesture of defiance and freedom, a divine madness . . ."[109] It's like Bogdanov's Red Martians, sending the seeds of life into the universe.

In this paradise, Robinson broaches a rare topic: what does utopian ageing and death look like? Maya suffers from *jamais vu*.[110] Each day seems an exact repetition of another, an eternal return. Jackie, her personal powers fading, joins a voyage out of the solar system. Sax can no longer hold a train of thought long enough to document it. The longevity treatments keep these cyborg bodies in a zone of complexity between the too orderly and the too chaotic, but they have their limits.

This utopia even has its own kind of revolution. Earth invades Mars by sending unauthorized colonists; the "native" Martians respond by embracing them and absorbing them into their world. The most effective tactic, as in the two previous Martian revolutions, is "people in the streets."[111] In this post-colonial confrontation, the natives have a higher level not only of cultural but also of technical organization, and prevail.

Here are utopia's three achievements: "Nowhere on this world were people killing each other, nowhere were they desperate for shelter or food, nowhere were they scared for their kids."[112] Perhaps nothing should be said of the good life beyond the principle that nobody should go hungry. Not every possibility for "development" need be opened up. As in Platonov, the more labor dug into nature, the more nature presses down in return.

On Mars, not every kind of development is pursued. Sax withdraws his support for terraforming at any price when he destroys the soletta. The question in Robinson is not the refusal but the *selection* among kinds of development. The value of science fiction as a form is in organizing blocks of possible causation.[113] It is a laboratory of substitutions for the basic metaphor itself. Robinson's writing is rich in causational models: the coriolis effect, flocking algorithms, punctuated equilibrium, cascading recombinant chaos, and so on. *The Mars Trilogy* is particularly rich in geological causal substitutions. Science fiction is, or at least can be, a method for testing out new basic metaphors. In Robinson's hands, it is a dialogic procedure. Characters play out different organizational practices and corresponding ideologies, particularly ones that work out various basic metaphors and their attendant chains of substitution.

While in a very different key, Robinson shares with Platonov a sense that a revolutionary praxis has to be more than a religion, rather than less. Extracting a surplus from recalcitrant nature makes life possible, and this in turn is the condition of existence, in Platonov's terms, of the soul. But it is no guarantee of one. Utopian life only poses more completely the problem of how one is to live. This is what makes *Blue Mars* the most interesting of the volumes. It is a kind of *meta-utopia*. It is a détournement made of many utopias—some marked by the place names to which Coyote travels—but not a synthesis of them. It stages the conflicts; it respects their incommensurability.

Platonov documents all too vividly how the struggle for life under acute and trying circumstances can fail, how disorganization accumulates, how information is lost forever and in the process a whole ontology collapses in on itself. It is not that Robinson holds out hope for another fate. Rather, it is that he practices a different kind of realism. One that tests different causal sequences—like Sax running the climate simulator from different starting conditions over and over (if one can pardon the analogy). Based on language, it is a tektology that is much more open than "the craft of constrained storytelling," as Haraway calls it, of the sciences. And yet it is still bounded by the way labor might actually organize the world.[114]

At least one version of this "dialectic," if that is what it still is, finds in catastrophic moments the possibility of new kinds of organization. It is not so much a leap beyond material circumstances as a march right into them. It has happened before. Robinson is fascinated by the proposition that a previous era of climate change—the Ice Ages—forced forward momentum in human biological but also cultural evolution. In his tektological laboratory, climate crisis might be the moment for the *accelerando* as one possible causal sequence.[115]

Tektology in Robinson is a turn toward those sciences and technical knowledges that can ground an understanding and a praxis that combine work on a resistant objective world and the resistant subjectivity of politics and culture. He has found a form in which the incommensurable statements from both technical and organizational labor can meet on the same page without being reduced one to the other. It's a "laboratory of history" for thinking the twenty-first-century condition.[116]

Conclusion

The sheer scale of the misanthropocene. Our minds feel small and inert. Once every fragment seemed to bear within it the whole. Now the whole being too large for the mind to see stands before us always as a fragment.

—Joshua Clover and Juliana Spahr

The earnest enthusiasms of youth later come to seem like follies, but are even more enthusiastically embraced as follies, when everything else in everyday life has to be lived so much in earnest. The past is where the lightness lives. It can be the same with the historical past, although there the temptation to nostalgia, while no less earnest, is far more foolish.

As a young militant, I worked for a time in the regional party headquarters, a neat and austere place, with a bookshop, library, meeting rooms, and an offset printing press—an imposing thing I never learned to work. In the front office, portraits of Marx and Lenin stared down from their nails on the wall. It struck me as odd that in so well organized an office the portraits were hung off-kilter, rather than symmetrically mounted.

One day I noticed that while there were two portraits on the wall, of Marx and Lenin, there were three nails. When I remarked on this, it was explained to me that sometime during Khrushchev's thaw, Stalin's portrait had come down. The nail from which it once hung was still there.

The Communist Party of Australia was an unusual one.[1] When the Soviet Union invaded Czechoslovakia in 1968, those who supported the crushing of the "Prague Spring" found themselves in a minority. The majority continued under the name of the Communist Party, which of course ceased to have "fraternal ties" with its Soviet counterpart. So Stalin's portrait had come down, but not those of Marx or Lenin, who were taught in the party school, together with Antonio Gramsci and even Leon Trotsky. I sat in party school next to a metalworker with a finger missing and dirt under his nine nails.

The break with Moscow broke the rudder of ideological certainty, setting the party slowly but surely adrift. Yet it remained, even in the late 1970s, a real party: a power in the trade unions, an affective node within several influential social movements, with an inter-generational and inter-class culture, and a presence on the campuses. It was still just possible to imagine that the party was at least a small part of a vast alliance of humans in struggle, even if increasingly submerged within it. It had spawned at least one innovative tactic in the 1970s. Upon gaining control of the Builders Laborers' Federation, the union would not only "Black Ban" working on sites in struggle against the employers. It would also "Green Ban" sites deemed environmentally harmful.[2]

Around the corner from the District Party Office in my home town was the office of the Trade Union Environment Centre. It was run by party members, although apparently there had nearly been a split. The short walk between the two headquarters mapped the distance between these two factions. At the Centre, books by Barry Commoner were pressed into my hands.[3] It was here that I met the famous instigators of the Green Bans when they visited. At the Centre was an exciting sense of starting to think completely anew about what the conceptual basis of politics might become. The Centre thought it had escaped out from under those dusty portraits.

The most interesting thing to me in the District Party Office was the offset printing press. It was about the size of a washing-machine but considerably noisier. Sometimes I would assist the comrade printer who worked with it. Like a character out of Platonov, he understood machines. The principles of its operation were simple and even I grasped them quickly. But the machine was old, and the real work lay in gently tweaking the feeding of the paper, the pressure of the rollers, the precise interactions of ink and solvent. The machine was sensitive not just to different kinds of paper and ink but to temperature and humidity.

It was a delicate thing, but when the comrade printer turned it on, all the lights in the building would dim. Once, it tripped the circuit breaker, plunging the Party Office into an inky darkness. The power of this thing to make texts still depended on a whole network of objects, barely perceptible, until you crashed the system.[4]

It was a quiet day in the Office. I was minding the bookstore and reading an old edition of Lenin borrowed from the library in the back. It was a handsome two-volume set published in Moscow, I forget in which year. I don't remember which text I was reading, but upon turning the page, I was surprised to discover that half of it was neatly covered by a blank white sheet that had been pasted over half a paragraph. Even then I could grasp what this shocking discovery meant. Someone had become a non-person, in that brief period between the editing of this edition and its printing.

In one way or another, Bogdanov and Platonov were both non-people as far as Marxist-Leninist thought was concerned. Lenin himself did his best to minimize the significance of Bogdanov. Perversely enough, he lived on mostly through Lenin's virulent denunciation of him in *Materialism and Empirio-criticism*. None of Platonov's most extraordinary works of the 1920s and 1930s were printed until many years later.

These are all obscured pages, and not just in the now defunct Soviet orthodoxy. They were obscure to the Western Marxist tradition until quite recently as well. I'm no scholar of Russian literature or of Soviet history. My only claim to a relevant competence came from party school, long ago. It is to a non-standard Marxism that I want to restore them. But I do claim that these other Marxist passages can open onto a way of organizing knowledge in the present, in anticipation of the Carbon Liberation Front's more novel effects.

It is hard to orient oneself, let alone a movement, as an intellectual orphan. It helps to have some elective kin and kind, and some legends of thought-in-action. The New Left remade the intellectual past, but that new past is now past as well, and we need others. Bogdanov and Platonov hint at where some might lie buried. But Marxism hangs in the shadow of the histories those portraits on the wall efface.

One of the great virtues of the Marxist tradition used to be its indifference to the formal constraints of traditional disciplinary knowledge. It sought an organic rigor independent of that game. Starting with Marx and Engels themselves, at their best Marxists developed a working method for traversing disciplinary boundaries and for combining lessons learned from a range of practices, from scientific experiment to the struggles of everyday life.

Sometimes Marxism was misconstrued as a dogma applicable to all fields of knowledge and practice. As a corrective, the current known as Western Marxism restored an earnest philosophical rigor to Marxist inquiry.[5] But this came at the price, in the long run, of giving up the interstitial practice of networking between knowledges, in favor of a retreat back into the traditional field of philosophy as the university delimits it.

Subsumed within professional academic practice, Marxism falls prey to a kind of agenda-drift. It becomes more interested in the game within the scholarly field than in situations impinging from without. This got so bad that by the early twenty-first century you could read the leading inheritors of the Western Marxist tradition in vain for any hint that the fate of "modernity" had come to turn on the liberation of carbon.[6]

What flourished instead was an obsession with the detritus left behind by an obsolete bourgeois public sphere. Western Marxism and its heirs got caught up in the languages of the cultural, the political, or even the old theological superstructures. It substituted metaphors from its own intellectual labor practices onto the world, producing worldviews rich in the doings of philosophy or linguistics or psychoanalysis, but not those of cyborg labor or contemporary sciences. It's a question then of either abandoning the shade of Western Marxism to its tomfoolery, or reinventing it as a critical tradition for labor to confront that within which it is entangled.

Labor is the mingling of many things, most of them not human. Where Bogdanov talks of the labor point of view, this is something of an inhuman perspective, almost already a cyborg point of view, in which the human organism and its machines interleave in an apparatus. It's like the comrade printer and his press, or Platonov's engineers and their machines, or Robinson's scientists and their labs.

Labor is a prism through which to construct a version of Marx that does not disappear into the cultural, political, or theological problem of the subject.[7] It is not so much that it is objective, however. It is not about making a claim to have the true method. Rather, it is about the struggle of and within the realm of things, of how things organize themselves and how they might—through labor—become otherwise. The turn toward the object, as something that exceeds subjectivity in scale, can undo the damage done by the fascination with the great molar dramas, which appear as the clash of superhuman subjects, but subjects nonetheless.

On the other hand, it isn't progress to make the object a mere object of contemplation. This is the old sensuous materialism that Marx so decisively left. Rather, the labor point of view is a field of sensations, of a mediating apparatus, of a molecular process, which both feeds the appetites of collective human needs, but also opens up rifts in tektological wholes. It might be better to craft an inconsistent field of thought from the labor point of view than a consistent line centered on some avatar of the object or subject—as contemporary philosophy is still wont to do.

It's time for other stories. One thing, strangely, that the Soviet Union and its American Cold War nemesis had in common was a clear understanding that any narrative for a whole way of life has to *scale*.[8] It had to work for millions, even billions. The challenge then is to take the desire for alternatives from the romantic anti-capitalists and wed it to the grand scale on which capitalist realism imagines itself now to be the only discourse.

There used to be a third species of narrative, which took Marx's thought to be the seed-stock for a critique of the bedtime stories of both the superpowers, and claimed the same world historical remit. It went under several names, including Western Marxism and critical theory.[9] It used to think big, now it rarely does. It has not proven as sharp as one might like in confronting the problem of the metabolic rift. Critical theory became *hypocritical theory.*

One of the aims in *Molecular Red* has been to take two steps back into relatively neglected parts of the critical theory tradition to take three steps forward again, into the Anthropocene breach. That tradition still has the advantage of not taking capitalism itself to be a natural given thing. Our story takes place within the archives of mutating Marxisms, but requires a series of *reversals of perspective* that steer it away from some of its hypocritical habits.[10]

First—and last: *from bourgeois to proletarian.* Hypocritical theory is in love with the lovely things of its own class—bourgeois things. It makes a fetish of leaders, idolizing Lenin or Mao. It doesn't want to talk about workers; it wants to deal only with the representatives. Or: it finds excuses to remain within the detritus of a lost bourgeois culture—Wagner, Hegel, and Mallarmé. Or: it takes refuge in theology, as if only the Gods could save us. Or: it defaults into disciplinary loyalties and border skirmishes, as if no critique of its organization of intellectual labor need be ventured.

Second: *from high theory to low theory.* Rather than imagine theory as a policing faculty flying high as a drone over all the others, a low theory is interstitial, its labor communicative rather than controlling. Its method is some species of détournement, such as tektology or the factory of literature or dada. It refracts affects, perceptions, and concepts from one domain of labor to another using whatever apparatus is to hand. The verification of whether a concept holds, or a story applies, is specific to each labor process. Theory proposes; practice disposes. It does not set its own agenda but detects those emerging in key situations and alerts each field to the agendas of the others.

Third: *from schism to system.* Hypocritical theory got rather interested in splits and rifts, voids and aporias, but not metabolic ones. It is interested in nonidentity, supplements, incommensurability, how internally divided our subjectivity is, and how antagonisms structure politics. But its substitutions begin from the political or cultural superstructures, and it starts to imagine that "division goes all the way down."[11] It loses sight of the feedback loops which reticulate through the levels of social and natural existence. One would not want to impose the opposite metaphor, however, where everything consists of autotelic, autopoetic, homeostatic, self-governing systems. Totalities turn out in practice to be rather less total. Haraway: "Nothing is connected to everything; everything is connected to something."[12]

Fourth: *from molar to molecular.* Perhaps it's not just a matter of seeing the molar and molecular as two scales, one superimposed on the other, but of shifting the balance of perception much more to the molecular. For it is the molecular scale which corresponds best to the labor point of view. If nature is that which resists labor, it does so in a granular way. The molar is the language of management. It's the dialogue of ideas, in which the experience of those who organize labor substitutes for the experience of those whose labor organizes the material world directly.

Fifth: *from human to inhuman.* The language of molar drama is usually reserved for human subjects, even if they are collective ones, or for a drama of Man against Nature, or of Man against the Gods. While in Guattari's hands the idea of the molecular is often just a metaphor, it is one that could indeed extend all the way to the molecular scale of organization. We lack a language for our complicity with anonymous materials, and their complicity with each other.[13] Attention could better be focused on the inhuman apparatus via which the sensation of the nonhuman world is mediated.

Sixth: *from superstructure to base.* It was convenient for Marxists trained in the humanities to take their professional specialization to be the source of a basic metaphor, and to imagine the superstructure as autonomous or even as leading some "cultural revolution" independently or in parallel to the struggles of labor at the base. That was before the infrastructure of intellectual life itself started to change beyond all recognition. In the twenty-first century, even academic labor is becoming as precarious, as digitized, as algorithmic as any other. And if that infrastructure is changing, then others probably are too, and the whole question of what now constitutes an infrastructure has to be revisited.[14]

Seven: *from genteel to vulgar.* For a long time it was obligatory to say that one's critical method, whatever it was, had nothing to do with *vulgar Marxism.*[15] But now perhaps what we need is a pungent dose of vulgarity. The vulgar, after all, is the common, the ordinary, the multitudinous, the abundant, the coarse, and the indecent. All of which, to my mind, are, if not good things, then not bad things, and certainly pertinent things. This is the lesson I retain from party school.

Vulgar Marxism is usually taken, among other things, to mean a rather simplistic model of how the economic base "determines" the political and cultural superstructure. Its basic metaphors are either determinist, economistic, mechanical, or evolutionary. Curiously, these basic metaphors did actually come from the more advanced forms of labor and science of their time. A vulgar Marxism for today might look to the analogous sources of our own time.

What we might call by contrast a *genteel Marxism* insists on the relative—if not absolute—autonomy of the cultural and political superstructure.[16] And when it comes to the infrastructure, it privileges the *relations* of production over the *forces* of production. The relations of production are assumed to be described in essence by Marx, even if their phenomenal form changes from time to time. The qualitative breaks between different forces of production, from steam and steel to oil and aluminum to silicon and solar, get little or no attention.

This mode of production—is it still even capitalist or something worse?[17] It goes on and on as if there were no limit. It is as if the "real" Platonic form that was capital had detached itself from appearances, from the hard matter of everyday life, and revealed their falsity. These worldly things, this whole Earth, falls short of the one that capital imagines as its plaything. It has commanded already, and in advance, more Earths than this one. There is not enough base for its gleaming superstructures, not even if capital were to annex Mars as well. A latter-day Platonov might notice that it is in the imagination of *capital* that the super-structures are all that matter. From the point of view of labor, which lies beneath it and provides the surplus on which it feeds, no amount of effort could ever dig a pit big enough to found its vaulting ambitions.

But let's not depress ourselves too much. Rather, let's ask: how might the surplus of time, of information, of life itself, be organized differently? That might be a task for a no longer quite so hypocritical theory. There might still be a role for the things theory traditionally teaches, such as the arts of reading, even if a more constructive rather than suspicious mode of reading might be what the times require, and as a way to read a different kind of text.[18] Let's use the time and information and everyday life still available to us to begin the task, quietly but in good cheer, of thinking otherwise, of working and experimenting. Let's begin with a close (or close enough) reading of texts that come like stray artifacts, extracted from Voschev's bag.

It is time to leave the twenty-first century. The metabolic rift that wakes from the Carbon Liberation Front is not the only challenge to the biosphere. It is more enveloping than the comrades at the Trade Union Environment Centre could have imagined. The term Anthropocene, as taken up by Paul Crutzen and others in the earth sciences, splices two roots together, *anthropos* and *kainos*. Anthropos: that with the face of "man," that which looks up. Kainos: that which is not just a new unit of time but a new quality or form. What would this mean to Bogdanov? He would refuse the authoritarian causality lurking in anthropos, that residue of the sky-God, and insist instead on making it mean collective labor. The kainos of labor in the twenty-first century is labor as intra-action, entanglement, the tragedy of the totality.

As someone who does texts rather than things, I am tempted to reject the term Anthropocene. Naming things ought to be the prerogative of us professional wordsmiths. Why accept a name some scientists came up with? And can't we have a more aspirational name? I want a name for what the kainos ought to be, not what it is.[19] And in any case, it's too anthropocentric. All of the interesting and useful movements in the humanities since the late twentieth century have critiqued and dissented from the theologies of the human.

But then I wonder what the comrades at the Trade Union Environment Centre might have thought of it. Most of them were what Bogdanov called technical workers. They had a bit of that idealism of the young Platonov, the idea that engineering was about making a better world through applying physics to materials, tools to tasks. They were struggling for a sense of a good technology.[20] I imagine that for them the Anthropocene would have been something of a shock, in that it introduces the effects of labor into the situation in advance. What labor confronts is not just nature pristine, but nature always and already worked-over by labor. It's actually already there in Platonov, if you look. When work stops in Chevengur, a strange Anthropocene nature emerges, the grasses working out their own proportions—nature *after* labor.

The anthropos in Anthropocene might do unexpected work for those trained in the sciences or technical fields. Perhaps it is kainos that could be usefully confusing for humanists, social scientists, or for those few of us who remain who were trained at party school. What might it mean to think the qualitatively new, but where what is new is not defined by the communist horizon? It is striking how much even the anti-communists of the Cold War era took the model of a new kainos, against which any other had to be thought, to be "communism." Their neoliberal successors too.

This kainos, whether thought in, against, or after the communist horizon, is usually thought as a new *social* relation. To the extent that it is thought as a relation to nature, it is as a victory that made Platonovian struggles in and against nature obsolete. The Anthropocene, by contrast, calls for thinking something that is not even defeat. Nonhuman kainos is then as provocative a thing to think for those whose training is all about organizing the human as anthropos is for those whose training is in organizing the nonhuman.

Or such might be a way to make the most of something Bogdanov would surely have appreciated: that new experiences often have to be thought within the basic metaphors that already exist. Anthropocene it is, then. For now. A bad name for a bad time, thus not unfit. Haraway: "We need another figure, a thousand names of something else, to erupt out of the Anthropocene into another, big enough story."[21] It's a task not just of naming, but of doing, of making new kinds of labor for a new kind of nature.

There is still some low theory work to do, to transmit the metaphor of the Anthropocene between domains, but in that process, those labor processes will change it. Rather than "interrogate" Crutzen's Anthropocene—and where did *that* metaphor come from?—perhaps it is better to see it as what it is: a brilliant hack. The Anthropocene introduces the labor point of view—in the broadest possible sense—into *geology*. Perhaps the challenge is then to find analogous but different ways to hack other specialized domains of knowledge, to orient them to the situation and the tasks at hand.

Let's invent new metaphors! Personally, I like the *#misanthropocene*, but don't expect it to catch on. Jason Moore prefers the *Capitalocene,* Jussi Parikka the *Anthrobscene.* Kate Raworth suggests *Manthropocene*, given the gender make-up of the Anthropocene Working Group considering it as a name for a geological era. Donna Haraway offers to name it the *Chthulucene*, a more chthonic version of Cthulhu, the octopoid monster of H. P. Lovecraft's weird stories. "Chthulucene does not close in on itself; it does not round off; its contact zones are ubiquitous and continuously spin out loopy tendrils."[22]

Haraway notes the strikingly parallel evolution of new metaphorical tools in *both* humanities and biologies, where competitive individualism is no longer a given. In Bogdanovite terms, perhaps it is because in both domains, producing knowledge got strangely complex, collaborative, and mediated by apparatuses. A new breed of basic metaphor is at least partly at work and in play, one which in the biologies could be described as a "multi-species becoming-with."

Haraway wants to both "justify and trouble" the language of the Anthropocene. As Edwards does with climate science, she insists on the embeddedness in an infrastructure that makes the global appear as a work-object to those natural scientists for whom the Anthropocene makes sense as a metaphor. She points to the limits of its basic metaphors, which still think one-sidedly of competition between populations or genes, where success equals reproduction. More symbiotic—dare we say comradely?—kinds of life hardly figure in such metaphors. But perhaps, as Haraway says, "we are all lichens now"—cyborg lichens.[23]

After Robinson, the task is not debating names or trading stories, but making comradely alliances. Is not Crutzen one of those curious scientist-intellectuals that Robinson's fiction trains us to look out for? Crutzen and his colleagues in the earth sciences have flagged something that needs to shape the agenda for knowledge, culture, and organization. For those of us seeking to respond from the left, I think the authors presented in *Molecular Red* offer some of the best ways of *processing* that information. Bogdanov and Platonov would not really be surprised by the Anthropocene. They were vulgar enough to think aspects of it already.

So let's pop the following tools into the dillybag for future use:

Something like an *empirio-monism* has its uses, because it is a way of doing theory that directs the tendency to spin out webs of metaphoric language to the task at hand. It steers the language arts toward agendas arising out of working processes, including those of sciences. It is agnostic about which metaphors best explain the real, but it sees all of them as substitutions which derive from the forms of labor and apparatus of the time.

Something like *proletkult* has its uses, as the project for the self-organization of the labor point of view. It filters research into past culture and knowledge through the organizational needs of the present. Those needs put pressure on the traditional category of labor, opening it toward feminist standpoints, not to mention our queer cyborg entanglements.

Something like a tektology has its uses, as a way of coordinating labor other than through exchange or hierarchy, or the new infrastructure of corporatized "networks." It communicates between labor processes poetically and qualitatively. It is a training of the metaphoric wiliness of language toward particular applications which correspond to and with advances in labor technique.

Lastly, something like the *utopia* of *Red Star* has its uses, in motivating those working in separate fields to think beyond the fetishistic habits of the local and toward comradely goals. In the absence of a single counter-hegemonic ideology, perhaps something like a meta-utopia might be more useful, and more fun. Meta-utopia offers not so much an imaginary solution to real problems as a real problematizing of how to navigate the differences between the imaginal that corresponds to each particular labor points of view.[24]

And so, to conclude with the slogan with which we began. It might be the slogan of a Cyborg International. One which already possesses in imagination the means and the will to undo the workings of the Anthropocene. One with nothing for it but to build the new living world within the ruins of the old one. We all know this civilization can't last. Let's make another.

WORKINGS OF THE WORLD UNTIE! YOU HAVE A WIN TO WORLD!

Endnotes

PREFACE

1 Paul Crutzen, "'Geology of Mankind," *Nature*, Vol. 415, No. 23, January 2002. The term Anthropocene was probably coined by Eugene Stoermer. See also Vaclav Smil, *Harvesting the Biosphere: What We Have Taken from Nature*, Cambridge, MA: MIT Press, 2013.

2 Jan Zalasiewicz, Mark Williams, Will Steffen, and Paul Crutzen, "'The New World of the Anthropocene," *Environmental Science and Technology Viewpoint*, Vol. 44, No. 7, 2010, pp. 2228–31.

3 Ian Svenonius, *Psychic Soviet*, Chicago, IL: Drag City, 2006. For a tour of the ruins of the twentieth-century West, see the Center for Land Use Interpretation, *Overlook: Exploring the Internal Fringes of America*, London: Thames & Hudson, 2006.

4 Tom Bissell, "'Eternal Winter," *Harpers Magazine*, April 2002, Vol. 304, No. 1823. See also Rob Ferguson, *The Devil and the Disappearing Sea*, Vancouver: Raincoast Books, 2003.

5 I am indebted to the work of John Bellamy Foster for the significance of Marx's thinking about metabolic rift. See John Bellamy Foster, *Marx's Ecology: Materialism and Nature*, New York: Monthly Review Press, 2000. See also the work of Jason Moore for a different elaboration of the concept.

6 See Esther Leslie, *Synthetic Worlds: Nature, Art and the Chemical Industry*, London: Reaktion Books, 2006, a terrific account of German romanticism, dada, and critical theory, in the context of early twentieth-century Germany's great contribution to modern capitalism: the chemical industry.

7 See John Bellamy Foster et al., *The Ecological Rift*, New York: Monthly Review Books, 2010. The rifts mentioned there include not only climate change but

also ocean acidification, stratospheric ozone depletion, nitrogen and phosphorous cycles, fresh water shortages, loss of biodiversity and accumulated chemical pollution, which together might be described as the Anthropocene.

8 On terraforming, see Kim Stanley Robinson, *Red Mars*, New York: Bantam Books, 1993, to be discussed later in this book. See also M. M. Averner and R. D. MacElroy, *On the Habitability of Mars: An Approach to Planetary Ecosynthesis*, NASA SP-414, 1976.

9 Karl Marx and Friedrich Engels, "'Manifesto of the Communist Party," in Karl Marx, *The Revolutions of 1848*, London: Verso, 2010, p. 70. See also Marshall Berman, *All That Is Solid Melts Into Air: The Experience of Modernity*, New York: Penguin, 1988. Of course, much of the resonance of this phrase is an artifact of translation: "Alles Ständische und Stehende verdampft": All that stands steams into statements.

10 Elmar Altvater, *The Future of the Market*, London: Verso, 1993. Altvater is also useful in showing why the Soviet planning system could not compete against the West, without in the process becoming the latter's cheerleader. In both cases, the attempt to make labor more "'efficient'" was fossil-fueled.

11 For a quick review, see Kerry Emmanuel, *What We Know About Climate Change*, Cambridge, MA: Boston Review Books, 2007, or the poignantly titled "'Summary for Policymakers" to the Intergovernmental Panel on Climate Change, *Climate Change 2013: The Physical Science Basis*, New York: Cambridge University Press, 2014, pp. 3–32. For some context, see Bill McKibben (ed.), *The Global Warming Reader*, New York: O/R Books, 2011. Naturally, the Carbon Liberation Front was articulated with other (non)social movements, methane liberation, for example. In the last chapter of *Gamer Theory*, Cambridge, MA: Harvard University Press, 2007, I use methane as the molecular fulcrum for a critical theory of the totality.

12 On climate deniers, see Naomi Oreskes, *Merchants of Doubt*, New York: Bloomsbury, 2011.

13 See Andrew Ross, *Bird On Fire*, Oxford: Oxford University Press, 2011, for an excellent case study on "green" politics and consumerism which spatially displaces problems onto the less powerful without solving them.

14 See John Bellamy Foster, *The Ecological Revolution*, New York: Monthly Review Press, 2009; Allan Stoekl's *Bataille's Peak: Energy, Religion, and Postsustainability*, Minneapolis: University of Minnesota Press, 2007, is particularly effective on the carbon footprint measuring obsession.

15 Rebecca Comay, *Mourning Sickness: Hegel and the French Revolution*, Stanford, CA: Stanford University Press, 2012. Or perhaps the revolution in Haiti: See Susan Buck-Morss, *Hegel, Haiti and Universal History*, Pittsburgh: Pittsburgh University Press, 2009.

16 Vladimir Vernadsky, *The Biosphere*, New York: Springer Verlag, 1998; Vaclav Smil, *The Earth's Biosphere: Evolution, Dynamics, and Change*, Cambridge, MA: MIT Press, 2003.

17 As an exemplar, see Eric Hobsbawm, *The Age of Empire*, New York: Vintage, 1987, and *The Age of Extremes*, New York: Vintage, 1994.

18 Félix Guattari, *The Anti-Oedipus Papers*, Los Angeles: Semiotext(e), 2006, p. 418. The molar and molecular concepts were adapted by Guattari and Gilles Deleuze from Gilbert Simondon. See also Félix Guattari, *Three Ecologies*, London: Continuum, 2008, for a succinct statement of Guattari's ecological post-politics; and Manuel DeLanda, *A Thousand Years of Non-Linear History*, New York: Zone Books, 2000, for a wonderfully literal-minded approach to the molecular.

19 On low theory see Judith Halberstam, *The Queer Art of Failure*, Durham, NC: Duke University Press, pp. 15–18.

20 Although I am grateful to some humanities scholars who have focused their attention on such things. See Dipesh Chakrabarty, "The Climate of History: Four Theses," *Critical Inquiry*, No. 35, Winter 2009; Nicholas Mirzoeff, "Visualizing the Anthropocene," *Public Culture*, Vol. 26, No. 2, 2014; Henry Sussman (ed.), *Impasses of the Post-Global: Theory in the Era of Climate Change*, Ann Arbor, MI: Open Humanities Press, 2012.

21 This would map both my agreement and disagreement with the "acceleration-ists." See Robin Mackay and Armen Avanessian (eds.), *#Accelerate: The Accelerationist Reader*, Falmouth: Urbanomic, 2014; *e-flux journal*, Vol. 46, June 2013, at e-flux.com; and Gean Moreno (ed.), *Dark Trajectories: Politics of the Outside*, Miami, FL: [NAME] Publications, 2013.

22 "There is another world, and it is this one," was a slogan much used in the anti-globalization movement. It probably comes from Paul Éluard, *Donner à voir*, published in 1939, which can be found in his *Oeuvres completes*, Vol. 1, Paris: Gallimard, 1968, p. 986.

23 Mark Fisher, *Capitalist Realism: Is There No Alternative?*, Winchester: Zero Books, 2009. The term could be traced back to German artists such as Sigmar Polke and others from the mid 1960s.

24 See Amy Wending, *Karl Marx on Technology and Alienation*, Basingstoke: Palgrave Macmillan, 2011.

1. Alexander Bogdanov

1 Robert Service, *Lenin: A Biography*, New York: Pan Macmillan, 2000, p. 190.

2 See Dominic Pettman, *Human Error: Species Being and Media Machines*, Minneapolis, MN: University of Minnesota Press, 2011, and Giorgio Agamben, *The Open: Man and Animal*, Stanford, CA: Stanford University Press, 2004. The concept of population, incidentally, is also handy for not making too much of set theory.

3 Bogdanov is in some respects close to the syndicalists, but less prone to a fasci-nation with the mythic power of the proletariat as it is than with the evolution

of the organization of labor from the labor point of view. See Robert Chadwell Williams, *The Other Bolsheviks*, Bloomington: Indiana University Press, 1986.

4 See Timothy Morton, *Ecology Without Nature: Rethinking Environmental Aesthetics*, Cambridge, MA: Harvard University Press, 2007.

5 George Haupt and Jean-Jacques Marie, *Makers of the Russian Revolution*, Ithaca, NY: Cornell University Press, 1974, pp. 285, 175.

6 A. Bodganoff, *A Short Course of Economic Science*, revised edition, London: Communist Party of Great Britain, 1925. It went through nine Russian editions between 1897 and 1909, and was revived and revised again in 1919. There are even two English editions, in 1923 and this one in 1925. Much to Lenin's annoyance, Bogdanov's pedagogic texts were not without their influence both before 1917 and after.

7 Nicolai Berdyaev, *Dream and Reality: An Essay in Autobiography*, New York: Collier, 1962.

8 Williams, *The Other Bolsheviks*, p. 35.

9 For a representative range of views on Bogdanov's clash with Lenin, see the contributions to *The Russian Review*, Vol. 49, 1990, by John Eric Marot, Aileen Kelly, Andrezej Walicki, John Biggart, and Avraham Yassour. I am less interested in the historical question of whether Bogdanovism was a genuine challenge to the authoritarian streak in Lenin's conception of the party, and more in what might be extracted from the Bogdanovite position that is of use in the present.

10 George Plekhanov, *Selected Works*, Vol. 5, Honolulu: University Press of the Pacific, 2004, p. 687.

11 For a defense of orthodox dialectical materialist philosophy of science, see Helena Sheehan, *Marxism and the Philosophy of Science*, Amherst, NY: Prometheus Books, 1993; and Loren Graham, *Science, Philosophy and Human Behavior in the Soviet Union*, New York: Columbia University Press, 1987. On the other hand, one could attempt to build a contemporary philosophy out of contemporary physical science. See Karen Barad, *Meeting the Universe Halfway: Quantum Physics and the Entanglement of Matter and Meaning*, Durham, NC: Duke University Press, 2007, to be discussed in Part II.

12 Williams, *The Other Bolsheviks*, p. 138. Dominique Lecourt has tried to rescue the reputation of Lenin's text; see his *Une crise et sens enjeux*, Paris: Maspero, 1973, but to my mind it does not survive the devastating criticism of Anton Pannekoek, *Lenin as Philosopher*, London: Merlin Press, 1975. Pannekoek gives only a qualified defense of the Machist-Marxists, however.

13 Gilles Deleuze, *Spinoza: Practical Philosophy*, San Francisco: City Lights, 2001, Ch. 6.

14 Stuart Hall, "Old and New Identities, Old and New Ethnicities," in Anthony D. King (ed.), *Culture, Globalization and the World System*, Minneapolis, MN: University of Minnesota Press, 1991, p. 42. Like Judith "Jack" Halberstam, I take this as the turn-off to a low theory.

15 See Vittorio Strada, *L'Altra Rivolutzione*, Capri: Editioni La Conchiglida, 1994.

16 Quoted in Viktor Shklovsky, *Mayakovsky and His Circle*, London: Pluto Press, 1974, p. 117.

17 On Mars as a literary trope, see Robert Markley, *Dying Planet: Mars in Science and the Imagination*, Durham, NC: Duke University Press, 2005.

18 Alexander Bogdanov, *Red Star: The First Bolshevik Utopia*, trans. Charles Rougle, ed. Loren Graham and Richard Stites, Bloomington: Indiana University Press, 1984, p. 186. I am indebted throughout also to the additional texts in this volume by Stites and Graham. For a helpful account of the Russian context, see Anthony Anemone, "Utopia, Dystopia and Science Fiction: The Speculative Urge in Early Soviet Culture," in Rosa Ferré (ed.), *Red Cavalry: Creation and Power in Soviet Russia*, Madrid: La Casa Encendida, pp. 238–53.

19 This might mark the difference between Bogdanov and the "God Builders" Gorky and Lunacharsky. Bogdanov responded to the affective problem discovered by George Sorel, the question of motivation for the worker, not with God Building, but with an open-ended fiction of possible futures. See Anindita Banerjee, *We Modern People: Science Fiction and the Making of Russian Modernity*, Middletown, CT: Wesleyan, 2012, pp. 84–5.

20 Alexandra Kollontai, *Selected Writings*, ed. Alix Holt, New York: Norton, 1980. On blood in Bogdanov's early essays and fiction, see Douglas Greenfield, "Revenants and Revolutionaries," *Slavic and East European Journal*, Vol. 50, No. 4, 2006.

21 Bogdanov anticipates the technological production of surplus life out of the human body. See Rebecca Skloot, *The Immortal Life of Henrietta Lacks*, New York: Broadway, 2011. The story of how cancer cell tissue from Lacks's body became the basis for a whole biomedical industry, from which her descendents never benefited, and about which they did not even know, is emblematic of what Melinda Cooper calls surplus life, and the extraction of value from it, more than Bogdanov's more utopian idea about what Platonov would call "shared life." See Melinda Cooper, *Life as Surplus: Biotechnology and Capitalism in the Neoliberal Era*, Seattle, WA: University of Washington Press, 2008.

22 Bogdanov, *Red Star*, p. 65.

23 See Mark Poster, *The Mode of Information*, Cambridge: Polity, 1990; Paul Cockshott and Allin Cottrell, *Towards a New Socialism*, London: Coronet Books, 1993; Nick Dyer-Witheford, *Cyber-Marx: Cycles and Circuits of Struggle in High Technology Capitalism*, Champaign, IL: University of Illinois Press, 1999; Eden Medina, *Cybernetic Revolutionaries: Technology and Politics in Allende's Chile*, Cambridge, MA: MIT Press, 2011.

24 Bogdanov, *Red Star*, p. 79. See H. G. Wells, *A Modern Utopia*, London: Penguin Modern Classics, 2005, p. 11. There is of course a strong tradition of science fiction writing in Russia, utopian and otherwise, which arose even

before its more metropolitan counterparts. See Banerjee, *We Modern People: Science Fiction and the Making of Russian Modernity.*

25 Bogdanov, *Red Star*, p. 79, emphasis added. Compare to Jean-Paul Sartre, *Critique of Dialectical Reason*, London: Verso, pp. 162ff. There Sartre uses the example of the cutting of forests in China as a kind of counter-finality. The desired finality of increasing arable land results in the counter-finality of flooding and erosion. But Sartre sees this as a contradiction between individual and group praxis, whereas for Bogdanov deforestation is a problem of collective labor. Nevertheless Sartre's concepts of counter-finality and the practico-inert seem promising keys to thinking the era of climate change.

26 Eduard Brückner, *The Sources and Consequences of Climate Change and Climate Variability*, ed. Nico Stehr, Amsterdam: Kluwer, 2010. Brückner argued that deforestation could cause climate change as early as 1889.

27 Bogdanov, *Red Star*, p. 80, emphasis added.

28 This sets Bogdanov apart from all of those other currents that stress the proletarian point of view, of which the most influential in his own time was Sorel's syndicalism. See John Stanley (ed.), *From Georges Sorel: Essays in Socialism and Philosophy*, Piscataway, NJ: Transaction Publishers, 1987.

29 Alexander Bogdanov, *Essays in Tektology: The General Science of Organization*, second edition, Seaside CA: Intersystems Publications, 1984, p. 35. Bogdanov borrows the term tektology from Ernst Haeckel, the German follower of Darwin. See Robert Richards, *The Tragic Sense of Life: Ernst Haeckel and the Struggle Over Evolutionary Thought*, Chicago, IL: University of Chicago Press, 2009, for a vigorous defense of Haeckel. In Haeckel's work, tektology concerns the question of what constitutes an individual organism—a non-obvious question in certain species he studied, such as sponges. Haeckel's monism, descended from that of Goethe, was a strong influence on Bogdanov.

30 See Paul N. Edwards, *A Vast Machine: Computer Models, Climate Data, and the Politics of Global Warming*, Cambridge, MA: MIT Press, 2010, discussed further in Part II.

31 Nikolai Danielson, who had corresponded with Marx and Engels, translated *Capital* into Russian. V. A. Barazov and I. I. Skvortsov-Stepanov retranslated *Capital* under Bogdanov's supervision between 1907 and 1910, after Bogdanov took over the job from Lenin. The last edition with Barazov and Bogdanov's names on it is in 1930. See Andrei Belykh, "Bogdanov's Tektology and Economic Theory," in John Biggart et al. (eds.), *Alexander Bogdanov and the Origins of Systems Thinking in Russia*, Aldershot: Ashgate, 1998, p. 143. See also Ilmari Susiluoto, *The Origins and Development of Systems Thinking in the Soviet Union*, Helsinki: Suomalainen Tiedeakatemia, 1982, p. 43.

32 K. M. Jensen, *Beyond Marx and Mach: Aleksandr Bogdanov's Philosophy of Living Experience*, Dordrecht: Reidel, 1978, p. 32. I am indebted to Jensen for much of this section.

33 Here I agree with a point Bernard Stiegler has made: Foucault privileges the study of military and religious practices of power/knowledge, but there are others, and indeed labor movement practices of worker education are a signal omission.

34 The classic text is Guy Debord and Gil Wolman, "A User's Guide to Détournement," in Ken Knabb (ed.) *Situationist International Anthology*, Berkeley, CA: Bureau of Public Secrets, 2006, pp. 14–20. See also McKenzie Wark, *The Beach Beneath the Street*, London: Verso, 2011, pp. 33–45.

35 One could relate this to Ray Brassier's invocation of Sellars' distinction between folk and scientific images of thought, although the differences will also become apparent. See Ray Brassier, *Nihil Unbound: Enlightenment and Extinction*, Basingstoke: Palgrave Macmillan, 2010.

36 Alexander Bogdanov, *The Philosophy of Living Experience*, trans. David G. Rowley, forthcoming, ms, p. 6.

37 Ibid., p. 12.

38 See David K. Naugle, *Worldview: The History of a Concept*, Grand Rapids, MI: Eerdmans, 2002. Bogdanov derives the term "worldview" from Dilthey, although his understanding of their origins and purpose is quite different. Bogdanov is mentioned in Karl Mannheim, *Ideology and Utopia: An Introduction to the Sociology of Knowledge*, Orlando, FL: Harcourt, 1955, p. 331, as a forerunner to the sociology of knowledge, most likely for his organizational theory of worldviews.

39 Bogdanov, *The Philosophy of Living Experience*, ms, pp. 9–10.

40 Ibid., p. 12.

41 Bogdanov adopted the concept of the basic metaphor from the philologist and Sanskrit scholar Max Müller. See the remarks by Goveli in Biggart et al. (eds.) *Alexander Bogdanov and the Origins of Systems Thinking in Russia*, p. 106.

42 Bogdanov, *The Philosophy of Living Experience*, ms, p. 32. Bogdanov only tested his theory of the homology between worldviews and social formations on "Western" examples, but see Joseph Needham, *Science and Civilization in China, Vol.2: History of Scientific Thought*, Cambridge: Cambridge University Press, 1969.

43 The relation between exchange relations and Greek philosophy was later developed, probably independently, by George Derwent Thomson, Benjamin Farrington, and Alfred Sohn-Rethel.

44 Bogdanov, *The Philosophy of Living Experience*, ms, p. 28.

45 From Ben Woodward's interview with Slavoj Žižek, in Levi Bryant et al. (eds.) *The Speculative Turn*, Melbourne: re:press, 2011, p. 407.

46 Bogdanov, *The Philosophy of Living Experience*, ms, p. 32.

47 See J. D. Bernal, *Science in History*, Vol. 2, Cambridge, MA: MIT Press, 1971, p. 575ff.

48 Cited in Jensen, *Beyond Marx and Mach*, p. 47.

49 See Alexander Galloway, *Laruelle: Against the Digital*, Minneapolis, MN: University of Minnesota Press, 2014, which uses the work of François Laruelle for a critique of exchange with the other as a general model of philosophical thought.

50 Karl Marx, "Concerning Feuerbach," in *Early Writings*, Harmondsworth: Penguin, 1973, p. 421. This is the most cited text of Marx or Engels in Bogdanov. See Vadim Sadovsky, "From Empiriomonism to Tektology," in Biggart et al. (eds.), *Alexander Bogdanov and the Origins of Systems Thinking in Russia*, p. 44.

51 On the evolution of the concept of substitution in Bogdanov, see Daniela Steila, "From Experience to Organization," in Vesa Oittinen (ed.), *Aleksandr Bogdanov Revisited*, Helsinki: Aleksanteri Institute, 2009, pp. 151ff.

52 The apparatus has received quite a bit of attention in science studies. See for example Andrew Pickering, *The Mangle of Practice: Time, Agency and Science*, Chicago, IL: University of Chicago Press, 1995.

53 Quentin Meillassoux, *After Finitude: An Essay on the Necessity of Contingency*, London: Continuum, p. 52.

54 See McKenzie Wark, *A Hacker Manifesto*, Cambridge, MA: Harvard University Press, 2004.

55 Cited in Jensen, *Beyond Marx and Mach*, p. 72.

56 Bernal, *Science in History*, Vol. 3, pp. 804ff.

57 John Blackmore, *Ernst Mach: His Life, Work and Influence*, Berkeley: University of California Press, 1972.

58 Cited in Jensen, *Beyond Marx and Mach*, p. 98.

59 More could be said about the Feuerbachian side of Bogdanov. See Ludwig Feuerbach, *The Fiery Brook: Selected Writings*, trans. Zawar Hanfi, London: Verso, 2012.

60 Jensen, *Beyond Marx and Mach*, p. 105.

61 See Joseph Dietzgen, *The Nature of Human Brain Work: An Introduction to Dialectics*, Oakland, CA: PM Press, 2010.

62 Jensen, *Beyond Marx and Mach*, p. 109.

63 Cited in Jensen, *Beyond Marx and Mach*, p. 112.

64 Cited in ibid., p. 119.

65 Cited in ibid., p. 122.

66 Guy Debord, *In Girum Imus Nocte Et Consumumur Igni*, trans. Lucy Forsyth, London: Pelagian Press, 1991, p. 24.

67 See Yunir Urmantsev, "Tektology and GST: A Comparative Analysis," in Biggart et al. (eds.), *Alexander Bogdanov and the Origins of Systems Thinking in Russia*, p. 237, and Parmenov's remarks on p. 210. The discussion there concerns whether tektology is a theory or a science, whereas I maintain that what is essential to it is neither. Tektology is a collaborative poetic method of generating theories and coordinating their scientific verification or refutation.

68 Cited in Jensen, *Beyond Marx and Mach*, p. 133. Bogdanov can usefully be compared here to Alfred Sohn-Rethel, *Intellectual and Manual Labor*, London: Macmillan, 1983.

69 See Edwards, *A Vast Machine*, discussed further in Part II. In some ways Bogdanov anticipates Bruno Latour, but in one way not: Bogdanov would not identify modernity with reason, but with labor. If, for Latour, we have never

been modern in that the network of relations even in science does not conform to the model of reason, then for Bogdanov we have been modern since the nineteenth century, in that labor is organized pretty much as Marx describes it, via the wage relation. There is an ethnographic dimension to Bogdanov, in that he does not measure historical worldviews via an imaginary external standard of reason. But he does see a cumulative process via which worldviews of more and more generality succeed each other in time.

70 Cited in Jensen, *Beyond Marx and Mach*, p. 136.

71 For a recent example, see Ian Bogost, *Unit Operations*, Cambridge, MA: MIT Press, 2006, pp. 38–43, where Bogost writes about the idea of "object oriented ontology" in programming. "To negotiate the conflicting demands of protecting proprietary symbolic code and leasing that code to thousands of independent developers, the notion of component objects was born." Or in other words, while the application of object oriented ontology (OOO) to the design of software is a matter of protecting intellectual property, when OOO becomes a philosophical movement premised on the notion that objects withdraw, not only from subjects but from each other, the roots of this metaphor in the current organization of property relations is quietly forgotten. But it does not then seem unreasonable to interpret OOO as a philosophy in which objects protect their intellectual property from each other. This argument generally elicits puzzlement or fury from the advocates of OOO, who, regardless of their merits as original thinkers and allies in the overcoming of a rather stale phenomenology, have simply forgotten how to debug their own code when it comes to its implication in the particular organizational forms of the times. Which is something of a shortcoming in a movement with rather cosmic aspirations.

72 Cited in Jensen, *Beyond Marx and Mach*, p. 151.

73 See the classic studies by David Noble, *America By Design: Science, Technology, and the Rise of Corporate Capitalism*, New York: Alfred Knopf, 1977; and *The Forces of Production: A Social History of Industrial Automation*, Oxford: Oxford University Press, 1986.

74 Marcel van der Linden, *Western Marxism and the Soviet Union: A Survey of Critical Theories and Debates Since 1917*, Chicago, IL: Haymarket Books, 2009. Two first-hand, critical accounts from the left: Maxim Gorky, *Untimely Thoughts*, New Haven, CT: Yale University Press, 1998; N. N. Sukhanov, *The Russian Revolution 1917: A Personal Record*, Princeton, NJ: Princeton University Press, 1994.

75 Dietrich Grille, *Lenin's Rivale: Bogdanov und Seine Philosophie*, Cologne: Verlag Wissenschaft und Politik, 1966. This is the standard biography of Bogdanov. On the figure of the old mole, see Georges Bataille, *Visions of Excess*, Minneapolis, MN: University of Minnesota Press, 1985, pp. 32ff.

76 Alexander Bogdanov, "The Workers' Artistic Heritage," *The Labour Monthly*, September 1924, pp. 549–97, available at www.marxists.org, from which the following quotations are taken. See also See also Yehoshua Yahkot, *The*

Suppression of Philosophy in the USSR: The 1920s and 1930s, Oak Park, MI: Mehring Books, 2012, pp. 208ff.

77 And what different stories one can tell by making the (dis)organizing struggles of Ophelia the central character? See Kate Zambreno's *Green Girl*, New York: Harper Perennial, 2014; and *Heroines*, Los Angeles: Semiotext(e), 2012.

78 Zenovia Sochor, *Revolution and Culture*, Ithaca, NY: Cornell University Press, 1988, pp. 81–99.

79 Raymond Williams, *Marxism and Literature*, Oxford: Oxford University Press, 1978, pp. 128ff.

80 On Marx's practice of détournement, see Keston Sutherland, *Stupefaction*, Calcutta: Seagull Books, 2011.

81 Bogdanov, "The Workers' Artistic Heritage."

82 See Sheila Fitzpatrick, *The Commissariat of Enlightenment*, Cambridge: Cambridge University Press, 2002. Lunacharsky was also Bogdanov's brother-in-law.

83 Bogdanov, *Essays in Tektology*, p. 135.

84 See, for a start, Karl Marx, *Dispatches from the New York Tribune: Selected Journalism of Karl Marx*, ed. Francis Wheen, London: Penguin, 2008.

85 See Maurice Blanchot, *The Unavowable Community*, New York: Station Hill Press, 1988. In this regard Zamyatin's dystopian novel *We* misses its mark a little.

86 Here Bogdanov breaks from syndicalism. See George Sorel, *Reflections on Violence*, Cambridge: Cambridge University Press, 1999. It also puts some distance between him and workerist or autonomist thought, which tends to be based on the working class as it is, rather than in terms of its organizational mission to come.

87 Henri Lefebvre, *The Critique of Everyday Life*, Vol. 1, London: Verso, 2008.

88 A line of thought much extended in Boris Arvatov, "Everyday Life and the Culture of the Thing," trans. Christina Kiaer, *October*, Vol. 81, 1997, pp. 119–28.

89 See A. Bogdanov and I. Stepanov, *Kurs Politiceskoj Ekonomii*, Moscow, 1919.

90 Susiluoto, *The Origins of Systems Thinking in the Soviet Union*, p. 59.

91 Cited in ibid., p. 63.

92 Leon Trotsky, *Art and Revolution*, London: Pathfinder Press, 1992.

93 For example, Osip Brik argues for the uses to the revolution of formalism in poetics, since it deals with the "laws of poetic production" rather than merely agitating for proletarian spirit with the old bourgeois forms. But he does not get far beyond the poetics of the production of poetry, and certainly does not grasp production as poesis itself. See Osik Brik, "The So-called Formalist Method," in Catriona Kelly (ed.) *Utopias*, Harmondsworth: Penguin, 1999, pp. 76–8.

94 Lynn Mally, *Culture of the Future: The Proletkult Movement*, Berkeley: University of California Press, 1990.

95 See Victor Serge, *Memoirs of a Revolutionist*, New York: NYRB Classics, 2012, pp. 94–6. The Soviet secret police changed its name a few times, but for simplicity it is referred to in this text throughout as the "Cheka."

96 But see Mark D. Steinberg, *Proletarian Imagination: Self, Modernity, and the Sacred in Russia 1910–1925*, Ithaca, NY: Cornell University Press, 2002.

97 Bogdanov, *Essays on Tektology*, p. 2, see also p. 105. See Robert Fussell, *The Great War and Modern Memory*, Oxford: Oxford University Press, 2000.

98 Bogdanov, *Essays on Tektology*, p. 34. On Clausewitz and his relevance to conceiving of revolution as situation and organization rather than as a leap of faith, see McKenzie Wark, *The Spectacle of Disintegration*, London: Verso, 2012.

99 See Peter Dudley (ed.), *Bogdanov's Tektology Book 1*, ed. Vadim Sadovsky and Vladimir Kelle, Center for Systems Studies, University of Hull, 1996.

100 Sheehan, *Marxism and the Philosophy of Science*, p. 161.

101 See Jussi Parikka, *Insect Media: An Archaeology of Animals and Technology*, Minneapolis, MN: University of Minnesota Press, 2010. One could think the organ as a pharmakon.

102 Bogdanov, *Essays in Tektology*, p. 187.

103 Ibid., p. 126.

104 Ibid., p. 74.

105 See Sochor, *Revolution and Culture*, pp. 81ff.

106 Bogdanov, *Essays in Tektology*, p. 142. See Melissa Gregg et al. (eds.), *The Affect Theory Reader*, Durham, NC: Duke University Press, 2010.

107 Bogdanov, *Essays in Tektology*, p. 33.

108 Ibid., p. 94.

109 Ibid., p. 122, emphasis changed.

110 Ibid., p. 46; cf. p. 167. On false analogies, see p. 168. Bogdanov's extensive notes from the general science journals *Priroda* and *Uspekkhi Fizicheskikh Nauk* of 1913–1918 survive. See Simona Poustilnik, "Biological Ideas in Bogdanov," in Biggart et al. (eds.), *Alexander Bogdanov and the Origins of Systems Thinking in Russia*, p. 64. On "the socialism of science," see Simona Poustilnik, "Tektology in the Context of Intellectual Thought in Russia," in Oittinen (ed.), *Aleksandr Bogdanov Revisited*, pp. 119ff.

111 Ernst Mach, *Contributions to the Analysis of Sensations*, La Salle, IL: Open Court, 1897.

112 Ludwig Noiré, *The Origin and Philosophy of Language*, Ithaca, NY: Cornell University Press, 2009. On Noiré and Bogdanov, see James White, "Sources and Precursors of Bogdanov's Tektology," in Biggart et al. (eds.), *Alexander Bogdanov and the Origins of Systems Thinking in Russia*, pp. 30–4.

113 Bogdanov, *Essays in Tektology*, p. 60.

114 Ibid., pp. 3–5.

115 Ibid., p. 61.

116 Patricia Railing (ed.), *Victory Over the Sun*, London: Artists Bookworks, 2009. A futurist work of 1913 which for Groys sums up the ambitions of the

avant-garde. See Boris Groys, *The Total Art of Stalinism*, London: Verso, 2011. Groys' thesis on the continuity of the avant-gardes and socialist realism is controversial, but from a Bogdanovite point of view, not unreasonable.

117 On abstract labor see I. I. Rubin, *Essays on Marx's Theory of Value*, New Delhi: Aakar Books, 2007. Rubin was one of the great Marxist economic thinkers, a contemporary of Bukharin's, and who met a similar if less public fate.

118 Bogdanov, *Essays in Tektology*, p. 25. On technology transfer and steam power, see Bernal, *Science in History*, Vol. 2.

119 Bogdanov, *Essays in Tektology*, p. 35. The influence of Bogdanov on Arvatov is evident here.

120 Ibid., p. 66.

121 Ibid., p. 43.

122 Ibid., p. 60.

123 Asger Jorn proposed the same critique of dualism. See Wark, *The Beach Beneath the Street*, pp. 45–61. Both Jorn and Bogdanov are radical monists. The difference is that Bogdanov assimilates aesthetic to technical organization; Jorn assimilates technical to aesthetic practice.

124 In his classic work *Marx After Sraffa*, London: Verso, 1981, Ian Steedman showed how Marx's economics could be reconstructed without the category of surplus value. The demonstration is persuasive. However, the seemingly superfluous double concepts in Marx point toward a double reality: the commodity economy on the one hand, and the metabolic relation of collective labor to nature as resource on the other.

125 Bogdanov, *Essays in Tektology*, p. 61.

126 Ibid., p. 48.

127 Hayden White, *Metahistory: The Historical Imagination in the Nineteenth Century*, Baltimore: Johns Hopkins University Press, 1975, offers a more elaborate typology of historical narrative forms. In White's terms, Bogdanov puts the metaphorical to work for something other than an ironic historical mode.

128 Bogdanov, *Essays in Tektology*, p. 65. See John Hutnyk, *Bad Marxism*, London: Pluto Press, 2004. Bogdanov is maybe good-bad in relation to Hutnyk's terms, in his orientation to praxis. The metaphoric / metonymic schema is taken from Roman Jacobson, "Two Aspects of Language and Two Types of Aphasic Disturbances," in *On Language*, Cambridge, MA: Harvard University Press, 1995. A more thorough rhetorical analysis of Marx can be found in Thomas Keenan, *Fables of Responsibility*, Stanford, CA: Stanford University Press, 1997.

129 Karl Marx, *Capital*, Vol. 1, New York: Vintage Books, 1977, p. 638, emphasis added.

130 Brett Clark and John Bellamy Foster, "Ecological Imperialism and the Global Metabolic Rift: Unequal Exchange and the Guano/Nitrates Trade," *International Journal of Comparative Sociology*, Vol. 50, Nos. 3–4, 2009, pp. 311–34.

131 Bogdanov, *Essays in Tektology*, p. 98.

132 Karl Marx, *Capital*, Vol. 3, New York: Vintage Books, 1981, p. 949, emphasis added.

133 Mike Davis, *Planet of Slums*, London: Verso, 2006.

134 Bogdanov, *Essays in Tektology*, p. 73.

135 Ibid., p. 71.

136 Ibid., p. 72.

137 Bogdanov translates selection as "podbor" rather than "otbor," which gives more the sense of "assemblage" than "selection." See the remarks by Simona Poustilnik in Biggart et al. (eds.), *Alexander Bogdanov and the Origins of Systems Thinking in Russia*, pp. 112–16; and Simona Poustilnik, "Tektology in the Context of Intellectual Thought," in Oittinen (ed.), *Aleksandr Bogdanov Revisited*, pp. 112–18. He was not alone among Russian interpreters of Darwin in thinking evolution in a way that was remote from Malthus or Spencer. See for example Kropotkin's *Mutual Aid*. Given the extreme environment of much of the Russian continent, surviving against the elements rather than competing against other individuals of one's own species or against another species does become more of a factor. See Stephen Jay Gould, "Kropotkin Was No Crackpot," *Natural History*, No. 106, 1997, pp. 12–21.

138 Bogdanov, *Essays in Tektology*, p. 172.

139 Ibid., p. 75. See Franco Moretti, *Graphs, Maps and Trees: Abstract Models for Literary History*, London: Verso, 2007. See also Lev Manovich, "Trending: The Promises and Challenges of Big Social Data," in Matthew Gold (ed.), *Debates in the Digital Humanities*, Minneapolis, MN: University of Minnesota Press, 2012.

140 Bogdanov, *Essays in Tektology*, p. 71.

141 Bogdanov prefigures a few tendencies in twenty-first-century design thinking. See Janine Benvus, *Biomimicry*, New York: William Morrow, 2002; Michael Braungart and William McDonough, *Cradle to Cradle: Remaking the Way We Make*, New York: North Point Press, 2002; Tony Fry, *Design as Politics*, London: Berg Publishers, 2011; Carl DiSalvo, *Adversarial Design*, Cambridge, MA: MIT Press, 2012.

142 Bogdanov, *Essays in Tektology*, p. 75.

143 Ibid., p. 90.

144 Ibid., p. 101.

145 Ibid., p. 105.

146 Ibid., p. 89.

147 Ibid., p. 90.

148 Ibid., p. 89.

149 Ibid., p. 91.

150 Ibid., p. 74.

151 Ibid., p. 130, emphasis added. On the similarities and differences between Vernadsky's concept of the biosphere and Bogdanov's see Peter Plyutto,

"Pioneers in Systems Thinking," in Biggart et al. (eds.) *Alexander Bogdanov and the Origins of Systems Thinking in Russia*, pp. 74–82.

152 On symbiosis in Bogdanov, see Alexander Ogurtsov, "Bogdanov and the Idea of Co-Evolution," in Biggart et al. (eds.), *Alexander Bogdanov and the Origins of Systems Thinking in Russia*, pp. 254–5. For a more contemporary account, see Lyn Margulis, *Symbiotic Planet: A New Look At Evolution*, New York: Basic Books, 2008.

153 Bogdanov, *Essays in Tektology*, p. 130.

154 Bogdanov, *Essays in Tektology*, p. 97.

155 Ibid., p. 189.

156 Ibid., p. 170.

157 Nikolai Krementsov, *A Martian Stranded on Earth: Alexander Bogdanov, Blood Transfusions, and Proletarian Science*, Chicago, IL: University of Chicago Press, 2011. Alexander Bogdanov, *The Struggle for Viability*, trans. Douglas Huestis, Tuscon, AZ: Xibris, 2001.

158 Nikolai Bukharin, "On the Life of A. A. Bogdanov," trans. Evgeni V. Pavlov, *Platypus Review*, No. 57, 2013.

159 Sheila Fitzpatrick, *The Cultural Front*, Ithaca, NY: Cornell University Press, 1992.

160 See N. I. Vavilov, *Five Continents*, St. Petersburg International Plant Genetics Research Laboratory, 1997. Much has been written about the Lysenko affair. See David Joravsky, *The Lysenko Affair*, Cambridge, MA: Harvard University Press, 1970. In Loren Graham's *Science, Philosophy and Human Behavior in the Soviet Union*, we find a defender of genetics calling the Lysenkoites "Machists" but in a rather crude sense, meaning deniers of the structure of the gene, and adherents to what can be observed about the genesis of plant life (p. 122).

161 This is basically the program of Perry Anderson, *Considerations on Western Marxism*, London: Verso, 1976.

162 Bogdanov, *Essays in Tektology*, p. 166.

163 Ibid., p. 162, emphasis added.

164 On Bogdanov and systems theory, see Arran Gare, "Alexander Bogdanov and Systems Theory," *Democracy and Nature*, Vol. 6, No. 3, 2000. I take sympoesis from Donna Haraway's conference paper, "Staying With the Trouble: Paper for Isabelle Stengers," Cerisy, 2013.

165 Gilles Deleuze and Félix Guattari, *What Is Philosophy?*, London: Verso, 1994, pp. 61–85. Deleuze is a little too anxious to separate the philosophical personae from "merely" literary ones, a distinction of no importance to low theory, which has nothing invested in the notion of philosophy as a supposedly higher discourse. Donna Haraway shows in her critique of Deleuze and Guattari's conceptual personae of the wolf-pack that philosophical personae can actually be rather less helpful than ones from other fields, in this case from an actual knowledge of wolves. See Donna Haraway, *When Species Meet*, Minneapolis, MN: University of Minnesota Press, 2008, p. 29.

2. Adrey Platonov

1 Andrei Platonov, *Chevengur*, trans. Anthony Olcott, Ann Arbor, MI: Ardis, 1978. The first three chapters are available in a more recent translation in Robert Chandler (ed.), *The Portable Platonov*, Moscow: Glas New Russian Writing, 1999. I am grateful to all those who have labored so hard to translate Platonov, particularly Robert Chandler and his collaborators.

2 On the interzone between the rural and industrial, see T. J. Clark, *The Painting of Modern Life*, New York: Knopf, 1985, pp. 147ff.

3 Joseph Stalin, "Speech to the First All-Union Conference of Stakhanovites," November 17, 1935, *Collected Works*, Vol. 14, London: Red Star Press, 1978.

4 I am particularly indebted to Thomas Seifrid, *Andrei Platonov*, Cambridge: Cambridge University Press, 1992, on all Platonov matters, but I think he rather overestimates the extent to which Bogdanov shared the utopian optimism of his Proletkult followers. In this respect I think Platonov is in solidarity with Bogdanov against Proletkult. Platonov's use (or perhaps détournement) of Russian cosmist writing is a topic I leave aside. See George M. Young, *The Russian Cosmists: The Esoteric Futurism of Nikolai Federov and His Followers*, Oxford: Oxford University Press, 2012.

5 Platonov, "Fourteen Little Red Huts," in Chandler (ed.), *The Portable Platonov*, p. 136.

6 See Robert Paul Wolff, *Moneybags Must Be So Lucky: On the Literary Structure of Capital*, Amherst, MA: University of Massachusetts Press, 1988.

7 Platonov, "Fourteen Little Red Huts," pp. 156 and 132.

8 Lefebvre, *Critique of Everyday Life*, Vol. 1, p. 5. This is from the 1958 introduction.

9 Raoul Vaneigem, *The Revolution of Everyday Life*, London: Rebel Press, 2001, p. 26.

10 Guy Debord, *Society of the Spectacle*, New York: Zone Books, 1991, p. 146, s. 209.

11 Andrei Platonov, "Among Animals and Plants," in *Soul*, trans. Robert and Elizabeth Chandler et al., New York: NYRB Classics, 2007, p. 169; also in *The New Yorker*, October 22, 2007. The Soviet-era writers Boris Pilniak and Victor Shklovsky are alluded to on this same page—two supposedly "modernist" writers who practiced their own versions of détournement. On Lautréamont and literary communism, see Tom McDonough, *The Beautiful Language of My Century*, Cambridge, MA: MIT Press, 2007, pp. 13–53.

12 Maxim Gorky, *My Universities*, Harmondsworth: Penguin Books, 1988, p. 34.

13 Anatoly Lunacharsky, *Revolutionary Silhouettes*, New York: Hill & Wang, 1967, p. 13. On Lunacharsky's post-revolutionary career, see Fitzpatrick, *Commissariat of Enlightenment*, p. 202.

14 From a letter Platonov wrote to his publisher in 1922, quoted in Tatyana Tolstaya, "Introduction," to Andrei Platonov, *The Fierce and Beautiful World*, New York: NYRB Classics, 2000, p. xvi.

15 "The idea of the sublime that is suggested is one of overcoming the physical limits of the collective workers who will build it. The latter are required to sacrifice themselves, as sensory beings, in order to build a new world for the proletarian masses. In proportion as their own physical selves are diminished, the collective is enhanced in symbolic form." Susan Buck-Morss, *Dreamworld and Catastrophe: The Passing of Mass Utopia in East and West*, Cambridge, MA: MIT Press, 2000, p. 181.

16 Viktor Shklovsky, *Third Factory*, Normal, IL: Dalkey Archive, 2002, pp. 77–80.

17 Platonov's Tambov experience is perhaps behind his story "The Locks of Epiphan," about an engineer working on a canal-building project for Peter the Great. The story is a compact demonstration of some aspects of Platonov's method. It is constructed around a pun between the Russian words for utopia and drowning, and around two appearances of the figure of the "hole." The canal fails when a hole is dug too deep; the engineer is sodomized by his executioner before his death. Like Raymond Roussel, Platonov often seems to construct texts "structurally," out of homophones or homologies of figure. See Raymond Roussel, *How I Wrote Certain of My Books*, Boston: Exact Change, 2005. Not the least interest of Platonov is the way he combines *both* documentary realism and extremes of formalist method.

18 E. P. Thompson coined the phrase. See "History from Below," *Times Literary Supplement*, April 7, 1966, pp. 279–80. History from below the below is how I see the work of Thompson's former student, Peter Linebaugh, such as *The London Hanged*, London: Verso, 2006. Linebaugh traces the imposition of new forms of wage and property relation on the (sub)proletarian body by force.

19 See Davis, *Planet of Slums*. Platonov's characters are often only marginally connected to industrialization. Development happens elsewhere, off in the distance. As Davis shows, this is now a majority experience.

20 T. J. Clark mentions Platonov in passing as one of the authors he would recruit to his version of a left politics in a tragic key, but Clark's tragedy falls short of the tragedy of the totality which for Bogdanov would characterize a proletarian culture. See T. J. Clark, "For a Left With No Future," *New Left Review*, No. 74, March–April 2012.

21 On reading Marx's *Capital* as a novel, see Marshall Berman, *Adventures in Marxism*, London: Verso, 2001. On reading Platonov's major works as a great series of Marxist historical novels, one cannot but quote, in a sly way, the concluding remarks from 1937 of Georg Lukács, *The Historical Novel*, Lincoln: University of Nebraska Press, 1983, p. 350: "The historical novel of our time . . . must above all negate, radically and sharply, its immediate predecessor and eradicate the latter's traditions from its own work. The necessary approximation to the classical type of historical novel which occurs in this connection will . . . by no means take the form of a simple renaissance, a

simple affirmation of these classical traditions, but, if one will allow me this phrase from Hegel's terminology, a renewal in the form of the negation of the negation." It may also be worth noting that many of Platonov's reviews and even some stories were published in a journal for which Lukács was on the editorial board.

22 See Slavoj Žižek, *Repeating Lenin*, Zagreb: Arkzin, 2001, for a rather striking reading of Lenin's "leap of faith."

23 Platonov, *Chevengur*, p. 27.

24 Ibid., p. 30. See also Jonathan Flatley, *Affective Mapping: Melancholia and the Politics of Modernism*, Cambridge, MA: Harvard University Press, 2008, for a subtle reading of these scenes.

25 Platonov, *Chevengur*, p. 38. See Rolf Hellebust, *Flesh to Metal: Soviet Literature and the Alchemy of Revolution*, Ithaca, NY: Cornell University Press, 2003, pp. 120ff.

26 Platonov, *Chevengur*, p. 43.

27 Ibid., p. 125.

28 Ibid., p. 45. The superlative document of the (left) Menshevik point of view is surely Sukharnov's *The Russian Revolution*. Sukharnov was the editor of Gorky's paper and a delegate to the executive committee of the Soviet in St. Petersburg at the time of the February Revolution. While he missed the revolution itself, the Bolshevik spirit in the early years of the Soviet experiment are most ably captured by Victor Serge in his *Memoirs of a Revolutionary*.

29 Platonov, *Chevengur*, p. 45. One can compare the first part of *Chevengur* with the version of October 1917 in the provinces of Platonov's friend, the more well-known writer Boris Pilniak, in *The Naked Year*, Ann Arbor, MI: Ardis, 1975. To Pilniak's later cost, he portrays the spontaneous quality of revolution, rather than the party in command.

30 Platonov, *Chevengur*, p. 63. Forming communes was not an uncommon phenomena. Even Victor Serge tried it. See his *Memoirs of a Revolutionary*, pp. 172ff. See also Richard Stites, *Revolutionary Dreams: Utopian Vision and Experimental Life in the Russian Revolution*, Oxford: Oxford University Press, 1989, pp. 205ff.

31 Platonov, *Chevengur*, p. 65.

32 Ibid., p. 68. This fictional experience of the war and revolution can be compared to Eduard Dune's first-hand account, *Notes of a Red Guard*, Champaign, IL: University of Illinois Press, 1993.

33 Platonov, *Chevengur*, p. 78. On the most famous of the backwoods anarchists, see Alexandre Skirda, *Nestor Makhno, Anarchy's Cossack: The Struggle for Free Soviets in the Ukraine 1917–1921*, Oakland, CA: AK Press, 2003.

34 Platonov, *Chevengur*, p. 109. Kopenkin and Rosa would lend itself to a psycho-analytic reading, obviously, but let's not go there. Instead: "Ah, Rosa Luxemburg. How the ghosts of these and similar women haunt the minds of left-wing men! (Not so much the women.)" Doris Lessing, *Walking in the Shade*, New York: Harper, 1997, p. 219.

35 Platonov, *Chevengur*, p. 89.

36 Ibid., p. 96. One might compare this with Charles Fourier, *The Theory of the Four Movements*, Cambridge: Cambridge University Press, 1996, pp. 47ff, where cultivation leads to a benign global warming.

37 Compare to "clapped out barracks train" in Platonov, *Foundation Pit*, trans. Robert Chandler, Elizabeth Chandler, and Olga Meerson, New York: NYRB Classics, 2009, p. 146. The "locomotive of history" is from Karl Marx, "The Class Struggles in France," Ch. 3, at marxists.org. On part-objects, see Brian Massumi, *Parables for the Virtual*, Durham, NC: Duke University Press, 2002.

38 See Sheila Fitzpatrick, *Stalin's Peasants*, Oxford: Oxford University Press, 1996, pp. 5ff on peasant subaltern resistance to the Bolsheviks in the 1920s and 1930s. See also John MacKay, *Four Russian Serf Narratives*, Madison: University of Wisconsin Press, 2009.

39 Platonov, *Chevengur*, p. 110. On Kronstadt, see Serge, *Memoirs of a Revolutionary*, pp. 147–53. For a recent, and extensive, study of this controversial event, see Israel Getzler, *Kronstadt 1917–1921: The Fate of a Soviet Democracy*, Cambridge: Cambridge University Press, 2002.

40 Platonov, *Chevengur*, p. 113. For a more affirmative portrait of Trotsky in the civil war, see Isaac Deutscher, *The Prophet Armed*, London: Verso, 2009.

41 Platonov, *Chevengur*, pp. 115–17. These scenes seem like something out of Nikolai Leskov, *The Enchanted Wanderer*, New York: Melville House, 2012.

42 Platonov, *Chevengur*, pp. 125–6. See Alexandre Kojève, *Introduction to the Reading of Hegel*, Ithaca, NY: Cornell University Press, 1969, pp. 130ff.

43 Platonov, *Chevengur*, p. 137. Compare to the brilliant satire of the NEP period in Ilya Petrov and Evgeny Petrov, *The Golden Calf: A Novel*, Rochester, NY: Open Letter, 2009.

44 Andrey Platonov, "The Factory of Literature," trans. Anna Kalashyan, *Public Seminar*, January 6, 2014, at www.publicseminar.org.

45 Platonov, *Chevengur*, p. 141. For a refreshingly vulgar account of the relation between energy and politics, see Timothy Mitchell, *Carbon Democracy*, London: Verso, 2013.

46 Platonov, *Chevengur*, pp. 148, 145.

47 Platonov, *Chevengur*, p. 148. See Marx, "Critique of the Gotha Program," at www.marxists.org.

48 See Slavoj Žižek, *Living in End Times*, London: Verso, 2010, p. 374. Žižek thinks this gnostic-materialist current of the revolution is somehow distinct from Bolshevism proper, as well as being what "mature Stalinism," as he calls it, reacts against. But by Žižek's own account, Lenin participates in a mystic leap beyond material constraints. What is absent from Žižek's brief remarks on Platonov is an awareness not so much of his gnostic as of his materialist sensibility, his relentless attention to the tektological envelope of the body and its grim persistence against a resistant nature.

49 On the concentrated spectacle, see Debord, *Society of the Spectacle*, s. 63–4.

50 Platonov, *Chevengur*, p. 179. Chevengur could indeed be a place of carnival. See Natalia Skradol, "Non-working, Communism and Carnival," *Slavonic and East European Review*, Vol. 87, No. 4, 2009, pp. 610–28.

51 Platonov, *Chevengur*, p. 165. See Fitzpatrick, *Stalin's Peasants*, pp. 247ff on score-settling in the villages.

52 Platonov, *Chevengur*, p. 170. According to Stites, *Revolutionary Dreams*, pp. 124ff, it was not uncommon for peasants, in taking over estates, to insist that everyone share in the seizure and redistribution. On God-Building, see Maxim Gorky, *A Confession*, New York: Everett & Co., 1910.

53 Platonov, *Chevengur*, p. 156. According to Stites, *Revolutionary Dreams*, pp. 207ff, peasants rarely formed communes on their own. Communes like Chevengur were more likely the product of the landless and former soldiers, and did indeed attract displaced women. Here we diverge from Fredric Jameson's reading of Chevengur as a peasant utopia.

54 Platonov, *Chevengur*, pp. 157–8. "Never work!" was an early slogan of Guy Debord's, but the classic statement of the anti-work position is by Marx's son-in-law. See Paul Lafargue, *The Right to Be Lazy*, Oakland, CA: AK Press, 2011.

55 Platonov, *Chevengur*, p. 172. The sun recalls the utopia of Tommaso Campanella, *The City of the Sun*, Berkeley: University of California Press, 1981.

56 Boris Pilniak, *Mahogany and Other Stories*, Ann Arbor, MI: Ardis, 1993, p. 125. Pilniak was executed in 1938.

57 Platonov, *Chevengur*, pp. 176, 259, 273. On Platonov's ability to at once evoke the leap and undercut it, see Angela Livingstone, "Half-Worlds and Horizons in Platonov's *Chevengur*," *Slavonica*, Vol. 9, No. 2, 2003.

58 Platonov, *Chevengur*, p. 207.

59 Ibid., p. 197. See also *Foundation Pit*, p. 24 on the sun.

60 Platonov, *Chevengur*, p. 198.

61 Platonov, *Chevengur*, pp. 211, 270. For the other side of this story, see Shelia Fitzpatrick and Yuri Slezkine (eds.), *In The Shadow of Revolution: Life Stories of Russian Women From 1917 to the Second World War*, Princeton, NJ: Princeton University Press, 2000.

62 Platonov, *Chevengur*, p. 280. See Eliot Borenstein, *Men Without Women: Masculinity and Revolution in Russian Fiction, 1917–1929*, Durham, NC: Duke University Press, 2001.

63 Platonov, *Chevengur*, p. 314. See Seifrid, *Platonov*, p. 119.

64 Platonov, *Chevengur*, p. 236.

65 Ibid., p. 239.

66 On productivism, see Christina Kiaer, *Imagine No Possessions: The Socialist Objects of Russian Constructivism*, Cambridge, MA: MIT Press, 2008. Solar energy was in use in Egypt by 1913, so Gopner and Dvanov's interest in it is far from fanciful.

67 Platonov, *Chevengur*, p. 283.
68 Platonov, *Chevengur*, p. 227. See Morton, *Ecology Without Nature*. For Morton, "Nature" has too much history to function as a concept, and so he tries to rethink ecology without nature as referent. After Bogdanov, I think there might be some use value in the different ways in which nature as a concept is constructed out of different encounters with resistance by particular regimes of labor. Morton is also resistant to monism, imagining that it wishes away the problem of ecology, but as both Bogdanov and even more so Platonov show, a monism is no neat and tidy unity.
69 Platonov, *Chevengur*, pp. 294–5. Serbinov is troubled by a split between desire (meaning) and drive (passionate veins). Outside the purely psychoanalytic realm, the split between desire and drive is central to a whole line of thought that perhaps begins with Alexandre Kojève's *Introduction to the Reading of Hegel*. To lapse "back" from desire to drive is to fall out of history. This reading is still alive and well in Bernard Stiegler. But perhaps one can go the other way, as is suggested by Hiroki Azuma, *Otaku: Japan's Database Animals*, Minneapolis, MN: University of Minnesota Press, 2009. A richer and more interesting historical thought may emerge out of taking material drives seriously rather than the more theological "desires," or rather refusing the whole dualism—and hence I prefer the term appetites.
70 See Ivan Chtcheglov, "Formulary for a New Urbanism," in Tom McDonough, *Situationists and the City*, London: Verso, 2009, pp. 32–41. For a reappraisal of Soviet utopian architecture, see Owen Hatherley, *Militant Modernism*, Winchester: Zero Books, 2009, pp. 43ff.
71 Platonov, *Chevengur*, p. 310.
72 Ibid., p. 327.
73 Platonov's is one of the few contemporary accounts, but see also Vassily Grossman, *Everything Flows*, New York: NYRB Classics, 2009, pp. 115ff, and Fitzpatrick, *Stalin's Peasants*. In light of those two works, nothing in *Foundation Pit* about the forced collectivization seems at all surreal or fantastic.
74 The "production" novel is a sort of prototype for socialist realism, a bit too bogged down in statistics and not yet fully informed by the communist horizon. Key texts include certain editions of Fyodor Gladkov's *Cement*. Pilniak's *Mahogany* may also be a détournement of *Chevengur*, and *Foundation Pit* of Pilniak's revision of *Mahogany* along socialist realist lines. See Thomas Seifrid, *A Companion to Andrei Platonov's* The Foundation Pit, Brighton, MA: Academic Studies Press, 2009, p. 55.
75 Carey Gilliam, "Sweet Times for Cows," *Reuters*, September 23, 2012, at www.reuters.com. Or in other words, our own industrial food system might not survive all that much longer than Stalin's. See Michael Pollan, "The Food Movement, Rising," *New York Review of Books*, June 10, 2010.
76 Platonov, *Foundation Pit*, pp. 7, 44. The following line is of course from Debord's *Society of the Spectacle*, s. 9. The contents of Voschev's bag reads like

what Ian Bogost calls a "Latour litany." See his *Alien Phenomenology, Or What It Is To Be a Thing*, Minneapolis, MN: University of Minnesota Press, 2012. While for Bogost the kipple to be found littering the landscape of New Mexico has a certain aesthetic dimension; for Platonov, the leaf and other detritus work in a more critical way, as tokens of a tektology always falling short of the organization of the material world. Voschev's leaf might rather point forward to a kind of salvage-punk operation which finds other ways of valuing the detritus of failed organization. See Evan Calder Williams, *Combined and Uneven Apocalypse*, Winchester: Zero Books, 2011.

77 Platonov, *Foundation Pit*, pp. 4, 9, 13. See John Scott, *Behind the Urals: An American Worker in Russia's City of Steel*, Bloomington: Indiana University Press, 1989, for a point of comparison to Platonov on conditions in the Soviet construction industry.

78 Platonov, *Foundation Pit*, p. 19. Contrary to Chandler and Meerson, I don't see how this reduces Marx to "absurdity." See their note, *Foundation Pit*, p. 205.

79 Ibid., p. 33.

80 Ibid., p. 12.

81 Ibid., p. 132.

82 Ibid., p. 17.

83 Ibid., p. 43.

84 Ibid., pp. 59, 68. On the complexities of family and gender policy in Soviet times, see Wendy Goldman, *Women, the State and Revolution*, Cambridge: Cambridge University Press, 1993; and Eric Naiman, *Sex in Public: The Incarnation of Early Soviet Ideology*, Princeton, NJ: Princeton University Press, 1997.

85 Platonov, *Foundation Pit*, p. 65.

86 Ibid., p. 71.

87 Ibid., pp. 68, 52. On Stalin's appropriation of "cultural revolution" language for his own purposes, see Fitzpatrick, *The Cultural Front*, pp. 115ff.

88 Seifrid speculates that General Line Collective Farm refers to Eisenstein's film, generally known by the name *The General Line*. See Seifrid, *Companion*, p. 178.

89 Platonov, *Foundation Pit*, pp. 99, 78. See Sheila Fitzpatrick, *Everyday Stalinism*, Oxford: Oxford University Press, 1999, pp. 35ff, on the figure of the "activist."

90 Platonov, *Foundation Pit*, p. 98.

91 Ibid., p. 113. The critical analysis of the Soviet political economy was and remains a vexed issue in Marxist thought. This reading is premised on that of the Socialism or Barbarism group. See Cornelius Castoriadis, *Political and Social Writings*, Vol. 1, Minneapolis, MN: University of Minnesota Press, 1988.

92 Platonov, *Foundation Pit*, p. 109.

93 Ibid., p. 86. The becoming animal of a human also occurs in the story "Rubbish Wind," set in Nazi Germany. As for the folkloric bear in the smithy:

"Steel" and "Hammerer" refer to the nom de guerre of Stalin and Molotov respectively. On Platonov and becoming animal, see Oxana Timofeeva, *History of Animals: An Essay on Negativity, Immanence and Freedom*, Maastricht: Jan Van Eyck Academie, 2012.

94 Platonov, *Foundation Pit*, pp. 99, 103. Joseph Stalin, "Concerning the Policy of Liquidating the Kulaks as a Class" (January 21, 1930), in *Collected Works*, Vol. 12, Moscow: Foreign Languages Publishing House, 1955, pp. 184–9.

95 Platonov, *Foundation Pit*, pp. 105, 119. For context, see Joseph Stalin, "Dizzy With Success" (March 2, 1930), in ibid., pp. 197–205.

96 Platonov, *Foundation Pit*, p. 123.

97 Ibid., pp. 123, 147.

98 Ibid., p. 142.

99 On the Stalinist urbanism of the 1930s, see Katerina Clark, *Moscow the Fourth Rome: Stalinism, Cosmopolitanism, and the Evolution of Soviet Culture, 1931–1941*, Cambridge, MA: Harvard University Press, 2011.

100 On Stalin and the technical intellectuals, see Loren Graham, *The Ghost of the Executed Engineer*, Cambridge, MA: Harvard University Press, 1993. Graham claims in that text that Bogdanov's *Red Star* was a favorite work of Stalin's, and gives as his source Boris Souvarine, *Stalin*, trans. C.L.R. James, New York: Longmans, 1939, p. 504. What Souvarine actually says is that Bukharin invoked *Red Star* in writing about Lenin's electrification plan.

101 Andrey Platonov, *Happy Moscow*, trans. Robert and Elizabeth Chandler et al., London: Harvill Press, 2001, p. 83. On the image of abundance see Fitzpatrick, *Everyday Stalinism*, pp. 89ff. Fredric Jameson, in *The Seeds of Time*, New York: Columbia University Press, 1994, emphasizes rather the non-commodified basis of Soviet culture.

102 Platonov, *Happy Moscow*, pp. 44, 45. On engineers of human souls, see A. A. Zdanov, "On Literature," in *On Literature, Music and Philosophy*, London: Lawrence & Wishart, 1950. See also Boris Kagarlitsky, *The Thinking Reed: Intellectuals and the Soviet State*, London: Verso, 1988, p. 136.

103 Platonov, *Happy Moscow*, p. 26. See the thoughts of the remarkable minor character Muldbauer, pp. 40, 50. A cruel optimism is a misrecognition of a promise as an achievement, where an object comes to stand for a whole world, and the loss of that object would mean the loss of the whole world. The cruelty lies in the pleasure deriving solely from maintaining a relation to the object when the object itself is not pleasurable. Berlant's critique is of the capitalist realism of the overdeveloped world, but it appears to fit the opening scenes of *Happy Moscow* in interesting ways as well. See Lauren Berlant, *Cruel Optimism*, Durham, NC: Duke University Press, 2011.

104 Platonov, *Happy Moscow*, p. 12.

105 Ibid., p. 6. This configuration of the woman wandering the space of the city as a space of her own appetites anticipates Situationist International co-founder Michèle Bernstein's 1960s novels, *All The Kings Horses*, Los Angeles:

Semiotext(e), 2008, and *The Night*, London: Book Works, 2013. See Wark, *The Beach Beneath the Street*, pp. 75–83.

106 Platonov, *Happy Moscow*, p. 17.

107 Ibid., pp. 45, 46.

108 Ibid., p. 87.

109 Ibid., p. 11. Platonov also worked in Weights and Measures, where he invented an electric scale. See Seifrid, *Companion*, p. 5.

110 Platonov, *Happy Moscow*, p. 30. Nikolai Krementsov, *A Martian Stranded on Earth*, pp. 55ff, writes of the exhaustion of the Bolshevik ruling class and its interest in longevity treatments.

111 Platonov, *Happy Moscow*, p. 37.

112 Ibid., p. 70.

113 Ibid., p. 74.

114 Ibid., p. 89. On consciousness as an evolutionary mistake, see Peter Watts, *Blindsight*, New York: Tor Books, 2008.

115 Platonov, *Happy Moscow*, p. 71.

116 Ibid., p. 55.

117 Ibid.

118 Ibid., p. 61. See also Platonov's story "Fro," included in *Soul*. Contra Masha Tupitsyn, *Love Dog*, Los Angeles: Penny-Ante, 2013.

119 Platonov, *Happy Moscow*, p. 68.

120 Ibid., p. 75.

121 Ibid., p. 120. "Heart of a heartless world" is Marx's other phrase, besides "opium of the people," for religion, in the "Introduction to A Contribution to the Critique of Hegel's Philosophy of Right," at marxists.org.

122 Which is not as far-fetched as it sounds. See Sheila Fitzpatrick, *Tear Off the Masks! Identity and Imposture in Twentieth-Century Russia*, Princeton, NJ: Princeton University Press, 2005.

123 Platonov, *Happy Moscow*, p. 121. This might be an example of what Marco De Seriis calls the "improper name."

124 Ibid., pp. 126–7. See Theodor Adorno, "Extorted Reconciliation," in *Notes on Literature*, Vol. 1, New York: Columbia University Press, 1991.

125 Platonov, *Happy Moscow*, p. 81.

126 Ibid., p. 82.

127 Ibid., p. 92.

128 The dérive as thought and practiced by the Situationists is, like Moscow's, outside the division between labor time and leisure time. See Guy Debord, "Theory of the Dérive," in Knabb (ed.) *Situationist International Anthology*, pp. 62–7.

129 Jameson, *The Seeds of Time*, p. 120. See also the extraordinary schizoanalytic essay on Platonov by Valery Pogoroda, "The Eunuch of the Soul," in Thomas Lahusen and Gene Kuperman (eds.), *Late Soviet Culture*, Durham, NC: Duke University Press, 1993, pp. 187ff.

130 Joseph Stalin, "Report to the Seventeenth Party Congress of the Work of the Central Committee of the CPSU" (January 26, 1934), in *Collected Works*, Vol. 13, Moscow: Foreign Languages Publishing House, 1954, section 3; Joseph Stalin, "Conference of the Avant-Gardist Kolkhozine Men and Women of Tajikstan and of Turkmenistan with the Directors of the Party and the State" (December 4, 1935), *Works*, Vol. 14, London: Red Star Press, 1978.

131 Platonov's *The Fierce and Beautiful World* contains a translation under the name "Dzhan" of a Khrushchev-era edition. Platonov's *Soul* is based on the complete text. On Soviet adventure novels, usually set in the arctic rather than the far east, see Katerina Clark, *The Soviet Novel*, Bloomington: Indiana University Press, 2000, p. 91ff.

132 Platonov, *Soul*, p. 141. This rather parallels Kojève's dialectic of master and slave in his *Introduction to the Reading of Hegel*.

133 Platonov, *Soul*, p. 35. See Herman Melville, *Bartleby the Scrivener: A Story of Wall Street*, New York: Melville House, 2003. Extensive commentary on Bartleby was begun by Slavoj Žižek, *The Parallax View*, Cambridge, MA: MIT Press, 2003, pp. 342ff.

134 Platonov, *Soul*, pp. 103, 106.

135 Ibid., pp. 9, 11, 19.

136 Ibid., p. 21.

137 Ibid., p. 27, 46.

138 Platonov, *Soul*, p. 42.

139 Jesus says in Matthew 8:22: "Let the dead bury the dead," a phrase once détourned also by Marx. Stalin wrote in 1917, concerning Gorky and others who opposed the Bolshevik seizure of power: "The revolution is not disposed to either pity or to bury its dead." But for the base materialist Nur, "the dead can only be buried by the living." Platonov, *Soul*, p. 53; Karl Marx, "Letter from Marx to Ruge," May 1843, marxists.org; Joseph Stalin, "Strong Bulls of Basan Have Beset Me Round" (October 1917), in *Collected Works*, Vol. 3. H. G. Wells also uses it in *A Modern Utopia*, Ch. 3, s. 3.

140 Platonov, *Soul*, p. 53.

141 See Plato, *The Laws*, Book VII.

142 Platonov, *Soul*, p. 55. See also the comparison of memory in Benjamin and Platonov in Timofeeva, *History of Animals*.

143 Platonov, *Soul*, pp. 57, 61. On the ambient, see Morton, *Ecology Without Nature*.

144 Platonov, *Soul*, p. 76.

145 Ibid., p. 69.

146 Ibid., p. 75.

147 Ibid., p. 92.

148 Ibid., p. 92. On bare life, see Giorgio Agamben, *Homo Sacer: Sovereign Power and Bare Life*, Stanford, CA: Stanford University Press, 1998. In Agamben, the emphasis is on the sovereign power to decide what counts as political life and

what is bare life, outside the law. In Platonov, it is all the other way around. It is bare life in the sense of shared life and its appetites that is the base upon which the superstructures of a legally protected life might be based. *Soul* is among other things about the material basis of political life. Platonov's question is about how securing the material basis of the appetites might found an everyday life not subject to the sovereign's arbitrary violence.

149 Platonov, *Soul*, p. 103.

150 Ibid., pp. 108, 112.

151 Ibid., p. 121. Here Platonov seems to me a useful corrective to the somewhat euphoric revival of the figure of "communism" by younger theorists. While I support their critique of the apolitical and cultural turns in intellectual life, for me Platonov—who never abandoned his "fidelity" to it—nevertheless offers a much richer and historical sense of what a praxis might still be, as a "more interesting grief." See Bruno Bosteels, *The Actuality of Communism*, London: Verso, 2011; Jodi Dean, *The Communist Horizon*, London: Verso, 2012. The latter title immediately recalls Platonov's peasant, who accuses the party of taking both land and sky, and leaving the peasant *nothing but* the horizon.

152 Platonov, *Soul*, p. 127. This theme of the tactically expendable (but not sacrificial) avant-garde of the party I owe to Richard Barbrook. See his *Class Wargames: Ludic Subversion Against Spectacular Capialism*, London: Minor Compostions, 2014.

153 See George Bataille, *The Accursed Share*, New York: Zone Books, 1991, on the theme of the gift and a general economy.

154 See "Two Crumbs," in Andrey Platonov, *The Return and Other Stories*, trans. Robert and Elizabeth Chandler and Angela Livingstone, London: Harvill Press, 1999; see also Robert Chandler et al., *Russian Magic Tales from Pushkin to Platonov*, New York: Penguin Books, 2013; and Robert Chandler, *The Magic Ring and Other Russian Folktales*, London: Faber, 1979, for a selection of Platonov's versions of folk tales.

155 Andrei Platonov, "'The First Socialist Tragedy," *New Left Review*, No. 69, 2011, pp. 31–2. The figure of a nature pressing down even more as labor undermines it is also at work in Platonov's brilliant story "The Epifan Locks," in *The Return and Other Stories*.

156 Species-being has to be understood here, after Darwin, as a population, rather than an essence. Marx perhaps never quite outgrew the pre-scientific notion of species-being he inherited from Feuerbach, but one can rethink the category of species-being in a non-essential way. See Norman Geras, *Marx and Human Nature*, London: Verso, 1985.

157 See Raymond Williams, *Modern Tragedy*, Peterborough: Broadview, 2006. For Williams, the crucial question is: whose tragedy?

158 Here I am paraphrasing the unilateral causality of "determination in the last instance," or DLI, as understood by François Laruelle, *Introduction au non-Marxisme*, Paris: PUF, 2000, pp. 39ff. (My thanks also to Alexander

Galloway for letting me read his manuscript on Laruelle.) Whatever its other merits, Laruelle's DLI is a perfect analog for the experience of climate change. It is something of a détournement of Althusser, but where no exchange from the superstructure is possible with the base.

159 The "relative autonomy of the superstructures" and "determination in the last instance" are key concepts in Louis Althusser, "Ideology and Ideological State Apparatuses," *Lenin and Philosophy*, London: New Left Books, 1977. "The people make meaning, but not with the means of their own choosing" is of course a détournement of Marx's "Eighteenth Brumaire."

160 Kenneth Goldsmith, *Uncreative Writing: Managing Language in the Digital Age*, New York: Columbia University Press, 2013; Vanessa Place, *Tragodia* (3 vols.), Los Angeles: Blanc Press, 2010–11; Lev Manovich, "Cultural Analytics," at http://manovich.net; Kathleen Fitzpatrick, *Planned Obsolescence: Publishing, Technology, and the Future of the Academy*, New York: NYU Press, 2011.

161 Platonov, "The Factory of Literature," at www.publicseminar.org; Walter Benjamin, *The Arcades Project*, Cambridge, MA: Harvard University Press, 2002.

162 See Yuri Tsivian (ed.), *Lines of Resistance: Dziga Vertov in the Twenties*, Bloomington: Indiana University Press, 2005.

163 See Kathy Acker and Sylvère Lotringer, *Hannibal Lecter, My Father*, New York: Semiotext(e), 1991.

164 Compare to Ilya Ehrenberg, *Life of the Automobile*, London: Serpent's Tail, 1976.

165 One might think here also of collaborative, anonymous action in our own times. See Gabriella Coleman, *Hacker, Hoaxer, Whistleblower, Spy*, London: Verso, 2014.

166 Anne Balsamo, *Designing Culture: The Technological Imagination at Work*, Durham, NC: Duke University Press, 2011; Nick Hubble, *Mass Observation and Everyday Life*, Basingstoke: Palgrave Macmillan, 2011; *Viewpoint*, No. 3, 2013, "Special Issue on Worker's Inquiry," at viewpointmag.com.

3. Cyborg Donna Haraway

1 Alexis Madrigal, "American Aqueduct," *Atlantic Magazine*, February 24, 2014.

2 For the critique of the California Ideology, see Richard Barbrook and Andy Cameron, "The California Ideology," *Science as Culture*, Vol. 6, No. 1, 1996, pp. 44–72. For its history, see Fred Turner, *From Counterculture to Cyberculture: Stewart Brand and the Rise of Digital Utopianism*, Chicago, IL: University of Chicago Press, 2006.

3 Compare here two trilogies of novels by Kim Stanley Robinson. In *Three Californias* (1984–90), the Sierras are still a locus to which to retreat, even in

a dystopian future California of megamalls. However, in the *Science on the Capital* books (2004–7) even the mountains are no longer the sign of an ecology, but are rather marked already by climate change. See also Mike Davis, *Ecology of Fear*, New York: Vintage, 1999.

4 See for example Brassier, *Nihil Unbound*; Meillassoux, *After Finitude*; or, alternately, in a more vitalist mode, Rosi Braidotti, *Metamorphosis: Towards a Materialist Theory of Becoming*, Cambridge: Polity, 2002.

5 Not entirely silent. See Kenneth Michael Stokes, *Paradigm Lost: A Cultural and Systems Theoretical Critique of Political Economy*, Armonk, NY: M. E. Sharpe, 1995; Kenneth Michael Stokes, *Man and Biosphere: Toward a Coevolutionary Political Economy*, Armonk, NY: M. E. Sharpe, 1994.

6 Paul Feyerabend, *Knowledge, Science and Relativism*, Cambridge: Cambridge University Press, 1999, p. 129.

7 Paul Feyerabend, *Killing Time*, Chicago, IL: University of Chicago Press, 1996, p. 18, cf. p. 73.

8 See Feyerabend's interesting but unsatisfactory comments responding to Hilary Rose in *Killing Time*, pp. 148–50.

9 Feyerabend, *Knowledge, Science and Relativism*, p. 114. For a critique of Feyerabend's reading of Mach, see Klaus Hentschel, "On Feyerabend's Version of Mach's Theory of Research and its Relation to Einstein," *Studies in the History and Philosophy of Science*, No. 16, 1985, pp. 387–94.

10 This line of argument in Quentin Meillassoux perhaps has its origins in Maurice Merleau-Ponty. See, for example, *Adventures of the Dialectic*, Evanston, IL: Northwestern University Press, 1973.

11 On the ludic aspect of laboratory life, see Hans-Jorg Rheinberger, *Towards a History of Epistemic Things*, Stanford, CA: Stanford University Press, 1997.

12 For a deconstructive approach to science studies, see Vicki Kirby, *Quantum Anthropologies: Life at Large*, Durham, NC: Duke University Press, 2011.

13 V. I. Lenin, *Collected Works*, Vol. 14, Moscow: Progress Publishers, 1972.

14 Actually its full title is Ernst Mach, *The Analysis of Sensations, and the Relation of the Psychical and the Physical*, Mineola, NY: Dover, 1959.

15 Feyerabend, *Knowledge, Science and Relativism*, p. 133.

16 See Feyerabend, *Killing Time*, p. 72.

17 Paul Feyerabend, *Farewell to Reason*, London: Verso, 1987, p. 200.

18 Paul Feyerabend, *Against Method*, London: Verso, 1996, p. xiv.

19 Feyerabend, *Knowledge, Science and Relativism*, p. 132.

20 Peter Galison, *Einstein's Clocks, Poincaré's Maps: Empires of Time*, New York: Norton, 2003. See also Lee Smolin, *Time Reborn*, Boston: Houghton Mifflin, 2013. Smolin thinks the restoration of time as a real sensation has not gone far enough. Far be it for me to assess the scientific claims of this book, but I note with interest how it substitutes "selection" from evolutionary biology into an evolutionary cosmology.

21 Paul Feyerabend, "Consolations for the Specialist," in Imre Lakatos and Alan Musgrave (eds.) *Criticism and the Growth of Knowledge*, Cambridge: Cambridge University Press, 1970, p. 229.

22 Donna Haraway, "Introduction," *The Haraway Reader*, New York: Routledge, 2004, p. 1.

23 Georg Lukács, *History and Class Consciousness*, London: Merlin Press, 1971, p. 1.

24 Ibid., p. 4. The strand of Machist-Marxism Lukács has in mind stems from Friedrich Adler: scientist, social democrat, friend of Einstein. Adler assassinated the Austrian President Count von Stürgkh in 1916 in a vain attempt to end the war. Released from prison in 1918 he was active in the workers' councils during the short-lived German revolution.

25 Some useful background reading: Fred Kaplan, *The Wizards of Armageddon*, Stanford, CA: Stanford University Press, 1991; Stephen Levy, *Hackers*, Sebastopol, CA: O'Reilly, 2010; George Dyson, *Turing's Cathedral: The Origins of the Digital Universe*, New York: Vintage, 2012; John Gertner, *The Idea Factory: Bell Labs and the Great Age of American Innovation*, New York: Penguin, 2012.

26 See Paul R. Josephson, *Lenin's Laureat: Zhores Alferov's Life in Communist Science*, Cambridge, MA: MIT Press, 2010.

27 Donna Haraway, *Simians, Cyborgs, and Women*, London: Routledge, 1991, p. 172. For secondary literature on Haraway, see Nick Mansfield, *Subjectivity*, New York: NYU Press, 2000; Joseph Schneider, *Donna Haraway: Live Theory*, London: Bloomsbury, 2005; Arthur Kroker, *Body Drift*, Minneapolis, MN: University of Minnesota Press, 2012; Margaret Grebowicz and Helen Merrick, *Beyond the Cyborg*, New York: Columbia University Press, 2013; Gill Kirkup et al. (eds.), *The Gendered Cyborg: A Reader*, London: Routledge, 2000.

28 Haraway, *Simians, Cyborgs, and Women*, p. 23. See Sandra Harding, "A Socially Relevant Philosophy of Science? Resources from Standpoint Theory's Controversiality," *Hypatia*, Vol. 19, No. 1, 2004, pp. 25–47. Then watch standpoint theory work its way back into mainstream science and technology studies (or not): John Law, "On the Subject of the Object: Narrative, Technology and Interpellation," *Configurations*, Vol. 8, No. 1, 2000, pp. 1–29.

29 Shulamith Firestone, *Dialectic of Sex: The Case for Feminist Revolution*, New York: Farrar, Strauss and Giroux, 2013. See Haraway, *Simians, Cyborgs, and Women*, pp. 9ff.

30 See for example, John Roemer (ed.), *Analytic Marxism*, Cambridge: Cambridge University Press, 1986, which restores what one might think of as the kind of Marxism represented by Bukharin rather than Bogdanov.

31 Paul Alexander Juutilainen (dir.), *Herbert's Hippopotamus: A Story About Revolution in Paradise*, Cinema Guild, 1996; Andrew Feenberg, *The Critical Theory of Technology*, Oxford: Oxford University Press, 1991.

32 See Mary Wyer et al. (eds.), *Women, Science, and Technology: A Reader in Feminist Science Studies*, New York: Routledge, 2013; Maralee Mayberry et al. (eds.), *Feminist Science Studies: A New Generation*, New York: Routledge, 2001.

33 Donna Haraway, *Primate Visions: Gender, Race, and Nature in the World of Modern Science*, New York: Routledge, 1989, p. 257. To give just one influential example: Starhawk, *The Fifth Sacred Thing*, New York: Bantam, 1994. I am indebted here to the essay on Mary Daly in Meghan Morris, *The Pirate's Fiancée*, London: Verso, 1988.

34 Haraway, *Primate Visions*, p. 310.

35 Sandra Harding, *Whose Science? Whose Knowledge? Thinking from Women's Lives*, Ithaca, NY: Cornell University Press, 1991.

36 Haraway, *Simians, Cyborgs, and Women*, p. 68.

37 Ruth Wilson Gilmore, *Golden Gulag: Prisons, Surplus, Crisis, and Opposition in Globalizing California*, Berkeley: University of California Press, 2007.

38 Haraway, *When Species Meet*, pp. 292–301.

39 Donna Haraway, *How Like a Leaf: An Interview With Thyrza Nichols Goodeve*, New York: Routledge, 2000, p. 42.

40 Donna Haraway, *Modest_Witness@Second_Millennium*, New York: Routledge, 1997, pp. 8, 134. Haraway's use of actor network theory and the work of Bruno Latour is often noted. Her relation to Marxism, less so. See Margaret Grebowicz and Helen Merrick, *Beyond the Cyborg: Adventures with Donna Haraway*, New York: Columbia University Press, 2013.

41 Haraway, "The Promises of Monsters," *The Haraway Reader*, p. 66.

42 Mark Neocleous, "The Political Economy of the Dead: Marx's Vampires," *History of Political Thought*, Vol. 24, No. 4, 2003.

43 Haraway, *Modest_Witness@Second_Millennium*, p. 94, cf. p. 143.

44 Haraway, *How Like a Leaf*, pp. 24, 151.

45 Haraway, *Modest_Witness@Second_Millennium*, p. 218.

46 Against the regime of race, Charlotte Perkins Gilman; against the regime of populations, Ursula Le Guin and Joanna Russ; against the regime of the gene, Octavia Butler and Marge Piercy.

47 Haraway, *Modest_Witness@Second_Millennium*, p. 233. Ernest Haeckel, whose secular and monist evolutionary theory was so central to Bogdanov, was certainly of his time in his acceptance of race categories.

48 Bogdanov, *The Struggle for Viability*.

49 Haraway, *Modest_Witness@Second_Millennium*, p. 237.

50 Ibid., p. 238.

51 Ibid., p. 242.

52 Ibid.

53 Haraway, *Primate Visions*, p. 157.

54 Haraway, *How Like a Leaf*, p. 152.

55 Haraway, *Modest_Witness@Second_Millennium*, p. 244. Cf. Eugene Thacker, *The Global Genome*, Cambridge, MA: MIT Press, 2005.

56 See also Richard Lewontin, *Biology as Ideology: The Doctrine of DNA*, New York: Harper, 1993, and *The Triple Helix: Gene, Organism, and Environment*, Cambridge, MA: Harvard University Press, 2002.

57 Haraway, *Modest_Witness@Second_Millennium*, p. 97.

58 The literature on the fetish is extensive. See William Pietz, "The Problem of the Fetish, I," *Res*, No. 9, 1985; "The Problem of the Fetish, II," *Res*, No. 13, 1987; "The Problem of the Fetish, IIIa," *Res*, No. 16, 1988; and Pietz, "The Spirit of Civilization," *Res*, No. 28, 1995; Emily Apter and William Pietz (eds.), *Fetish as Cultural Discourse*, Ithaca, NY: Cornell University Press, 1993; Emily Apter, *Feminising the Fetish*, Ithaca, NY: Cornell University Press, 1991.

59 Haraway, *Modest_Witness@Second_Millennium*, p. 98. On algorithm as fetish, see McKenzie Wark, *Gamer Theory*, Cambridge, MA: Harvard University Press, 2007.

60 Haraway, *Modest_Witness@Second_Millennium*, p. 136.

61 Haraway, *How Like a Leaf*, p. 92. Cf. Lukács, *History and Class Consciousness*, p. 83.

62 Haraway, *Modest_Witness@Second_Millennium*, p. 135.

63 Ibid., p. 146. Cf. Eugene Thacker, *Biomedia*, Minneapolis, MN: University of Minnesota Press, 2004.

64 Haraway, *Modest_Witness@Second_Millennium*, p. 148.

65 Ibid., p. 163.

66 Ibid., p. 7. Cf. James Boyle, *The Public Domain: Enclosing the Commons of the Mind*, New Haven, CT: Yale University Press, 2008.

67 Haraway, *Modest_Witness@Second_Millennium*, pp. 152, 174. See also Allucquère Rosanne Stone, *The War of Desire and Technology at the Close of the Mechanical Age*, Cambridge, MA: MIT Press, 1996; and Béatriz Préciado, *Testo Junkie*, New York: Feminist Press, 2013.

68 Skloot, *The Immortal Life of Henrietta Lacks*.

69 Haraway, *Modest_Witness@Second_Millennium*, p. 35.

70 David Noble, *A World Without Women: The Christian Clerical Culture of Western Science*, New York: Random House, 2013; Silvia Federici, *Caliban and the Witch: Women, the Body, and Primitive Accumulation*, New York: Autonomedia, 2004.

71 Haraway, *How Like a Leaf*, pp. 158, 162.

72 Haraway, *Modest_Witness@Second_Millennium*, p. 36.

73 Haraway, *Primate Visions*, p. 139. On the history of the figure of the cyborg, see Chris Hables-Gray et al. (eds.), *The Cyborg Handbook*, London: Routledge, 1995. A good twenty-first-century example of the cyborg figure might be Alex Rivera's film *Sleep Dealer* (2008).

74 Haraway, *Simians, Cyborgs, and Women*, p. 4. On the various version of Haraway's most famous text, and its reception, see Zoë Sofoulis, "Cyberquake: Haraway's Manifesto," in Darren Tofts et al. (eds.), *Prefiguring Cyberculture: An Intellectual History*, Cambridge, MA: MIT Press, 2002; and Joseph Schneider, "Haraway's Viral Cyborg," *WSQ: Women's Studies Quarterly*, Vol. 40, Nos. 1–2, 2012, pp. 294–300.

75 Haraway, *Simians, Cyborgs, and Women*, p. 149. On critical theory as heresy, see Alexander Galloway, Eugene Thacker, and McKenzie Wark, *Excommunication*, Chicago, IL: University of Chicago Press, 2013.

76 Haraway, *How Like a Leaf*, p. 103. On Haraway's reworking of the cyborg figure as science fiction, see Istvan Csicsery-Ronay, "The SF of Theory: Baudrillard and Haraway," *Science Fiction Studies*, Vol. 18, No. 3, 1991, pp. 389–404.

77 Haraway, *Simians, Cyborgs, and Women*, p. 152.

78 Haraway, *How Like a Leaf*, p. 129. See Paul Edwards, *The Closed World: Computers and the Politics of Discourse in Cold War America*, Cambridge, MA: MIT Press, 1996, for a history of the cyborg "fathers," such as they are.

79 Haraway, *The Haraway Reader*, p. 3.

80 Haraway, *Simians, Cyborgs, and Women*, p. 154.

81 Ibid., p. 161. Cf. Trebor Scholz (ed.) *Digital Labor: The Internet as Playground and Factory*, New York: Routledge, 2012; Christian Fuchs, *Digital Labour and Karl Marx*, London: Routledge, 2014.

82 Haraway, *Simians, Cyborgs, and Women*, p. 164. For an example of substituting code all the way to the cosmos, see Stephen Wolfram, *A New Kind of Science*, Champaign, IL: Wolfram Media, 2002.

83 Haraway, *Simians, Cyborgs, and Women*, p. 168. Cf. Julian Assange et al., *Cypherpunks*, New York: O/R Books, 2013.

84 Haraway, *Simians, Cyborgs, and Women*, pp. 169–72. Cf. Andrew Ross, *Nice Work if You Can Get It: Life and Labor in Precarious Times*, New York: NYU Press, 2010.

85 On the question of what an international might mean in these times, see Jacques Derrida, *Specters of Marx*, London: Routledge, 2006. See also Kathi Weeks, "The Critical Manifesto: Marx, Engels, Haraway, and Utopian Politics," *Utopian Studies*, Vol. 24, No. 2, 2013, pp. 216–31, for a comparison of the Communist and Cyborg Manifestoes as critical utopian texts.

86 See Wark, *The Spectacle of Disintegration*, on the uses of Charles Fourier's utopian writerly practice. I mentioned there his correspondence with Flora Tristan, whose work calls for a whole study in itself. See Flora Tristan, *The Worker's Union*, Champaign, IL: University of Illinois Press, 2007.

87 For example: Samuel Delany, *Tales of Nevèrÿon*, Middletown, CT: Wesleyan, 1993. Here Haraway connects up with a tendency in feminist screen theory. See Barbara Creed, *The Monstrous-Feminine*, London: Routledge, 1993; and Annette Kuhn (ed.), *Alien Zone: Cultural Theory and Science Fiction Cinema*, London: Verso, 1990.

88 Haraway, *Simians, Cyborgs, and Women*, p. 176. Critics such as N. Katherine and Nigel Thrift have added nuance to the cyborg as figure, but not so much to Haraway's political nous. See the special issue at *Theory, Culture and Society*, Vol. 23, No. 7–8, 2006.

89 Ibid., p. 186. Jackie Orr, "Materializing a Cyborg's Manifesto," *WSQ: Women's Studies Quarterly*, Vol. 40, No. 1–2, 2012, pp. 273–80, sees Haraway as

prefiguring the return of vitalist materialism in the twenty-first century, but here I think she is pointing a few degrees to the left of that.

90 In other words, the opposite of what Heidegger thinks in the world picture essay, in *The Question Concerning Technology and Other Essays*, New York: Harper, 1982. See Haraway, *How Like a Leaf*, pp. 20–3.

91 Robert Buderi, *The Invention that Changed the World*, New York: Simon and Schuster, 1996.

92 Sharon Traweek, *Beamtimes and Lifetimes*, Cambridge, MA: Harvard University Press, 1992.

93 Barad, *Meeting the Universe Halfway*, p. 29. Diffraction as trope comes from Haraway, "The Promises of Monsters," in *The Haraway Reader*.

94 Henri Lefebvre, *Introduction to Modernity*, London: Verso, 2012, pp. 127ff.

95 Andrew Brown, *J. D. Bernal: The Sage of Science*, Oxford: Oxford University Press, 2005, pp. 46ff.

96 Charles Sanders Peirce, *Philosophical Writings*, Mineola, NY: Dover Publications, 2011.

97 Barad, *Meeting the Universe Halfway*, p. 72.

98 Ibid., p. 88.

99 Ibid., p. 93. This was the lost opportunity of the so-called Sokal affair. The editors of *Social Text* and Sokal both misunderstood the procedure. Even "hard" science journals publish results that are merely interesting, as Sokal's "hoax" text might well have been. See *Social Text*, No. 46, 1996.

100 Ibid., p. 122, emphasis added.

101 Werner Heisenberg, *Physics and Philosophy: The Revolution in Modern Science*, New York: Harper, 2007, pp. 44ff.

102 Steven Shapin, *A Social History of Truth*, Chicago, IL: University of Chicago Press, 1995; Lorraine Daston and Peter Galison, *Objectivity*, New York: Zone Books, 2010.

103 Henry Folse, *The Philosophy of Niels Bohr*, London: Elsevier Science, 1985.

104 Barad, *Meeting the Universe Halfway*, p. 19.

105 Ibid., p. 114.

106 Ibid., p. 129.

107 Ibid., p. 143.

108 Ibid., p. 146.

109 Ibid., p. 169.

110 Ibid., p. 171.

111 Ibid., p. 175.

112 Ibid., p. 177.

113 Ibid., p. 178.

114 Ibid., p. 184.

115 Ibid., p. 140.

116 Ibid., p. 149. Such statements are in some quarters at least not as controversial as they once were. See Joseph Rouse, "Philosophy of Science and Science

Studies in the West: An Unrecognized Convergence," *East Asian Science, Technology and Society*, Vol. 5, No. 1, 2011, pp. 11–26, on Barad and Haraway's understanding of scientific practices in the context of contemporary science studies and philosophy of science.

117 Barad, *Meeting the Universe Halfway*, p. 179. See Nancy Cartwright, *Hunting Causes and Using Them*, Cambridge: Cambridge University Press, 2007, on the vexed question of causal models and metaphors.

118 Barad, *Meeting the Universe Halfway*, p. 153. *Meat-space* comes from the early novels of William Gibson.

119 See for example Rosi Braidotti, *The Posthuman*, Cambridge: Polity Press, 2013. This is a fine work in the vitalist materialist lineage, but not one that sticks close to the realism of sensation and the historical form of the apparatus.

120 Barad, *Meeting the Universe Halfway*, p. 142.

121 Karen Barad, "Nature's Queer Performativity," *Kvinder, Køn og forskning*, No. 1, 2012, pp. 25–53.

122 Platonov, "The Motherland of Electricity," in *Soul*, pp. 261–79.

123 Philip Mirowski, *Machine Dreams: Economics Becomes a Cyborg Science*, Cambridge: Cambridge University Press, 2002; Philip Mirowski, *Science-Mart: Privatizing American Science*, Cambridge, MA: Harvard University Press, 2011.

124 James Roger Fleming, *Historical Perspectives on Climate Change*, Oxford: Oxford University Press, 1998, p. 35.

125 Intergovernmental Panel on Climate Change, *Climate Change 2013: The Physical Science Basis*, Cambridge: Cambridge University Press, 2014.

126 Louis Althusser, "Preface to *Capital* Volume 1," in *Lenin and Philosophy*, New York: Monthly Review Press, 2001.

127 On third nature, see McKenzie Wark, *Telesthesia*, Cambridge: Polity Press, 2013.

128 William Ruddiman, *Plows, Plagues, and Petroluem: How Humans Took Control of Climate*, Princeton, NJ: Princeton University Press, 2010. The proposition of this book is that collective human labor has been altering climate for a very long time.

129 Of course there are more sophisticated figures of Gaia: see the interview with Isabelle Stengers in Etienne Turpin (ed.), *Architecture in the Anthropocene*, Ann Arbor, MI: Open Humanities Press, 2013, pp. 171–83; but they may still be variants on an exchange metaphor.

130 Richard Grove, *Ecology, Climate and Empire*, Isle of Harris: White Horse Press, 1998.

131 Karl Marx and Friedrich Engels, *The German Ideology*, Ch. 10, at www.marxists.org.

132 Edwards, *A Vast Machine*, p. 84.

133 Jean-Paul Sartre, *The War Diaries: Notebooks from a Phoney War 1939–1940*, London: Verso, 2011, pp. vii–viii. While not all Sartre's notebooks survived, it is curious how little interest he seems to have taken in what he was actually doing.

134 Edwards, *A Vast Machine*, p. 139. On military objectives and their consequences in computing, see David Golumbia, *The Cultural Logic of Computation*, Cambridge, MA: Harvard University Press, 2007.

135 Edwards, *A Vast Machine*, p. 139.

136 Ibid., p. 173.

137 For a pioneering work on satellites that merges media and infrastructure studies, see Lisa Parks, *Cultures in Orbit: Satellites and the Televisual*, Durham, NC: Duke University Press, 2005.

138 Edwards, *A Vast Machine*, p. 223. Cf. Paul Virilio and Sylvère Lotringer, *Pure War*, Los Angeles: Semiotext(e), 2008.

139 Edwards, *A Vast Machine*, p. 213.

140 Ibid., p. 253.

141 Ibid., p. 267. For a critical ethnographic approach to model-driven science, see Anna Tsing, *Friction: An Ethnography of Global Connection*, Princeton, NJ: Princeton University Press, 2005, pp. 101ff.

142 Lisa Gitelman (ed.), *Raw Data is an Oxymoron*, Cambridge, MA: MIT Press, 2012.

143 Edwards, *A Vast Machine*, p. 281.

144 James Bridle, "The New Aesthetic and its Politics," *booktwo.org*, June 12, 2013.

145 Edwards, *A Vast Machine*, p. 284.

146 Ibid., p. 301.

147 Ibid., p. 321.

148 Ibid., p. 401. See Naomi Oreskes and Erik Conway, *Merchants of Doubt*, London: Bloomsbury Press, 2010.

149 See Michel Löwy and Robert Sayre, *Romanticism Against the Tide of Modernity*, Durham, NC: Duke University Press, 2001, for a thorough account of the entanglements of Marxism and left-romanticisms. In *The Beach Beneath the Street* and *The Spectacle of Disintegration*, I developed out of Henri Lefebvre a conception of the romantic contribution to critique that did not long for something prior to, or anterior to, capitalism, but rather thought the practice of producing utopian impulses was internal to it.

150 See Kenneth Rexroth, *In the Sierra: Mountain Writings*, ed. Kim Stanley Robinson, New York: New Directions, 2012; Kim Stanley Robinson, *The Novels of Philip K. Dick*, Ann Arbor, MI: UMI Research Press, 1989.

4. Kim Stanley Robinson

1 Kim Stanley Robinson, *Red Mars*, New York: Bantam Books, 1993, p. 32; on Arkady and Alexander Bogdanov, see Kim Stanley Robinson, *Blue Mars*, New York: Bantam Books, 1996, p. 667. For a selection of key critical readings of Robinson's work as science fiction, see William Burling (ed.), *Kim Stanley Robinson Maps the Unimaginable*, Jefferson, NC: McFarland, 2009.

2 On Defoe, see Franco Moretti, *The Bourgeois: Between History and Literature*, London: Verso, 2013, pp. 25ff. I am rather bending his excellent formal analysis of *Crusoe* to my own purposes here.

3 On over-identification in theory and practice, see Alexei Monroe, *Interrogation Machine: Laibach and NSK*, Cambridge, MA: MIT Press, 2005.

4 A. J. Greimas, *On Meaning: Selected Writings in Semiotic Theory*, Minneapolis, MN: University of Minnesota Press, 1987. See the Foreword by Fredric Jameson. See also Robinson, *Red Mars*, p. 219; *Green Mars*, New York: Bantam Books, 1995, p. 368; *Blue Mars*, p. 53. See also Kim Stanley Robinson, *The Martians*, New York: Bantam Books, 2000, which contains not only chapters omitted from the *Mars Trilogy*, but intimations of quite different plot lines that could take place through the same literary space of possibility.

5 On Robinson's critical relation to the terraforming literature, see Robert Markley, *Dying Planet: Mars in Science and the Imagination*, Durham, NC: Duke University Press, 2005, pp. 355ff.

6 There is a nod to Brecht in *Blue Mars*, pp. 611ff. See Bertolt Brecht, *Brecht on Theater: The Development of An Aesthetic*, New York: Hill & Wang, 1977, p. 71. Darko Suvin's now-classic formula for science fiction is that it is estrangement plus cognition. For an elaboration see Soo-Young Chu, *Do Metaphors Dream of Electric Sheep: A Science Fictional Theory of Representation*, Cambridge, MA: Harvard University Press, 2010, and for a critique of it, see China Miéville's contribution to Mark Bould and China Miéville, *Red Planets: Marxism and Science Fiction*, Middletown, CT: Wesleyan, 2009.

7 Robinson, *Green Mars*, p. 376. On science fiction and ecology, see Gerry Canavan and Kim Stanley Robinson (eds.), *Green Planet: Ecology and Science Fiction*, Middletown, CT: Wesleyan, 2014.

8 Robinson, *Red Mars*, pp. 59–61.

9 Kim Stanley Robinson, *Antarctica*, New York: Bantam, 2002. On the study of actually existing utopias, see Erik Olin Wright, *Envisioning Real Utopias*, London: Verso, 2010.

10 Robinson, *Red Mars*, p. 89.

11 Ibid., p. 342, emphasis changed. Samuel Bowles and Herbert Gintis, *Cooperative Species: Human Reciprocity and Its Evolution*, Princeton, NJ: Princeton University Press, 2011, assesses the social science that would support this view.

12 On the critique of sacrifice, see Vaneigem, *The Revolution of Everyday Life*. If the Chevengurians all ate the scapegoat to share the guilt, on this Mars, nobody knows who was really responsible for the death of John Boone, and guilt is free floating and diffused. Both Frank and Maya are widely regarded as the guilty ones. In Bogdanov there is much less emphasis on sacrificing the bourgeoisie than on the affirmative task of organizing labor. Given how one sacrifice led to another in Bolshevik thinking, and in *Chevengur*, it's a salient point.

13 Robinson, *Red Mars*, p. 257. See Carl Abbott, "Homesteading on the Extraterrestrial Frontier," *Science Fiction Studies*, Vol. 32, 2005, pp. 240–64, which puts Robinson in the context of science fiction and other writing about homesteading the west.

14 Robinson, *Red Mars*, p. 314.

15 Ibid., p. 378.

16 Ibid., p. 293.

17 Ibid., pp. 266, 343.

18 Ibid., pp. 177–9.

19 See Bogost, *Alien Phenomenology*.

20 Robinson, *Blue Mars*, p. 97. On metaphysical concepts of life, see Eugene Thacker, *After Life*, Chicago, IL: University of Chicago Press, 2010.

21 Robinson, *Red Mars*, p. 471.

22 Robinson, *Blue Mars*, p. 55.

23 Robinson, *Green Mars*, p. 9, see also pp. 358–9; and *Red Mars*, pp. 211, 332, 228–9.

24 Almost a "Deleuzian" one. See *Blue Mars*, p. 640.

25 Robinson, *Red Mars*, p. 230.

26 Ibid., p. 347.

27 Ibid., p. 221. See Jeffrey Jerome Cohen (ed.), *Prismatic Ecology: Ecotheory Beyond Green*, Minneapolis, MN: University of Minnesota Press, 2013.

28 Robinson, *Red Mars*, pp. 323, 427.

29 Robinson, *Green Mars*, p. 223. One could read the three volumes, and the three revolutions, as being about David Graeber's three modes of social organization: hierarchy, exchange, communism, which incidentally could also be mapped onto Bogdanov's three basic metaphors. See David Graeber, *Debt: The First 5000 Years*, New York: Melville House, 2011.

30 Robinson, *Red Mars*, p. 465.

31 Ibid., p. 395.

32 Ibid., p. 403.

33 Ibid., pp. 457–8.

34 As in Knabb, *Situationist International Anthology*, p. 9.

35 See the standard accounts: Anderson, *Considerations on Western Marxism* (in which Bogdanov gets a footnote); Martin Jay, *Marxism and Totality*, Berkeley: University of California Press, 1986 (in which he is not mentioned at all).

36 Robinson, *Red Mars*, p. 460. Cf. *Green Mars*, p. 235.

37 Gramsci is the exception here. Ideology does have a positive organizing function for him. See Terry Eagleton, *Theories of Ideology*, London: Verso, 2007. On the influence of Bogdanov on the concept of ideology in Soviet philosophy, see Yakhot, *The Suppression of Philosophy in the USSR*, pp. 208–13. If the construction of affirmative ideology in the Soviet Union has a precursor, however, it isn't Bogdanov so much as his God-Building comrades Gorky and Lunacharsky.

38 Robinson, *Red Mars*, p. 474.

39 On the fused group, see Sartre, *Critique of Dialectical Reason*, Vol. 1. As Fredric Jameson notes, Marxism is short of middle-range theories of organization, even though it is rather rich on theories of macro-organization, and more recently, theories of the subject. In relation to which Bogdanov is interesting as offering a theory of *scale-independent* organization.

40 Robinson, *Red Mars*, p. 564.

41 Robinson, *Red Mars*, p. 556.

42 Meillassoux, *After Finitude*, p. 64.

43 Robinson, *Red Mars*, p. 550.

44 See Firestone, *Dialectic of Sex*. Paternity is always ambiguous in Hiroko's world, but his father appears to be Coyote. See Robinson, *The Martians*, p. 364.

45 Robinson, *Green Mars*, p. 15.

46 Ibid., p. 326. The ecotogene, or gestation outside the womb, is an idea popularized by Aldous Huxley, who got it from the Marxist biologist J. B. S. Haldane.

47 Guy Debord, *Comments on the Society of the Spectacle*, London: Verso, 1998, p. 11; Robinson, *Green Mars*, p. 488.

48 Ibid., p. 75.

49 Ibid., pp. 77–9. See Herman Daly and Joshua Farley, *Ecological Economics: Principles and Applications*, 2nd edition, Washington, DC: Island Press, 2010.

50 Robinson, *Green Mars*, p. 87. As a counterpoint to the *Mars Trilogy*, see Charlie Stross, *Accelerando*, New York: Ace Books, 2005. In contrast to Robinson, Stross builds on the language of techno-utopia and capitalist realism directly, and produces a bleaker accelerationist vision.

51 Robinson, *Green Mars*, pp. 291, 294.

52 Ibid., p. 35.

53 Ibid., p. 50.

54 Robinson, *Blue Mars*, p. 328. See Tom Moylan, "Utopia Is Where Our Lives Matter," *Utopian Studies*, Vol. 6, No. 2, 1995, pp. 1–24; Tom Moylan, *Demand the Impossible: Science Fiction and the Utopian Imagination*, London: Methuen, 1996. Moylan reads Robinson as continuing the critical utopian writing of the 1970s, with its interest in process and wariness of blueprints. Carol Franko, "Kim Stanley Robinson: *Mars Trilogy*," in David Seed (ed.), *A Companion to Science Fiction*, Oxford: Blackwell, 2005, p. 544, sees the *Mars Trilogy* as a "dynamic view of utopia." I think Robinson's innovation is a kind of *meta-utopia*, which creates textual spaces for the negotiation between different utopian desires and actions.

55 Robinson, *Green Mars*, p. 42. The ultimate impossibility of the pure gift is the subject of Jacques Derrida, *Given Time: I. Counterfeit Money*, Chicago, IL: University of Chicago Press, 1994. In the anthropological literature, the problem of potlatch is the gift that keeps on giving. Of pertinence here is David

Graeber, *Towards an Anthropological Theory of Value: The False Coin of Our Own Dreams*, Basingstoke: Palgrave, 2001, pp. 188ff.

56 Robinson, *Green Mars*, pp. 122–5. Cf. *The Martians*, p. 306. Punctuated Equilibrium is a theory of evolution co-authored by Niles Eldridge and Stephen Jay Gould.

57 Robinson, *Green Mars*, p. 126.

58 Ibid., p. 134.

59 Ibid., p. 144.

60 Ibid., p. 146.

61 See Mark C. Taylor, *After God*, Chicago, IL: University of Chicago Press, 2009.

62 Robinson, *Green Mars*, p. 321.

63 Ibid., p. 155. See Comte de Lautréamont, *Maldoror and the Complete Works*, Boston, MA: Exact Change Press, 1994, p. 159. The fan wiki is *Mangalawiki*, at kimstanleyrobinson.info. See Henry Jenkins, *Convergence Culture*, New York: NYU Press, 2008, on fan cultural production. Not the least reason to pay attention to Robinson, apart from literary merit, is that his *Mars Trilogy* has a significant and distinctive fan culture footprint.

64 Robinson, *Green Mars*, p. 185.

65 Robinson, *Blue Mars*, pp. 55–6.

66 See the alternate history stories included in Jonathan Strahan (ed.) *The Best of Kim Stanley Robinson*, San Francisco: Night Shade Books, 2010.

67 Robinson, *Green Mars*, pp. 185–6.

68 Ibid., p. 220; also *Red Mars*, p. 88.

69 Robinson, *Blue Mars*, p. 83.

70 Robinson, *Green Mars*, p. 204.

71 Ibid., p. 214. See Philip Mirowski, *The Effortless Economy of Science*, Durham, NC: Duke University Press, 2004, and Mirowski, *Science-Mart*.

72 Fredric Jameson, *Archaeologies of the Future*, London: Verso, 2005, p. 396. Here we differ from Jameson's reading. It is not just a question of revealing the political substrate to science, but vice versa as well.

73 On incommensurable discourse, see Jean-François Lyotard, *The Differend: Phrases in Dispute*, Minneapolis, MN: University of Minnesota Press, 1989.

74 Robinson, *Green Mars*, p. 221. Particularly noteworthy here is a short story by Robinson, "Selected Abstracts from the *Journal of Aerological Studies*," in *The Martians*, pp. 314–20. It's a story about a real meteor, ALH84001, which was found in Antarctica and probably originated on Mars, and may or may not contain evidence of life. Robert Markley has a brilliant analysis of the tensions in the scientific literature on this fossil in *Dying Planet*, pp. 323ff. Robinson continues the "scientific" debate, not to its resolution, but to its exhaustion. It's the kind of complex, empirically grounded science that refuses subsumption in model-making at which Sax eventually arrives.

75 Robinson, *Green Mars*, p. 189.

76 To cite standard works on the postcolonial and civil society, respectively: Gayatri Spivak, *Critique of Postcolonial Reason*, Cambridge, MA: Harvard University Press, 1999; Andrew Arato and Jean Cohen, *Civil Society and Political Theory*, Cambridge, MA: MIT Press, 1994.

77 Robinson, *Green Mars*, p. 389. On the commons as the mark of the truly popular constitutional document, see Peter Linebaugh, *The Magna Carta Manifesto: Liberties and Commons for All*, Berkeley: University of California Press, 2008.

78 Robinson, *Green Mars*, p. 481.

79 Robinson, *Green Mars*, p. 514.

80 Ibid., pp. 560, 543.

81 Ibid., pp. 508, 538, 553, 557.

82 Ibid., p. 580.

83 Robinson, *Blue Mars*, p. 594.

84 Ibid., p. 54.

85 Ibid., p. 120. See William J. Burling, "The Theoretical Foundation of Utopian Radical Democracy in Kim Stanley Robinson's *Blue Mars*," *Utopian Studies*, Vol. 16, No. 1, 2005, pp. 75–96, which reads Martian politics through the work of Ernesto Laclau and Chantal Mouffe.

86 Robinson, *Blue Mars*, p. 124. See Charles Fourier, *The Theory of the Four Movements*, Cambridge: Cambridge University Press, 1996. Robinson actually wrote a whole constitution for Mars, see *The Martians*, pp. 265–80.

87 Robinson, *Blue Mars*, pp. 143–4. See Walter Benn Michaels, "The Shape of the Signifier," *Critical Inquiry*, No. 27, 2001, pp. 266–83. Here Michaels attacks those, including Haraway, who he thinks are committed to "deconstructive" theses of the materiality of the signifier, and (same thing for him) the "primacy of the subject." He thinks there can be no conflicts of interpretation among subjects taken to speak incommensurable languages. But this is where Robinson's meta-utopia is an interesting "laboratory," for while it is populated by very different and incommensurable points of view, only in this case derived as much from their labors as their "subject positions," it is nevertheless possible to at least narrate the negotiation of their positions, which are constituted in relation to each other in part by practices of governance but also by verifiable knowledge procedures. It is possible, for example, to measure a volume of water or a quantity of off-gassing. It is revealing that Michaels's essay focuses on the names of Mars, and not on any of the other ways in which its characters know and measure and labor in and on and with it.

88 Robinson, *Blue Mars*, p. 172. See K. Daniel Cho, "Tumults of Utopia: Repetition and Revolution in Kim Stanley Robinson's *Mars Trilogy*," *Cultural Critique*, No. 75, 2010, pp. 65–81.

89 Robinson, *Blue Mars*, p. 213.

90 Ibid., p. 209.

91 Ibid., p. 270.

92 Ibid., p. 428. On the merits of the Athenian election by lottery, see Kojin Karatani, *Transcritique*, Cambridge, MA: MIT Press, 2003, pp. 182–4.

93 Robinson, *Blue Mars*, p. 332. In Robinson, the expansion of the molecular, even submolecular powers of science and its reorganization go together. See Colin Milburn, "Greener on the Other Side: Science Fiction and the Problem of Green Nanotechnology," *Configurations*, Vol. 20, 2012, pp. 53–87.

94 Robinson, *Blue Mars*, p. 370.

95 Ibid., p. 89. Robinson's interest in Thoreau is even clearer in the Science in the Capital Trilogy: *Forty Signs of Rain*, New York: Bantam, 2004; *Fifty Degrees Below*, New York: Bantam, 2005, and *Sixty Days and Counting*, New York: Bantam, 2007.

96 Robinson, *Blue Mars*, p. 400.

97 Ibid., p. 412.

98 Ibid., p. 656.

99 Ibid., p. 657.

100 Ibid., p. 669. Robinson has a clear grasp of the compromises and politicking involved in science even at its best. See "Sexual Dimorphism," in *The Martians*, which takes the junior scientist's point of view.

101 Robinson, *Blue Mars*, p. 393.

102 *The Martians*, p. 306.

103 Robinson, *Blue Mars*, p. 446. See Patrick Murphy, "Engineering Others, Engineering Ourselves: The Ethics of Terraforming and Aeroforming," *Journal of Ecocriticism*, Vol. 1, No. 1, pp. 54–9.

104 Robinson, *Blue Mars*, p. 411. See Eric Otto, "Kim Stanley Robinson's *Mars Trilogy* and the Leopoldian Land Ethic," *Utopian Studies*, Vol. 14, No. 2, 2003, pp. 118–35.

105 Robinson, *Blue Mars*, p. 454.

106 Ibid., p. 725. See the chapter on Constant in Wark, *The Beach Beneath the Street*, and Mark Wigley, *Constant's New Babylon: The Hyper-Architecture of Desire*, Rotterdam: 010 Publishers, 1998.

107 Robinson, *Blue Mars*, p. 505. See Gilles Deleuze, *Negotiations*, New York: Columbia University Press, 1995, p. 121: "All the new sports—surfing, windsurfing, hang-gliding—take the form of entering into an existing wave. There's no longer an origin as starting point, but a sort of putting-into-orbit. The key thing is how to get taken up in the motion of a big wave, a column of rising air, to 'get into something' instead of being the origin of an effort."

108 Robinson, *Blue Mars*, p. 507. Sex becomes rather more interesting in *2312*, a sequel of sorts to the *Mars Trilogy*, when humans have speciated and intra- and multi-gendered bodies proliferate.

109 Robinson, *Blue Mars*, p. 530. See also *2312*, pp. 150ff.

110 Robinson, *Blue Mars*, p. 617.

111 Ibid., p. 764.

112 Ibid., pp. 761. That no one should go hungry is from Theodor Adorno, *Minima Moralia*, London: New Left Books, 1973, pp. 155–7. Andrew Bird, *Denaturalizing Ecological Politics*, Toronto: University of Toronto Press, 2005.

113 A particularly fine example is the alternate history of Kim Stanley Robinson, *The Years of Rice and Salt*, New York: Random House, 2003.

114 Haraway, *Primate Visions*, p. 366.

115 Kim Stanley Robinson, *Shaman*, New York: Orbit, 2013, pursues the idea that it was a previous climate crisis that accelerated human development. On the accelerando, see *Blue Mars*, pp. 666ff, and also *2312*, pp. 276–9.

116 Kenneth Knoespel, "Reading and Revolution in the Horizon of Myth and History," *Configurations*, Vol. 20, 2012, p. 113.

CONCLUSION

1 On the formation and early history, see Stuart Macintyre, *The Reds*, Sydney: Allen & Unwin, 1988; Alastair Davidson, *The Communist Party of Australia: A Short History*, Stanford, CA: Hoover Institute Press, 1969. One thing I learned in the party was how to tell an anecdote, and as mine are in the Australian vernacular style, I should point out that they are true in essence but take certain liberties for narrative purposes.

2 See Meredith Burgmann and Verity Burgmann, *Green Bans, Red Union*, Sydney: University of New South Wales Press, 1998.

3 Most famously, Barry Commoner, *The Closing Circle: Nature, Man and Technology*, New York: Random House, 1971.

4 See Jane Bennett, *Vibrant Matter: A Political Ecology of Things*, Durham, NC: Duke University Press, 2010. The problem with this very interesting book is that on the one hand it insists on retaining the idea of a "politics" but on the other loses sight of the labor point of view.

5 Interestingly, in making his case for a turn to philosophical rigor in Marxist thought, Karl Korsch mentions as an example comments in the socialist periodical press about an article by Bogdanov on Ernst Mach. Where the German social democrats had considered philosophy unimportant on principle, Lenin had only maintained that attitude for tactical reasons. But Korsch considers the question of Bogdanov settled, and contrary to his own strictures on philosophical rigor, does not return to investigate. And so things have stood, more or less, for almost a century. See Karl Korsch, *Marxism and Philosophy*, London: Verso, 2013, p. 35. Lukács, in *History and Class Consciousness*, opens by marking off the distance between a revolutionary theory of the subject-object correlation from the "Machists," for whom reality follows natural laws that can't be grasped or modified by human action (p. 4). At this point in his career Lukács' strictures against science seem to rest on the example of David Ricardo! Of all the "canonic" writers in the Western Marxist tradition, only

Althusser offers much of an engagement. See Louis Althusser, *Philosophy and the Spontaneous Philosophy of the Scientists*, London: Verso, 2011. After modern physics put paid to the materialist metaphysics inherited from the eighteenth century, scientific "savants" produced rival theories such as Mach's, which "seduced" even qualified philosophers such as Bogdanov. It is hard to escape the notion that for Althusser, just as workers need the party of professional revolutionaries to tell them what to do, scientists need the academy of professional philosophers to tell them how to think.

6 See Razmig Keucheyan, *Left Hemisphere: Mapping Contemporary Theory*, London: Verso, 2013. What strikes this reader from Keucheyan's magnificent survey is the gap between the breath, depth, and relevance of Marxist work across the social sciences and the poverty of its philosophy. Not to mention the absence of work on the sciences.

7 For instance: Alain Badiou, *Theory of the Subject*, London: Continuum, 2009; Slavoj Žižek, *The Ticklish Subject: The Absent Center of Political Ontology*, London: Verso, 2009. Here I am much more inclined towards Maurizio Lazzarato, *Signs and Machines: Capitalism and the Production of Subjectivity*, Los Angeles: Semiotext(e), 2014, which accounts for both the production of subjective identities and the algorithmic control of non-subjective affects.

8 Soviet authors were fascinated by the United States. See Erika Wolf (ed.), *Ilf and Petrov's American Road Trip*, New York: Princeton Architectural Press, 2006; Vladimir Mayakovsky, *My Discovery of America*, London: Hesperus Press, 2005. In *Red Plenty*, Minneapolis, MN: Greywolf Press, 2012, Francis Sufford makes the excellent point that what both the United States and the Soviet Union had in common was a sense of the *scale* of modernity.

9 Richard Barbrook, *Imaginary Futures: From Thinking Machines to the Global Village*, London: Pluto Press, 2007, recounts the parallel stories of Western and Soviet grand narrative, and the attempt to create a third one answerable to neither.

10 Vaneigem, *The Revolution of Everyday Life*, p. 185. Vaneigem borrows the reversal of perspective from Bertolt Brecht's Herr Keuner stories.

11 Here we part company with Jodi Dean's *The Communist Horizon*, pp. 119ff. Not everything in the experience of labor is antagonism.

12 Haraway, "Staying With the Trouble: Paper for Isabelle Stengers." Haraway derives this in part from Thom Van Dooren, *Flight Ways: Life at the Edge of Extinction*, New York: Columbia University Press, 2014.

13 Reza Negarastani, *Cyclonopedia: Complicity with Anonymous Materials*, Melbourne: Re:press, 2009.

14 See Keller Easterling, *Extrastate: The Power of Infrastructure*, London: Verso, 2014; Benjamin Bratton, "The Black Stack," *e-flux journal*, No. 53, 2013, at www.e-flux.com.

15 See Eric Hobsbawm, *On History*, New York: The New Press, 1997, pp. 141ff.

16 A key moment is Althusser's formula of the "relative autonomy" of the

superstructures, which gave license to "Marxist" social scientists and humanities scholars to stay within the given disciplinary boundaries in which they were trained and to deploy the methods specific to their training. The political superstructure became the object of political philosophy, the ideological superstructure became the province of semiotics. The "determination in the last instance" by the economic was understood narrowly, as referring to a formalized version of Marx's critique of political economy—if at all. The encounter with nature was relegated to the pure sciences, or rather to the philosophy of the pure sciences. On the return of the repressed—the "determination in the last instance"—see Laruelle, *Introduction au non-marxisme*.

17 A question I raised in *Telesthesia*, pp. 101ff.

18 See Galloway's contribution to Galloway, Thacker, and Wark, *Excommunication*.

19 For a thorough critique, see Eileen Crist, "On the Poverty of Our Nomenclature," *Environmental Humanities*, No. 3, 2013. Her preferred term is *Ecozoic*, coined by ecotheologian Thomas Berry. But why should theologians still have the privilege of naming the kainos?

20 Influential among these comrades was the work of Mike Cooley, *Architect or Bee? The Human-Technology Relationship*, Slough: Langley Technical Services, 1980; and Hilary Wainwright and David Elliot, *The Lucas Plan*, London: Allison & Busby, 1982, which in retrospect seems perfectly congruent with proletkult.

21 Haraway, "Staying With the Trouble: Paper for Isabelle Stengers," p. 26.

22 See Jason Moore, "The Capitalocene," June 2014, at www.jasonmoore.com; Jussi Parikka, *The Anthrobscene*, Minneapolis: University of Minnesota Press, 2014. For "Manthropocene" see Andrew Revkin, "Never Mind the Anthropocene," *New York Times*, October 17, 2014. For Cthulhucene, see Haraway, "Staying With the Trouble." Haraway is less interested in Lovecraft than in the fact that a spider native to her part of California is named after Cthulhu. I borrow #misanthropocene from Joshua Clover and Julianna Spahr, *#misanthropocene: 24 Theses*, Commune Editions, 2014, at http://communeeditions.com, although like all such terms it appears to have been invented spontaneously several times.

23 Haraway attributes this slogan to Scott Gilbert et al., "A Symbiotic View of Life," *Quarterly Review of Biology*, Vol. 87, No. 4, 2012. The classic statement of symbiosis as a basic metaphor is Lynn Margulis, *Symbiotic Planet: A New Look At Evolution*, New York: Basic Books, 1998.

24 See Chiara Bottici, *Imaginal Politics: Images Beyond Imagination and the Imaginary*, New York: Columbia University Press, 2014. Bottici is building on Cornelius Castoriadis, *The Imaginary Institution of Society*, Cambridge, MA: MIT Press, 1998.

Index